Victoria and Albert at Home

By the same author

The Young Victoria

Albert's Victoria

The Widow of Windsor
(a trilogy of biographical novels about Queen Victoria)

Bertie

Edward
(two biographical novels about Edward VII)

The Last Kaiser
(a biography of William II, German Emperor)

Victoria and Albert at Home

Tyler Whittle

Routledge & Kegan Paul
London and Henley

First published in 1980
by Routledge & Kegan Paul Ltd,
39 Store Street, London WC1E 7DD and
Broadway House, Newtown Road,
Henley-on-Thames, Oxon RG9 1EN
Set in Bembo 10 on 12pt by
Rowland Phototypesetting Ltd,
Bury St Edmunds, Suffolk
and printed in Great Britain by
Unwin Brothers Ltd,
The Gresham Press, Old Woking, Surrey
A member of the Staples Printing Group
Plates printed by
The Scolar Press Ltd, Ilkley, Yorkshire
© Michael Tyler-Whittle 1980

British Library Cataloguing in Publication Data

Whittle, Tyler

Victoria and Albert at home.
1. Victoria, Queen of Great Britain –
Homes – England – Wight, Isle of
2. Osborne House
3. Victoria, Queen of Great Britain –
  Homes – Scotland
4. Balmoral Castle, Scot.
I. Title
941.081'092'4   DA555

ISBN 0 7100 0541 5

to Quentin and Susan Agnew

Contents

Author's note   xiii

Acknowledgments   xv

Genealogical table   xviii

1   A suitable seaside property   1
2   Negotiations   6
3   The Napoleonic Mr Cubitt   13
4   'How my beloved Albert enjoys it all'   16
5   Bricks and mortar   21
6   Two sides of the Cairngorms   32
7   A most determined Jacobite   37
8   A second private home   47
9   Great changes   57
10 Accommodation for at least a hundred   61
11 The elusive Mr Smith   65
12 'The work is terribly hard'   69
13 Topsy-turveydom   74
14 An old shoe for luck   77
15 A slow permeation of presence   87
16 'Our cheerful and unpalace-like rooms'   94
17 Fledglings from the nest   100
18 'So overwhelming a calamity'   105
19 The greatest depth of grief   114
20 More marriage and death   120
21 Apt to blaze   127
22 Almighty indiscretions   131
23 First independent steps   137
24 'Too foolish!!'   144
25 Titania and her ageing Puck   147

Contents

26 Prising open the oyster   153
27 The lot of 'essential daughter'   163
28 Triumph, exhaustion and anxiety   171
29 'Mud pies'   176
30 A champagne quality   184
31 No more boiled potatoes in the heather   190

Epilogue   198

Some sources consulted   199

Index   206

Illustrations

Plates

between pages 76 and 77
1 Brighton Pavilion, 1845. Water-colour by C. R. Stanley (reproduced by Gracious permission of Her Majesty the Queen)
2 Old Osborne House in October 1844. Water-colour by C. R. Stanley (reproduced by Gracious permission of Her Majesty the Queen)
3 New kitchens at Osborne designed by Thomas Cubitt (reproduced by Gracious permission of Her Majesty the Queen)
4 Part of Prince Albert's dressing-room at Osborne (Crown Copyright – reproduced with permission of the Controller of Her Majesty's Stationery Office)
5 The Queen's sitting-room in the completed Pavilion (Crown Copyright – reproduced with permission of the Controller of Her Majesty's Stationery Office)
6 Osborne in August 1847, during construction. A water-colour by W. L. Leitch (reproduced by Gracious permission of Her Majesty the Queen)
7 Contemporary picture in coloured sands of the completed Osborne House (reproduced by kind permission of Mrs Oliver Thynne; photo: R. S. Hildersley)
8 Tools, barrows and cart used by the Royal children in their gardens at Osborne, c. 1854 (Crown Copyright – reproduced with permission of the Controller of Her Majesty's Stationery Office)
9 The shore at Osborne (Crown Copyright – reproduced with permission of the Controller of Her Majesty's Stationery Office)
10 Thomas Cubitt, builder of Osborne. By an unknown artist (National Portrait Gallery)

11 William Smith, architect of Balmoral, 1861 (reproduced by kind permission of Miss Helen Smith; photo: R. S. Hildersley)

12 Old Balmoral Castle. A study in pioneer photography by George Washington Wilson

13 Prince Albert's dressing-room at Alt-na-Giuthasach, 1849. A water-colour by an unknown painter (reproduced by Gracious permission of Her Majesty the Queen)

14 New Balmoral under construction, 1854. A photograph taken by William Brookes, an enthusiastic English amateur (reproduced by kind permission of Colin Brookes-Smith; photo: R. S. Hildersley)

15 The drawing-room at Balmoral. A water-colour by J. Roberts (reproduced by Gracious permission of Her Majesty the Queen)

16 The Queen's dressing-room in the new Castle. A water-colour by J. Roberts, September 1857 (reproduced by Gracious permission of Her Majesty the Queen)

17 A photographic portrait of the Royal Family at Osborne, 1857 (in an *Early Album belonging to Albert Edward, Prince of Wales*) (reproduced by Gracious permission of Her Majesty the Queen)

18 Queen Victoria's Birthday Table at Osborne, 1861. A water-colour by J. Roberts (reproduced by Gracious permission of Her Majesty the Queen)

19 Rudolf Löhlein. A contemporary study (reproduced by Gracious permission of Her Majesty the Queen)

20 John Brown in 1860 (reproduced by Gracious permission of Her Majesty the Queen)

21 The first Garden Cottage at Balmoral. A water-colour showing the Queen working at her despatch boxes (reproduced by Gracious permission of Her Majesty the Queen)

22 The Glassalt Shiel. A water-colour by W. Simpson, 1882 (reproduced by Gracious permission of Her Majesty the Queen)

23 Benjamin Disraeli, Earl of Beaconsfield. A photograph by Messrs W. & D. Downey (reproduced by Gracious permission of Her Majesty the Queen)

24 Jane, Lady Churchill in 1862 (reproduced by Gracious permission of Her Majesty the Queen)

25 A Ghillies' Ball at Balmoral. A water-colour by W. Simpson (reproduced by Gracious permission of Her Majesty the Queen)

26 Balmoral Castle seen from the north side of the Dee. A picture drawn by Victor Prout and etched by Swain (reproduced by permission of Mr Dennis Hatfield Bullough)

27 The Queen in old age. Photograph by Milne of Ballater (reproduced by Gracious permission of Her Majesty the Queen)

28   The Munshi and nephew. Photograph by Milne of Ballater (re-
     produced by Gracious permission of Her Majesty the Queen)
29   Osborne House from the air (Crown Copyright – reproduced
     with permission of the Controller of Her Majesty's Stationery
     Office)

Plans

1   A simplified plan of the first floor at Osborne House
    after the Durbar Wing had been added   26–7
2   Block plan of the new Castle at Balmoral, showing its
    position in relation to the old Castle, and to the River Dee
    (after William Smith)   54
3   A ground-floor plan of the House Block at Balmoral
    (after William Smith)   55

(All three plans drawn by Ar. Angelo Cavaliere. Those of Balmoral
are based on photographs of William Smith's originals supplied by
the Royal Commission on Ancient Monuments, Scotland, the
originals being the property of the former firm of Messrs Rowand
Anderson, Kinninmonth and Paul, Edinburgh.)

Author's note

My aim has been to describe the siting, construction and decoration of these two great Victorian houses, and the additions and alterations made to them during the long life of the Queen. I have also given what I believe is an objective account of some of the more memorable family and political events that took place beside the Solent and the River Dee, and of the gradual process by which the buildings took on lives of their own and became homes.

Acknowledgments

For permitting the reproduction of their copyright material at no charge I am indebted to Miss Mary Griffiths, Mr Colin Brookes-Smith, Miss Helen Smith, Mrs Oliver Thynne, the Royal Commission on the Ancient and Historical Monuments of Scotland, and the former partnership of Edinburgh architects, Rowand Anderson, Kininmonth & Paul.

I should also like to thank Surgeon-Captain R. S. McDonald, R.N., House Governor of Osborne House, Mr Ian Gow of the Department of the Environment Inspectorate of Ancient Monuments, and the staffs of the Scottish Record Office, the North East of Scotland Library Service, Aberdeen University Library, Grampian Region Archives, Dyfed County Council Archives, City of Aberdeen Libraries Department, the Isle of Wight County Council Cultural Services, and the Hampshire County Library.

I owe much to the very large number of people who have kindly assisted in my researches; and, in particular, I wish to record my obligation and sincere thanks to H.R.H. Princess Alice Countess of Athlone, the late Admiral of the Fleet Earl Mountbatten of Burma, Mr Alick Bell, Mr Colin Brookes-Smith, the Reverend Professor Owen Chadwick, the Reverend Alan Coldwells, Lord Denham, Miss Frances Dimond, Mr R. G. Farnham, Mr Arnold Florance, Mr H. V. Godfrey, Mr D. Hatfield Bullough, Mr Geoffrey Head, Mr R. S. Hildersley, Miss Hermione Hobhouse, Mr Cecil Johnson, the Countess of Longford, Dr James Macaulay, Sir Robert Mackworth-Young, Mr John Matson, Miss Diane Morgan, Miss Anthea Morton-Saner, Mr T. C. M. O'Donovan, Miss Helen Smith, the late Mr Oliver Thynne, and Mr Harold Yates.

Finally I express my great gratitude to Architetto Angelo Cavaliere for his painstaking work based on the original plans of William Smith; and to those who read through the manuscript and gave unstintingly of their time to help me at all stages: Mr Alan Barnard, a notably rich source of information on Queen Victoria's family and Court; and Mr Edward Sibbick, whose unique knowledge of Osborne House, its history and its collections, he has shared with conspicuous generosity.

Tyler Whittle

Scala, Salerno
November, 1979

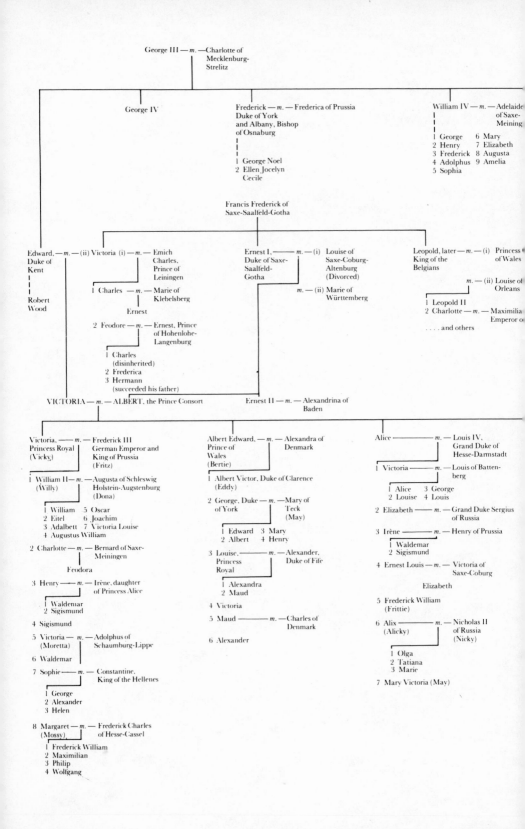

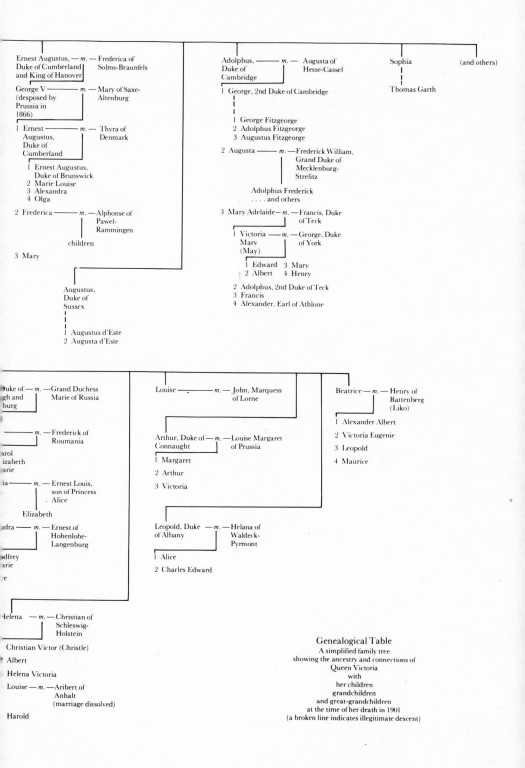

Ernest Augustus, — m. — Frederica of
Duke of Cumberland | Solms-Braunfels
and King of Hanover |

George V ——————— m. — Mary of Saxe-
(desposed by | Altenburg
Prussia in
1866)

1 Ernest ——————— m. — Thyra of
Augustus, | Denmark
Duke of
Cumberland

  1 Ernest Augustus,
    Duke of Brunswick
  2 Marie Louise
  3 Alexandra
  4 Olga

2 Frederica ——————— m. —Alphonse of
| Pawel-
| Rammingen
    children

3 Mary

Augustus,
Duke of
Sussex

1 Augustus d'Este
2 Augusta d'Este

Adolphus, ——— m. — Augusta of
Duke of | Hesse-Cassel
Cambridge

1 George, 2nd Duke of Cambridge

  1 George Fitzgeorge
  2 Adolphus Fitzgeorge
  3 Augustus Fitzgeorge

2 Augusta ——— m. —Frederick William,
| Grand Duke of
| Mecklenburg-
| Strelitz

  Adolphus Frederick
  . . . . and others

3 Mary Adelaide— m. —Francis, Duke
| of Teck

1 Victoria — m. —George, Duke
Mary | of York
(May)

  1 Edward 3 Mary
  2 Albert 4 Henry

2 Adolphus, 2nd Duke of Teck
3 Francis
4 Alexander, Earl of Athlone

Sophia   (and others)

Thomas Garth

Duke of — m. —Grand Duchess
gh and | Marie of Russia
burg

——————— m. — Frederick of
| Roumania
arol
izabeth
arie

ia ——— m. — Ernest Louis,
| son of Princess
. Alice

  Elizabeth

adra — m. — Ernest of
| Hohenlohe-
| Langenburg
dfrey
arie
e

Helena — m. — Christian of
| Schleswig-
| Holstein

Christian Victor (Christle)
Albert
Helena Victoria
Louise — m. —Aribert of
    Anhalt
    (marriage dissolved)
Harold

Louise — . — m. — John, Marquess
| of Lorne

Arthur, Duke of— m. —Louise Margaret
Connaught | of Prussia

1 Margaret
2 Arthur
3 Victoria

Leopold, Duke — m. —Helena of
of Albany | Waldeck-
| Pyrmont

1 Alice
2 Charles Edward

Beatrice — m. — Henry of
| Battenberg
| (Liko)

1 Alexander Albert
2 Victoria Eugenie
3 Leopold
4 Maurice

Genealogical Table
A simplified family tree
showing the ancestry and connections of
Queen Victoria
with
her children
grandchildren
and great-grandchildren
at the time of her death in 1901
(a broken line indicates illegitimate descent)

Chapter 1

A suitable seaside property

In the year 1843 a young couple made a decision of considerable importance. They were Victoria, Queen of Great Britain and Ireland, and her husband and first cousin, Prince Albert, Duke of Saxony and Prince of Saxe-Coburg-Gotha.

By coincidence both had been brought into the world by the same woman doctor, and at an early age each had been deprived of one parent. Queen Victoria had no recollection of her father who, during her infancy, had died penniless of pleurisy at a watering place, exclaiming: 'Do not forget me!' Nor was she greatly attached to her mother, Victoria, Duchess of Kent, who had schooled her harshly, kept her in isolation, and who had a soiled reputation on account of alleged misconduct with the Comptroller of her Household. Prince Albert numbered amongst his ancestors sovereigns named 'The Wise', 'The Pious' and 'The Magnanimous', but his father could have been justly named 'The Satyr'. His ill-hidden infidelities had moved his much younger wife to solace herself with another, and Prince Albert had been five when his mother was first separated and then divorced and went off to Paris to live with her lover. None the less the boy had had a reasonably happy childhood. Now, both were twenty-four years of age; she the elder by three months; they had been married for three years and they had three children of their own.

Queen Victoria was 5 feet tall, already showing traces of embonpoint, but neither these defects nor her sloping chin and slightly protuberant eyes lessened her physical attractions. Her hair shone, was parted in the centre and looped in side ringlets, and her complexion was good. Her irises were a bright light blue and her mouth sensitive to show moods and appetites. Her smile was rare but radiant. Prince Albert, too, was not tall, about 5 feet 7 inches, but, by all other standards, undoubtedly a handsome man. His figure was trim; he wore his blond hair fashionably long and had sufficient but not abundant side whiskers and a moustache. His dreamy eyes and the colour of his skin gave him a porcelain, delicate look. He held himself well.

The fate of these two had been chiefly schemed by one of their Coburg uncles, Leopold, first King of the Belgians, something of a fop with the old-fashioned habit of wearing a wig and high heels and raddling his cheeks, but with nothing foppish about his management of affairs. From the first he had seen great advantages to be gained by a marriage between Coburg and Great Britain and had worked with patience and astuteness to bring it about. His chief assistant in this was a man whom he had trusted for many years. Baron Stockmar was his physician, his political adviser, his friend, even on one occasion his procurer, and, in the course of time, he had become counsellor to many of the crowned heads of Europe. He was virtually Merlin at Queen Victoria's Court, with his own apartments at Windsor, the adviser who never failed either the Queen or her husband, and who was the arbiter in their quarrels.

Inevitably in the early stages the marriage had passed through crises. There had been clashes of temperament because the Prince could not be master in his own house. There had been rows over nurseries, about who should be their closest advisers, about such small matters as seating arrangements at the Opening of Parliament and whether the royal band should be wind or string. Stockmar had guided them from his tower through family, political, and constitutional problems; not perhaps with faultless judgment but always with the best interests of the Queen and the Prince in mind. He was essential to them for the Queen got on with very few of her family, and Prince Albert was too distant from his own at Coburg. Members of their Households could be and were of great assistance but both leaned most upon advice from Uncle Leopold at the Laeken palace or from his deputy, Baron Stockmar.

Except for elderly Lord Melbourne who, as the Queen's Prime Minister had enjoyed both her confidence and a rather pleasant old man's springtime of affection for his sovereign, the British aristocracy had not much regard for either the Queen who was more than three-quarters German or for her wholly German consort. But this was no new thing. Patricians have very seldom made great courtiers. Nevertheless the great nobles did their duty and invited the sovereign and the prince to enjoy their hospitality on progresses through the countryside.

In many of the houses where they were guests the royal couple met with comforts that they found enviable. Being practical, they had asked themselves why they should not have equal comforts in their own homes. Thinking and speaking in German as they did, they were striving for the scarcely translatable word *Gemütlichkeit* that the Queen was to render as 'cosiness'.

At first sight it appears strange that this quality should evade them in the houses placed at their disposal. A more careful look shows another picture. There were many royal establishments; none in Wales, two in Ireland, one in Scotland, the rest in England. However, one was a garrison, another the seat of Parliament, another the Court to which foreign envoys were accredited, and the great majority were Grace and Favour houses. Five were available for use but two of these were unsuitable. Holyrood House was dark and mouldering in the smokier parts of Edinburgh, and the Lodge of Trinity College, Cambridge had the disadvantage in that the Master had to be given due notice to turn out if it was required. Therefore only three were really free, and none were comfortable. Buckingham Palace was in theory regularly maintained; in practice it was patched up from time to time. The Prince Regent's exotic Marine Pavilion at Brighton had been encroached on by building speculators. In Berkshire there was Windsor, a Gothic castle renovated by Wyattville, with a park sprinkled with Grace and Favour lodges, 'a castellated conglomeration' known as Fort Belvedere, a cottage orné, a Chinese fishing temple, and Frogmore House. Windsor certainly had grandeur but equally certainly it had considerable disadvantages. Privacy was virtually impossible. Plumbing was rudimentary and the stench of ill-placed cesspits and the polluted Thames scarcely to be endured in summertime. It was not a comfortable home. Disraeli, with his talent for description, called the Castle 'that temple of the winds'.

Both the Queen and the Prince preferred Claremont at Esher, a large house built originally by Clive of India and bought by the Crown in 1816. The Queen only had the use of it by the kindness of her Uncle Leopold. He had married as his first wife Princess Charlotte of Wales, and had a life interest in the estate as part of the marriage settlement. She even had to obtain his permission to have the conservatory roof raised for the sake of a growing palm tree. It was not easy to enjoy *Gemütlichkeit* in someone else's house.

The year before, in 1842, the Queen and the Prince had planned a visit to Belgium, but owing to Court mourning on the death in a carriage accident of the brother of the Queen of the Belgians, the tour had to be cancelled and a visit to the northern kingdom had been substituted. Holyrood House had not been used because of the risk of infectious diseases in the capital, but they had enjoyed their holiday north of the Border and, for the first time, a piper was added to the Queen's Household.* When, twenty-six years later the Queen wrote an account

* Commended by the Marquis of Breadalbane, MacKay, the Queen's Piper arrived at the English Court early in 1843, and though it might be considered curious for pibrochs to be skirled at Buckingham Palace, Windsor, Claremont and Brighton, it is worth noticing that the Queen's uncle, the Duke of Sussex, took on MacKay's brother to be his piper at Kensington Palace.

of the visit in *Leaves from the Journal of our Life in the Highlands* she was looking back with the partial eyes of one deeply in love with Scotland. At the time it was not much more than a pleasant excursion, and she made no objection when Lord Melbourne, in his dry, Whiggish way agreed that the country was picturesque and its history romantic, adding: 'There is nothing to detract from it, except the very high opinion that the Scotch themselves entertain of it.' She would not have permitted such criticism of the Scots to go undefended in later years.

Besides a piper at Court one other change followed the holiday in Scotland. It had taken three and a half days to sail north aboard the *Royal George* to Leith; only forty-eight hours to steam south 'on board a large and very fast steamer, the *Trident*, belonging to the General Steam Navigation Company'. The Queen was not a very good sailor, the Prince a distinctly bad one. Almost directly after their return, the Prime Minister, Sir Robert Peel agreed to urge upon the Admiralty the necessity of providing the Queen with a steam yacht. Seven months later, in April 1843, the *Victoria and Albert* was launched. The steamer was of 1049 tons, driven by paddles, commanded by the Queen's cousin, a natural son of William IV, Lord Adolphus Fitzclarence, and the officers and crew of the *Royal George* were transferred to man her.

By 1843 a network of railways that was to be the envy of Europe was spreading over the British Isles, and the royal couple had already made a journey by the Great Western Railway from Windsor to London. But, as yet, railroads had not caught the imagination of travellers. The Queen's new paddle-steamer with a fine turn of speed opened large vistas even to those who were poor sailors, and in the summer of 1843 the Queen and the Prince went cruising, using Brighton as their base, and were fortunate in their weather. First they went to the Isle of Wight, putting in at Cowes, and went on as far as Falmouth. Then they crossed the Channel to visit the King and Queen of the French. Their third cruise was to Belgium. Thence they sailed to the Port of London and took a train on to Windsor. Invigorated by what she called 'the sailor-gypsy life', the Queen confessed to her Uncle that the '*voyages* and *visits* have made me think Windsor and its daily occurrences very dull'.

Evidently she enjoyed and benefited from living by the sea, but less and less did she care for the Pavilion. The Royal Crescent with its statue of the Prince Regent before it* and the whole area about the Pavilion was being swallowed up by the town. There was no longer a view of the sea from any of the windows and though the gardens were undeni- ably pretty, and the stables and riding house magnificent, Brighton's loyal subjects stared in at their monarch. Moreover, the Queen felt

* Battered by the sea, the figure had lost an arm and was generally considered to be a statue of Lord Nelson.

overwhelmed by the extravagant ornamentation. In places like the Chinese Corridor where there were huge figures of fishermen in silk robes with lanterns instead of carp attached to their rods, *Gemütlichkeit* was quite out of the question.

On an October day they made their decision. Brighton should be given up as quickly as possible and they would find an alternative marine residence. Moreover, if possible, it should belong to them. Like any other couple with a growing family they wished for a home of their own. Once more Sir Robert Peel was applied to. He was asked to institute private inquiries about the possibility of finding a suitable seaside property. The Prime Minister wasted no time. That same month he proposed two. Both were on the Isle of Wight.

Chapter 2

Negotiations

The first name of the turbot-shaped island cut off from the mainland by the Solent and Spithead was Ynys yr Wyth, a mouthful which the Greeks rendered as Ouichthis, the Romans as Vectis, the Saxons as Whitland, and the English as Wight. It was inhabited from the early Stone Age, conquered in turn by the Romans, Jutes, West Saxons and Normans. In the early middle ages for about two hundred years it was an independent sovereign country. Then Isabella, the Lady of the Island, sold it to Edward I. In the Island's first royal residence, Carisbrooke Castle, Charles I was the prisoner of his Parliament, and his daughter, the Princess Elizabeth, died there.

Queen Victoria had known the island since 1831, when she had stayed in the mock medieval Norris Castle with her mother and two Württemberg cousins, and they were visited by the young Queen of Portugal who was given the messy and smelly gift of an album of pressed seaweeds. One of her chief memories was that the sea and the shore had infinite fascination. There was boating and slithering about in the water. There were pools to explore at low water for shells and starfish, urchins and hermits, weeds and anemones, shrimps, sea-cucumbers and gooseberry sea-squirts. Both then, and in 1833 when she revisited Norris Castle, Victoria had ridden or been driven to many parts of the island that had endless interest because, although only measuring roughly 23 miles by 13, it had a large variety of physical features and presented any number of landscapes and seascapes of different colours and forms. There were parklands and coverts, water-meadows, fields under plough and fallow, furze and undulating downs. There were steep cliffs, a few coves and wide stretches where the land ran gently down to the sea. There were slow-flowing rivers and brooks and, close to the southern tip, therapeutic springs gushed from the ground that were said to be as effective as the chalybeate waters of

Tunbridge, Cheltenham and Buxton.* Dusty lanes connected the little towns and villages. Hedges and woods sheltered shy green wood-peckers, wrynecks and black redstarts, and chattering grasshopper warblers that competed with the nightingales long after dusk. The insects and wild plants were equally plenteous and beautiful; and, amongst the cloud of butterflies, were brimstones, skippers, wood whites, silver-studded blues, and the Island's speciality found nowhere else in Britain, Glanville's fritillary. Everywhere the air was soft and sometimes had a taste of iodine.

The island that the Queen recalled from her childhood was still very lovely and quiet when in October 1843 her Prime Minister discovered that the Osborne estate formerly called Austerborne, near to East Cowes and Norris Castle, was being offered for sale for £30,000.

The name cannot have pleased her because it was at Osborne Lodge that her mother's Comptroller had stayed with his family whenever they had been at Norris Castle, and whether or not she believed there had been a liaison between them, she certainly had no liking for her mother's Comptroller.† She was carrying her fourth child and instinc-tively wished to settle, and she also wanted to please her husband who blazed with enthusiasm for the idea.

On their cruise that summer the Prince had been enchanted by the Isle of Wight and, with his penchant for associations, had declared that the seascapes reminded him of the environs of Naples.‡ The only draw-back was the island's enervating climate but Osborne was at the most bracing part, lying close to the northern tip. Otherwise it was a perfect situation for a family home. Moreover he was well aware of the advantages of living cut off from the mainland. The more difficult the Royal Family was to reach, the more privacy it would enjoy, a point Tiberius had noted more than eighteen hundred years before on retiring to Capri, his isle of imperial voluptuousness, and which Sir Robert Peel might have been wise to consider – both for his own convenience and that of his successors. But it is almost certain that one of Osborne's great attractions to the Prince lay in the fact that any alterations and improvements would be under his direct personal supervision, and he would have endless opportunities to employ his talents as an organizer,

---

* The spa at Sandrock has since been swept away in landslides.
† It is interesting to note that, when they took possession of the property, Osborne Lodge was demolished and Osborne Cottage built on the site. This was used as an 'overflow' house for many years, and after the Queen's death Princess Beatrice lived there until 1912 when she went to live in Carisbrooke Castle. Osborne Cottage is now an old people's home.
‡ In Scotland, the year before, he had noted that many of the Scots resembled Germans, that one Perthshire mountain reminded him of Switzerland and another of Thüringen, and that Perth 'put him in mind of the situation of Basle'.

already arduously tested by taking the Queen's complex financial affairs in hand, reorganizing the Royal Household, itemizing the royal collections, and by improving the financial state of the Duchy of Cornwall, the appanage of the Prince of Wales. Naturally he hoped that Parliament might contribute to the cost but, through his careful management, there was already quite sufficient in the Queen's Privy Purse to realize their ambition for a private home without having to go cap in hand to anyone.

By strange coincidence it was another Lady Isabella who was selling island property to the sovereign of England. Barrington Pope Blachford, owner of the Osborne estate, had married Lady Isabella, youngest daughter of the 3rd Duke of Grafton, and in 1816 left her a widow with a boy and a girl in their infancy. In 1840 Lady Isabella's son had died at the age of twenty-six; and this was the cause of her decision to move to London.

It has come to be generally accepted that Lady Isabella was difficult to handle and tiresome over the negotiations. The Blachford Papers suggest there might be another point of view. They show, too, that through his solicitor, Mr Edward White, the Prince was, on the Queen's behalf, not too proud to try to strike a bargain.

The original asking price for the estate was £30,000. Negotiations were opened on 27 February 1844 when the royal agents offered to rent the property for a year's tenancy for £1,000 with an option to purchase for £28,000 'including the furniture but not works of art, pictures etc., the offer being subject to inspections of the property by the Prince'.

The Prince wasted no time. He crossed from Portsmouth and found a charming Georgian house with 200 acres of lawns and parkland that stretched down to the sea. The stabling and offices were to the rear. From the front windows of the house there were superb views of Spithead. He declared himself thoroughly satisfied with the site.

A year's lease was drawn up, and presumably the matter was then made public because on 16 March the *Illustrated London News* published an article about Osborne. It pointed out: 'Considerable additions must be made to the building to accommodate a large establishment . . . The first and second floors contain sixteen bed and sitting-rooms; very inadequate accommodation for a royal suite.' This anticipated the Prince's argument that only further investment would make the proposition viable, and can scarcely have pleased Lady Isabella's agents because the demerits of the house were bound to constitute a bargaining point in the negotiations that lay ahead.

However, for the moment the matter had to be left. The Prince's father had died at the end of January; an event received with mixed feelings in England. Victoria dutifully wrote a lament to Uncle

Leopold, but she had small cause to care for her father-in-law. He had bullied her into giving him a substantial income, and she must have found his philanderings embarrassing. Prince Albert wept bitterly but was not at the funeral though later, after his inspection of Osborne, he went to visit his brother, the new reigning Duke and an even more scandalous philanderer than their father, to see to family affairs.

In the Prince's suite were his Swiss confidential valet, Cart, who had looked after him since his childhood, a man of such strength that he had once doused a blazing bookcase by beating it with a marble table, and a second personal attendant, Rudolf Löhlein, a Coburger who, by repute and by close physical resemblance, was a half-brother, being a by-blow of the dead Duke Ernest.★

The Queen expected a child in August and could not accompany her husband. It was, therefore, the first time they had been separated in their married life and they felt it keenly. Each gave private instructions to Charles Eastlake for a picture to be painted as a surprise for the other. Eastlake accepted both secret commissions and held his tongue. The Queen gave the Prince 'The Sisters'. The Prince's gift to the Queen was of a group of four cherubs bearing lilies and the legend 'Heil und Segen' above an incense pot. The separation also caused a flow of letters. The Queen wrote to the King of the Belgians: 'the *thought* of *such a* separation is quite dreadful.' The Prince wrote to the Queen from Dover Harbour on 28 March: 'I reiterate my entreaty, "Bear up!"'' And, later that same day from Ostend after a bad crossing: 'I kept my seat on one spot all the way with my eyes shut.'

In a fortnight the Prince was home again to face a crowded year: entertaining Mendelssohn, the Emperor of Russia, the King of Saxony and the King of the French; helping the Queen through her customary depression after the birth of Prince Alfred; allegedly postponing a royal visit to Dublin on account of ill-feeling about the imprisonment of the Irish leader O'Connell and substituting another visit to Scotland.

On this second holiday north of the Border, they took Blair Castle as it had already become the custom for Highland landowners to let their homes to sportsmen from the south. The Queen had her piper play beneath her window to greet each day, began her collection of cairngorms and Scotch pearls, and was exuberant in her praise of the inhabitants, the sport, the sublime scenery, and walks with her husband – 'so rural and romantic, so unlike our daily *Windsor* walk'. The Prince also

★ In *Leaves* The Queen wrote a long note on Löhlein who, after the Prince Consort's death, became her own personal attendant. She described his father as 'fifty years Förster at Füllbach, close to Coburg'. Her courtiers, and particularly Sir Henry Ponsonby, first Equerry to the Prince and afterwards her Private Secretary for many years, were convinced he was half-brother to the Prince.

enjoyed himself, writing to his widowed step-mother: 'We are all well and live a somewhat primitive, yet romantic, mountain life, that acts as a tonic to the nerves, and gladdens the heart . . . . '. Romance was the thing. The Royals, as they were called by their Household and servants, were so enthusiastic that allegedly the *Morning Post* reported: 'Her Majesty has expressed a desire to take a permanent residence in the Highlands' and Sir James Clark, her favourite physician, had been asked to 'collect statistical details'.

It seems strange to those who live in a less ample age that the idea of a home in Scotland might have been in the Queen's mind even before Osborne was bought. Undoubtedly she had decided Scotland was to figure in her future holidays. Charles Greville, the Clerk to her Privy Council, was of the opinion her gadding about showed she had inherited the mental weakness of her paternal grandfather, George III; an odd idea in view of the fact that patricians and their sovereigns have always been peripatetic. Later in life Prince Albert himself was to aver that 'monotony of place' was 'prejudicial to the nervous system' and he certainly would not have been averse to leasing a deer forest. But his chief preoccupation that autumn was Osborne. In July he had appointed Ludwig Gruner, overall designer of the interior of the mound pavilion in Buckingham Palace Gardens, as 'adviser in art' for the embellishment of their island home.

On 10 October the royal couple moved as tenants into Osborne House. The Queen was delighted. She was sanguine, believing that with a few additions and improvements it could be made perfect. 'So complete and snug', she wrote in her Journal on the 15th, adding: 'The rooms are small.' Smallness was just what she wanted; a perfect setting for *Gemütlichkeit*.

The Prince was more realistic and aware of the need to make enlargements. The kitchens especially would have to be rebuilt. For the moment their two pastrycooks were obliged to go down to Wheeler's, the baker and grocer at East Cowes, to make use of his oven. Nevertheless Albert also much enjoyed that first holiday in old Osborne House. He wrote to his brother: 'We have retired to a small house in the Isle of Wight which we shall most likely buy . . . so that it will then belong to us and not to the inquisitive and often impudent people.'

Then came a cold splash; no less than a memorandum from the very man who had found Osborne for them urging cautious re-consideration. Should the option to purchase be taken up when the lease fell in? It was a bad time for the nation. The 'Hungry Forties' was already an expression that meant something. He expressed the doubt if Parliament could be moved to assist.

The Prince replied that it was his intention to make the proposition

viable, not only by improving the poorly maintained agricultural hold-
ings on the estate but also by buying more farms to bring it to an
economic size. As for the house, he noted that with a few alterations
such as new kitchens, a servants' dormitory, and the addition of some
rooms, it could be made into 'a very suitable and comfortable residence
for the Queen and the children and part of the suite'.

Peel would not have missed the significance of that word 'part', but
he was fond of the Prince and had every confidence in his acumen. He
was prepared, he said, to co-operate in any way he could, though he still
thought it unwise to expect anything in the form of a Parliamentary
grant.* Lord Lincoln, then Commissioner of Woods and Forests,† also
offered the help of his department and instructed Edward Blore, Architect of Buckingham Palace, to do a design for the alterations. There
is evidence in the British Museum that Blore did begin a design but he
soon gave place to a London master-builder who was required to go
down to the Isle of Wight and survey the house in detail. At Christ-
mastide he made his report to the Queen and the Prince at Windsor.
Urgent repairs and alterations to the old house could be put in hand at
once but rather than make extensive additions to accommodate even a
modified Royal Household, it would be wiser and, in the end, less
costly to replace the house with a new building altogether.

The Prince and the Queen considered this. They went off to stay with
the Duke of Buckingham at Stowe and afterwards with the Duke of
Wellington at Strathfieldsaye. They were not anxious for such
splendour, but they did want their home on the island. To the Prince
the idea of supervising the construction of an entirely new building
with formal and informal gardens, plantations, avenues and parks, in
addition to the improvement of the farmlands must have been irresist-
ibly attractive. Eventually it was agreed that Brighton Pavilion be sold
with those of its contents not needed for other royal establishments and
the money put towards the repair and enlargement of Buckingham
Palace, and that the Osborne estate be the Queen's private property
beyond any sort of ministerial control.

On 3 January 1845 the Queen's agents inquired from Lady Isabella's
agents if a lower price recommended by the Queen's valuers would be
acceptable. Presumably it was not. A long silence then tested the nerve
of both parties. Unknown to Lady Isabella, the Queen and the Prince
had a very uncomfortable time at the Pavilion that February. The loyal
subjects of Sussex not only stared on this occasion; they also jostled.

---

* No public funds were asked for. The Queen's Privy Purse paid for her new Royal
Marine Residence.
† This later became a greater part of the Ministry of Works that in turn became the
Department of the Environment.

Prince Albert wrote to the Prime Minister: 'We are more disgusted with Brighton than ever.' But, wisely, they said nothing in public and affected an indifference to the issue at Osborne with such success that in the Household it was generally believed that the Queen was no longer interested. The bluff was well maintained. By 3 March Lady Isabella had come to the conclusion that the option would not be taken up. She instructed her agents to prepare a new estate rent list. Then, suddenly, ten days later, the royal agents announced that the Queen was no longer prepared to offer for the property, but would Lady Isabella kindly say what sum less than £28,000 she was prepared to accept. The Blachford agents did not care for this bazaar bargaining. They replied that £28,000 was already well below the original asking price of £30,000; the Queen must speak out; Lady Isabella's price was still £28,000. It had an effect. Three days passed. On 20 March, the Prince's Treasurer and Private Secretary wrote personally to Lady Isabella to say he was commanded by Her Majesty to offer £26,000. Evidently the Queen was very confident that the price would be accepted because before any agreement had been reached, she wrote to her Uncle Leopold:

> You will, I am sure, be pleased to hear we have succeeded in purchasing *Osborne* . . . It sounds so snug and nice to have a place of *one's own*, quiet and retired, and free from all Woods and Forests and other charming Departments who are really the plague of one's life.

She was hardly being fair to her Prime Minister or to Lord Lincoln, both of whom had helped with the negotiations; but she was right to presume that with certain compromises, her offer would do. The furniture was taken at valuation, the purchase was considered settled on 1 May, and the final account came to £27,814 18s. 5d. But the Prince was not yet finished. He wanted more land. He needed Barton Manor for the lodging of important visitors and members of the Household, and certain other properties that were owned by Winchester College and leased for the next seventeen years. Peel obligingly had a private Act of Parliament passed so that the Queen could take possession, and the Winchester property passed to her for £18,000 and a rent charge of £113 16s. od. to the College and 13s. 4d. annually to the Bishop of Winchester.

By the time the Prince had finished making the estate an economic size it ran south all the way from the small Norris Castle property to a piece of sloping ground named Mount Misery. He set about planning improvements and alterations. As ever he was tireless.

Chapter 3

The Napoleonic
Mr Cubitt

The fact that no architect was employed in the creation of Osborne House enraged, and still enrages over-sensitive members of that profession. It 'confirms the suspicion' wrote Professor Henry Russell Hitchcock in the first volume of his *Early Victorian Architecture in Britain* 'that the Royal family had no real respect for the profession'.

The Royal Institute of British Architects that conferred diplomas to associates and fellows had been founded in 1834, but there were plenty of practising architects, such as Edward Blore who did not possess diplomas. Blore was trained as an architectural and topographical draughtsman, a scale or two down to those concerned with professional status, but he was still sufficiently competent to design Abbotsford for Sir Walter Scott, carry out other important commissions, and end as the appointed architect of Buckingham Palace. Moreover the *Oxford Dictionary* has a wider conception of what an architect is than Professor Hitchcock. Its definitions include 'a Master-builder', 'one who designs and frames any complex structure', and 'a builder-up'. All have to be capable of drawing up plans and general supervision of the work. To go so far as to accept John Ruskin's definition: 'No person who is not a great painter or sculptor *can* be an *architect*' would exclude a very large number of 'qualified' architects. Evidently the Prince's critics failed to notice that he did, in fact, have a high regard for the profession, but most if not all of the prominent architects of the day were already employed by the very Commission of Woods and Forests from which the Queen was so anxious to escape. They also overlooked the equally valid fact that the Prince himself, though necessarily an amateur, had a very wide knowledge of building construction, and his own collections and his appreciation of the royal collections showed that though, like everyone, he had blindspots, he was a man of taste. Furthermore, Thomas Cubitt, the man employed to build Osborne, was no common or garden builder. He was a very remarkable master-builder.

Cubitt was from Norfolk and had the wry sense of humour and

non-belligerent contrariness that has always marked Norfolk 'dumplings'. He married, fathered a family, and provided for them more than handsomely. His immense will that, at the time he drew it up, was the longest ever written, shows that he expected to be remembered as the founder of a large landed estate rather than by his work. In this he was disappointed. He passed through all the stages of his trade, as apprentice, journey-man and master, and his qualifications were more substantial than any degree or diploma. They included the draining of a sizeable boggy tract behind Buckingham Palace and laying out what is now recognized as one of the more splendid parts of London. It was first nicknamed for him Cubittopolis, then became Belgravia, and brought him a fortune as it did the principal landowner, the Marquis of Westminister. Later, amongst other enterprises, there was his development of Clapham and Pimlico, and, after his fine work at Osborne, he assisted the government in the sale of the Brighton Pavilion and the renovation of Buckingham Palace. In fact, his independent advice was frequently sought by the Commission of Woods and Forests and he gave evidence to many Parliamentary bodies. To describe such a man as 'a mere builder' was contentious. He was unique, a phenomenon of his trade, a master-builder and imaginative engineer whose schemes were for the improvement of whole areas rather than single buildings, and he was prepared to undertake all the work of construction not farm out parts of it to sub-contractors. Therefore he had in his employ a wide range of experts from glaziers to paper-hangers, and he had his own works at Thames Bank as a central repository for everything used in the trade.

As a man he was much liked by his employers and, more unusual at that time, by his employees. He was even liked by his competitors who could not fail to respect his position that far outranked theirs. They presented him with his portrait and a testimonial about the integrity of his character and the exceptional standard of his work. He was an extrovert; amiable and kindly until old age and increasing illness made him impatient and drove away his smile. At the time Prince Albert decided to commission him to attend to old Osborne House and afterwards build a new one, Cubitt was in his prime, eager to make original experiments in the improvement of building construction, willing to co-operate with other people's ideas, so dependable that his estimates and timetables could be entirely relied upon, a brilliant organizer who could phase the building so that at no time was the Royal Family prevented from being at Osborne, brisk and short of stature with unlimited ideas and energy and apparently imperturbable. The Queen and the Prince took at once to the Napoleonic Mr Cubitt.

The master-builder's reputation was already familiar to the Prince but they were also drawn together by other considerations. On the Queen's marriage her mother had gone to live for a time at Ingestre House, in the heart of 'Cubittopolis'.* And on the rare occasions when George Anson, the Prince's Private Secretary, could get away from Court, he lived in a Cubitt house. Though on first coming to England he had objected to having his own Private Secretary being chosen for him, the Prince had become devoted to Anson. Both enjoyed systematic hard work, chess, billiards, shooting, coursing with greyhounds, and hunting. They spent a great deal of time together and it has been claimed that Anson and Sir Robert Peel were the Prince's only intimate English friends. Therefore if Anson spoke warmly of the comforts of his house in Belgravia, the Prince was impressed. Indeed it was written into the specification for the building of the Pavilion at Osborne that it should 'be done with the best materials in a workmanlike manner and not inferior to the house belonging to Mr Anson in Eaton Place'.

The Prince wasted no time. When, on 29 March, 1845 the Queen's agents and the Queen agreed that the purchase should be considered settled on 1 May, he at once sent for the master-builder. He and Cubitt then went over Osborne House and Barton Manor and decided on urgent work that could be put in hand immediately. This was to include the building of a large modern kitchen and scullery; repairing the stables and providing servants' rooms above them; and, in the house, installing a water-closet and remaking some rooms with partition walls. Cubitt's men actually started work within the week. The Prince meanwhile visited the works at Thames Bank, selected wallpapers for the re-decoration of old Osborne, and discussed his plans with Cubitt in greater detail. He was anxious that the new Royal Marine Residence should suit both the soft outlines of the Isle of Wight and the changing texture of the sea. It must blend in with its surroundings and ultimately, by skilful planting, become an integral part of the scene. It was a tribute to his farsightedness that neither of his creations came to perfection in his short lifetime, nor until long after when the hardwood plantings had matured. Cubitt agreed with this policy of harmony and showed his patron Albert Gate Mansions, a complex that he had recently completed. That, and the Neapolitan sea-scapes of the Solent and Spithead helped to decide the general style of the new Osborne. It has been called 'Italianate', but though it had Italian aspects, it was really a happy marriage of 'Cubitt style' and the Prince's idea of a comfortable and fitting country house beside the sea. They created what was really an 'Osborne style' and many little 'Osbornes' proliferated over the countryside in the years that followed.

* Now 3, Belgrave Square, this house was leased by the late Duke and Duchess of Kent from 1934 until the Second World War.

Chapter 4

'How my beloved Albert enjoys it all'

To Lady Isabella Blachford Osborne had probably become a place of sorrow. Having sold it, she left the Isle of Wight for her London house and never returned. To the Queen and her husband although the house was small, and though they were instantly subjected to the discomforts of re-decoration, repairs and building by the energetic master-builder, it was essentially a family home, and for many years it was a place of peace and joy.

In the whirl of activity that followed their taking possession in May, 1845 the Queen was radiantly happy. She was touched by her warm welcome on the Island. One of the most widely-read of all the studies of the modern Royal Family published in the year of Queen Elizabeth II's Silver Jubilee contained a considerable number of errors, amongst them the absurd contention that Queen Victoria was engrossed by her 'public image'. Nothing could be further from the truth. As Queen Regnant she believed herself entirely apart, simply the Queen. She no more considered what people thought of her than did the Pennine Chain. Yet she did like neighbourliness and she appreciated the courtesy of the islanders in founding the Royal Victoria Yacht Club on her birthday, 24 May, to mark her arrival amongst them.* And her family was equally happy, especially the Prince who had seldom been so busy. Sometimes, in the past, the Queen had been apt to be overpossessive of his time, but she was not so on this occasion. She wrote in her Journal: 'It does my heart good to see how my beloved Albert enjoys it all.'

In fact, the Prince was not ecstatically rushing, Bunthorne-like, round Osborne thinking of nothing but improvements. His ordered life could not vary a great deal. Besides his exacting routine with state papers as unofficial Private Secretary to the Queen, he was also planning to take

* This was generally known as the Red Squadron as it flew the Red Ensign. The Royal Southern Yacht Club at Southampton flew the Blue Ensign; the Royal Yacht Squadron at Cowes, the White.

her to Coburg that summer on her first visit to Germany; preparing a
Concert of Ancient Music in London for which he had made himself
responsible; noting the progress after trials of a new screw-driven
tender to the Royal Yacht that travelled at 15 knots; and reporting to
Baron Stockmar: 'Osborne is bought, and with some adjoining farms,
which we have also bought, makes a domain of 1,500 acres in a ring
fence. The weather is frightfully cold and disagreeable, still both crops
and grass promise well.' In many ways the Prince was diffident and
Cubitt's engaging manner reassured him. They fully agreed about the
main works. Barton Manor, a much larger building than Osborne, was
a major priority because half its fifty-seven rooms were uninhabitable
and space was needed for guests and members of the Household. Cubitt
was to deal with it as quickly as possible without altering the Eliza-
bethan character of the house, and make special bricks to match the
originals. Restoration work was not in his line, but he was adaptable.
He was also to deal with the estate cottages and lodges that stood in need
of repair. And he gave practical advice with regard to the Prince's ideas
for the new building; that a wing be latched to the old house by a loggia
or covered corridor so that both could be used simultaneously, the new
part for the Royal Family, the old house for special guests and the ladies
of the Household, both served by Cubitt's new kitchens, stables and
servants' quarters.

The new part was to be symmetric with rooms arranged round a
grand staircase. The basement should house a heating apparatus, stores
and other necessary offices. The state apartments would be on the
ground floor. They would not be stately in the ordinary sense, merely
three large rooms, inter-connected in a U-shape; a billiard-room for the
gentlemen, a drawing-room for the Queen and her ladies, and a large
dining-room. Each room should give on to a hallway, but each should
also be loosely connected. The first two were separated only by pillars
so that two gentlemen could be seated during a game of billiards even
though the Queen was in hearing round the corner in the drawing-
room. Between the drawing-room and the dining-room was a partition
wall with wide and high double doors that were to be frequently left
open. On the first floor should be a governess's sitting-room and the
schoolroom so that a parental eye could be kept on progress, then the
Prince's and the Queen's apartments. Both were to have bathrooms, a
most unusual feature in royal establishments. The Prince's contained
cupboard space, a water-closet and a copper bath painted in imitation of
veined, white marble, and was to be next to his dressing- and sitting-
room, a repository for his clothes with a day bed, a desk for work, a
bookcase, and a pedal harmonium. This was to lead directly into the
Queen's sitting-room shared by them both for work and leisure, and it

was to have a shaded balcony outside the windows. The Queen's dressing-room should be beyond and contain a chest of drawers, a dressing table, a cheval looking-glass, and a bath exactly like the Prince's. In the same wall-space as the recess, and connected to both her dressing-room and her bedroom, should be a water-closet. On the floor above it was intended there should be day- and night-nurseries, and all the necessary rooms for young children and their attendants. The roof should be flat – paving stones laid on asphalt and leaded – and para-peted with a central chimney stack; and, in the south-west, a two-storied flag tower. In design it was to suggest an Italian *campanile* but its purpose was to carry the Royal Standard on a flagpole at the tower centre whenever the Queen was in residence. From the beginning the new building was named the Pavilion.

The Prince's plans were sketched out, sent up to Cubitt's draughts-men, returned for comment and modification, and a final draft sent back for copying.

Cubitt's management was breathtaking. He bustled, building his own brickworks about 3 miles from the site. He was a pioneer in pre-fabrication. Much of the material was made at Thames Bank in-cluding the casting of girders and most of the joinery. These were then shipped directly to Cowes. So were the dressed stones and slates for roof tanks from quarries. He was also ahead of his time in his com-prehensiveness. Ludwig Gruner had the loosest sort of general artistic direction. He would advise but not authorize like a sanctioning ar-chitect, and at this early stage he had virtually nothing to do. Apart from gilding and marbling work, the provision of furnishings, chan-deliers and encaustic tiles, Cubitt was prepared to provide and fix anything from sinks to lightning conductors. The baths and hot-water systems were not too great a matter for him, providing doormats and candle-boxes not too little. And he delighted the Prince by the care he took to make the Pavilion as fireproof as possible. The skirting 'boards' were to be cement. The wooden floors were laid on brick arches and iron girders. Bonds were of iron not wood. And, between each floor, there was an insulating layer of cockle shells that were both sound and fire-proof.

The master-builder's aim was to carry out the work as quickly as possible and indulge his patrons. The Queen had a great liking for the staircase at Claremont House. Therefore Cubitt had it copied exactly in the Pavilion at Osborne. The Prince had a knowledgeable interest in what was then called sanitation and more recently plumbing, and it was the subject of much discussion between them. Though water-closets had long been in existence very few were attached to any sort of drainage system. Mostly they were portable and required emptying.

Even the earth-closet had yet to be invented by an ingenious clergyman in 1860, and the optimus, syphonic and washdown closets were things of the distant future.* The knowledge of traps and cesspools was limited but the Prince was highly informed about sewage systems and had ideas for using effluent for agricultural purposes that greatly interested the builder. These, however, were at the theoretical stage and, for the present, a long drain was made from tiles baked on the estate that ran far out to sea beyond the low-tide mark. When the Prince's theories about the utilization of matured sewage reached the practical stage, the long drain fell into desuetude, but it was so well constructed that, were it necessary, it could, with some minor repairs, be put into use again today.

Caen stone, used for some of the great medieval monasteries and cathedrals had that year come back into fashion, and was being recommended by most architects. But Cubitt mistrusted it. Shrewdly he accepted the warning that the modern stone was not from the same quarries as the medieval stone and much softer. Under his advice the Prince ordered that the more costly Portland stone be used, but only for the loggia that joined the old house to the Pavilion, for the flooring of the ground-floor passages, the grand stairway, and the stone roof. Elsewhere a cement stucco, coloured by pigments poured into the mix, took the place of stone. Again, under the master-builder's advice, the Prince ordered other necessary economies. Modern plate glass should be used only in the principal rooms. Deal would do for most of the building, though oak and mahogany were contracted for in the state rooms. Instead of marble, cast-iron pillars should be plastered, the last layer a hard surface of Keen's cement rendered shiny from the plasterer's trowel, then painted with several coats of base colour, expertly marbled and finally varnished. This also served quite adequately for walls, plinths and, in fact, was so well done that to sight and touch only a true expert would know the difference.

Prince Albert has never been a hero to the British, but the charge that he showed parsimony in using artificial materials has made his detractors seem ludicrous. The Privy Purse was by no means bottomless. Moreover these practices were common at the time, much used by Thomas Cubitt, and the Prince's critics failed to take into account the number of unusual extras that were included to make the house just that much more comfortable.

It was due to the Prince that there were sufficient properly drained

* The primitive plumbing of the century is underlined by the fact that when Erskine Childers won a Clerkship to the House of Commons in 1893 he found that in the Palace of Westminster he and his colleagues were expected to use chamber pots embossed with the royal coat of arms.

water-closets in the final building. He also appreciated that although each room had its fireplace, scuttle, fender and fire-irons, no sizeable room could be kept warm, even with careful screening and window-hangings, if most of the heat roared up the chimney. Cubitt had a careful arrangement so that all the flues, lined or parged, as the custom was, with fresh cowmanure and mortar, led to the minimum of concealed chimney stacks, and that they drew well but not too well. Yet this was still insufficient for a large house in an exposed position. A secondary system was an extravagance but desirable. Therefore the Prince and Cubitt decided on a warm air apparatus. It was to operate from four-inch iron pipes slung between the basement ceiling and ground floor, filled with warm water from a boiler. The hot air rose from the pipes up wall flues to warm the floors of specially selected rooms and the corridors through brass grilles. As a further protection, each room was to have hinged wooden shutters that folded back into reveals during the day; and, in the state drawing-room the windows had moveable protectors with reflecting looking-glasses that pulled out from the wall on a metal track to prevent any possibility of draught. Yet another noteworthy extra and a very rare one, was the insertion of a brass lever into the window frames that could be used to pinch the two sashes together and prevent rattling in gusty winds. These, like the imaginative plumbing and other improvements, were regarded by the Prince as necessities to comfort rather than luxuries.

In many respects Osborne was unique amongst the English country houses of the 1840s.

Chapter 5

Bricks and mortar

Soon after formally taking possession of the property on 1 May, 1845 the foundations were dug. On 23 June the foundation stone was laid by the Queen. First she placed a glass box containing a record of the event and coins of that year in a hole in the ground. This she and her husband and their two eldest children cemented over and a large stone was lowered from a gyn to be tapped by all present. Cubitt's organization buzzed like a beehive. By September Barton Manor was largely repaired, a porter's lodge had been built, and the Pavilion only lacked a roof and the flag-tower.

A Privy Council was held at old Osborne House that month and the Clerk, Charles Greville, who was not much of an admirer of his royal mistress, made a note on the house: 'It was very ugly.' He took comfort in the fact that, though a great deal of money was being spent, it was not the nation's, and averred the Prince was unpopular locally because he had culled the Osborne herd of deer. Doubtless he was right. Prince Albert was never popular save with those who knew him well, and as a farmer trying to put a large run-down estate in order, it is unlikely that his culling was appreciated by the local poachers. At all events, by this time the Prince had come to the conclusion that, satisfactory as the Pavilion was, much more building was required.

The Queen always considered a Privy Councillorship as almost the equivalent of a peerage and the dignity of her Council required more than the little drawing-room of old Osborne. The Prince realized that a suitable Council Room would have to be built. He also appreciated that the two Households could not continue to camp out, as it were, in lodges and scattered places. The gentlemen would do very well at Barton, and they did until the end; but they must dine together when not at the Queen's dinner and the ladies must all be accommodated under one roof. There was also the question of visitors; and, of course, his mother-in-law.

Once a formidable lady, the Duchess of Kent had not led the happiest
of lives. At seventeen she married a childless widower twenty-four
years her senior who died at a critical time in the Napoleonic wars
leaving her with two children and the regency of a German pumper-
nickel court. Her second husband, the martinetish, penniless Duke of
Kent, was also older than she by nineteen years, passionately attached
to song-birds and musical devices, who gave her Victoria, then
widowed her a second time in a strange land to which she never became
accustomed and where, for years, she was at the centre of uproar. The
clamour had died, her Comptroller and alleged lover had been
pensioned off, and, as they became vacant, she was given the use of
Frogmore House and Clarence House in St James's. By her sixtieth
year, largely due to the patient persuasion of her son-in-law, she and
Victoria had become partially reconciled. She spoke so gutturally that
few could understand her, but those who did found her increasingly
amiable. It was in the natural order of things that she ought to visit
Osborne to see her grandchildren from time to time. But where could
she be put? She had not been considered when the Pavilion was planned. As the Queen's mother she could not be put in a lodge or a
farmhouse. She would have to have suitable accommodation in the new
building.

The Prince and Thomas Cubitt put their heads together. There was
no question of stopping work on estate restorations, nor of spoiling any
of the work already done, and the Pavilion must be left available for the
use of the Royal Family as much as possible during the new building
work. This would demand precise timing and systematic planning and
costing. Cubitt undertook to do all this.

The general plan was that the corridor or loggia that connected the
old Osborne House with the Pavilion should be extended by about 100
feet to the south-east. This would be glazed and make a long and wide
entrance hall, and above it would be a second open loggia. This should
form the base of two large wings; one, the Main Wing, sited roughly
where old Osborne House stood; the other, at least 50 feet behind,
named the Household Wing. The latter should be built first so that old
Osborne House and the Pavilion could continue to be used as a unit
until everything was ready for building the Main Wing. There should
be separate entrances so that the Pavilion always remained a family
establishment separate from the two new wings.

It was not without significance that at the farthest end of the
ground-floor of the Main Wing, apartments were designated for the
Duchess of Kent. In the end it turned out that, from her boudoir to the
door of the dining-room in the Pavilion, the Duchess had to walk
exactly 282 feet, that is, more than the length of four cricket pitches and

as long as some cathedrals. At such a distance she could enjoy independence and would not often intervene in the lives of her daughter and her grandchildren.

In November 1845 the Prince and Gruner and Cubitt held consultations about decorations and ornaments and furnishings. Surprisingly, in view of the later royal obsession with antlers, the Prince refused the offer of some horn furniture from his brother that same month.

In December the royal family was settled, or squashed, in old Osborne House, watching their new home being made by Cubitt's men, when a crisis overtook them.

All over Britain there had been disastrous harvests. The Irish, almost wholly dependent on horse potatoes grown the easy way on a raised bed, lost their entire maincrop and were threatened with famine. Peel wished to open the ports to foreign grain. His own party, protectors of British farmers against foreign interests, would not support him. He arrived at Osborne and resigned as Prime Minister. Overwrought at the thought of a change the Queen tactfully informed old Lord Melbourne that had he been in better health she would have sent for him. He confessed he had 'such a horror of the sea' that crossing from the mainland to Cowes was tantamount to a voyage across the Atlantic. His successor in the Whig leadership, Lord John Russell, had to be invited to form a government. Russell consulted his colleagues. On 19 December, knowing he had Peel in a vice, he told the Queen he could not form a ministry. She turned once more to Peel. It was political suicide but he felt obliged to continue in office. He announced the repeal of the corn laws to save the Irish and was cheered by the opposition. Up in the gallery, for the first time in his life, was Prince Albert to show his support of Peel. It was also the last time. The Tories were adamant that he keep his nose out of Parliament. The Queen, carrying her fifth child, was beside herself. The Prince soothed her and took measures with Cubitt to lessen the distress of unemployment on the island. They agreed that the building of some of the less essential lodges and cottages and outbuildings should come at a later stage in the programme so that local labourers would still have work when Cubitt's men had gone home. It now became the Prince's policy not to be in too great a haste about inessentials on the estate, to keep the work force of islanders as steady as possible, and temporarily turn them off when they could easily find work elsewhere at the hay and corn and potato harvests.

On 1 March, 1846 Thomas Cubitt took his patrons round the Pavilion. Already the ceilings and the Claremont staircase were in and he promised that, given good weather, the decorating, finishing and furnishing would be completed by the end of the summer. They were enchanted at the anticipation. But, though always busy with Osborne, the Prince was still determined that the worst features of Buckingham Palace be put right. It had been brought to his notice that a huge cesspool, planned to collect all the sewage of the metropolis, had been sited only 800 yards from the Palace. He strongly objected.

On 25 May, the day after the Queen's twenty-seventh birthday, she gave birth to her fifth child and third daughter, Helena. She recovered quickly and safely and scarcely had any of her usual post-natal depression. There were things to worry about, to be sure. Guests had proposed themselves for Osborne, amongst them her mother and her Aunt Louise, Queen of the Belgians with her intimate Lady-in-Waiting, Madame Vilain XIV.* This would make a press and Queen Adelaide and the Princess of Prussia were to be neighbours at Norris Castle and would have to be invited for luncheon or dinner. Moreover the prospect of losing Sir Robert as her Prime Minister was a daily threat. But not even these prospects daunted her. On 8 June she wrote in her Journal: 'Really when one is so happy & blessed in one's home life, as I am, Politics (provided my Country is safe) must take only a 2nd place.' And at Windsor for Ascot, just before leaving for Osborne, she livened up a ball by suddenly commanding that everyone present should join in the Sir Roger de Coverley. From the Queen's mother to the youngest Maid of Honour, all had to obey. 'The *pousette* in which they went round,' wrote Sarah, the Dowager Lady Lyttelton to her daughter, 'was too excellent as fun.'

Lady Lyttelton was Governess to the royal children; that is, she looked after their diet and health and superintended the nurseries and nurses, and the schoolroom and governesses; and she had great influence. She was an estimable widow with some odd relations. Lord Lucan, who was to be blamed for the loss of the Light Brigade at Balaclava, was her cousin. So was Lord Melbourne's wife who became Byron's mistress and then went mad. Her father was an amiable peer, the 3rd Earl Spencer; her mother a great beauty, but eccentric and bad tempered. Of her four brothers, one was a statesman, two were admirals, and the youngest threw aside the family living and became a Roman monk. As a young lady she had enjoyed spending the summer at fashionable Ryde on the Isle of Wight, and detested going to Brighton for the season there – 'nasty place.' She had married early, brought up five children, and after a year of widowhood had been appointed one of the Queen's Ladies of the Bedchamber. At Court she had become everyone's favourite, and was chosen to restore order when the royal nurseries got out of hand and there were emotional

---

* This curious name came into being through the choice of a certain M. Vilain during the reign of Louis XIV. On being offered a reward for services to the crown, he asked for no more than permission to add the same numeral as the King's to his surname.

scenes between physicians, nurses, nursery footmen, governesses and the royal parents. Even Baron Stockmar had failed in that area. Lady Lyttelton had courageously accepted the appointment, discharged the more unsatisfactory nursemaids, and from the moment of her arrival in the nurseries she showed a calmness that soothed away all troubles. Imperturbable, a woman of great common sense, by disposition kindly but firm, she was respected by the governesses under her super-intendence and dearly loved by her charges who nicknamed her 'Laddle'.

After a gap of thirty-eight years it must have been a great pleasure and seemed an extraordinary coincidence to her to be intimately connected with a move from the Brighton she had never cared for to the Isle of Wight she loved. Unlike the Clerk to the Privy Council, she approved of the Pavilion at Osborne. 'It seems to please all the people who see it: John Bulls and Jack Tars. It was a good notion of Her Majesty.'

She did not always approve. At the not-admitted age of fifty-five, who, in her lifetime, had seen the fashionable hour for dinner move from three in the afternoon to half-past eight at night, she felt she had the right to disagree occasionally with the young Queen and the young Prince. For example, she strongly objected to his coursing parties – for he took every opportunity to course his greyhounds after hares and expected everyone to go with him. And she begged to differ when he told his children they might pray sitting, like Presbyterian Scots or German Lutherans. Their Governess decreed that, as members of the Established Church, they should kneel.

But Lady Lyttelton's influence was by no means confined to the nurseries and schoolroom. She was the centre of the family, a con-fidante of the Queen to whom she acted almost as a permanent extra Lady of the Bedchamber, and the friend of the members of the House-hold in waiting. In her letters she described many aspects of life at Osborne from the summer of 1846. Being personally acquainted with the royal visitors who crammed into old Osborne House she was able to help the Queen entertain them. The Queen of the Belgians was her great friend, so was Madame Vilain XIV. She also helped entertain the Queen Dowager and the Princess of Prussia while deploring the stiff protocol that was inescapable when Prussians were about. Their visits she complained, were 'always the cause of lame legs and worn-out spirits to all officials past thirty'. She tried to play Blind Hookey with the Duchess of Kent for penny stakes, but not with much success. From her letters it is clear she got on very well with George Anson, and, on a walk to Whippingham Church one Sunday, she listened to and ap-proved of the Prince's plans for his labour force of Islanders. Most certainly she would have approved of the open-air dinner followed by

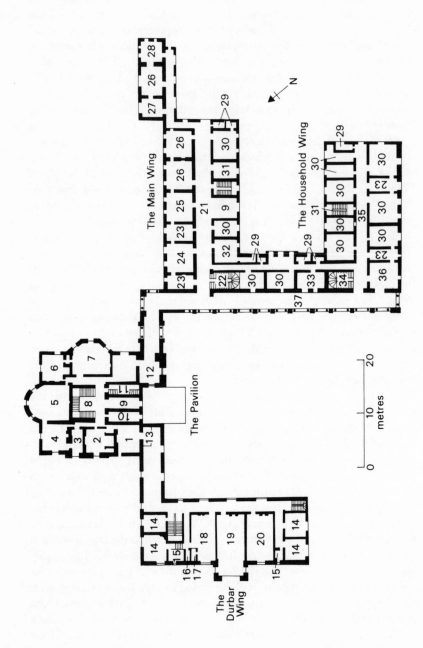

Key

The Pavilion
1 Governess's room (until Durbar Wing built)
2 Schoolroom
3 The Prince's bathroom and WC
4 The Prince's dressing-room
5 The Queen's sitting-room
6 The Queen's bathroom and dressing-room
7 The Queen's bedroom
8 The grand staircase
9 Vestibule
10 Page's bedroom
11 Service staircase
12 The flag tower
13 The Queen's lift

The Durbar Wing
14 Bedrooms
15 Bathrooms
16 WC
17 Bath in recess
18 Bedroom
19 Drawing-room
20 Dining-room

33 Master of the
    Household's bedroom
34 Principal stairs
35 Ladies' corridor
36 Household drawing-room
37 Arcade

The Main Wing and the Household Wing
21 Princesses' corridor
22 Principal staircase
23 Dressing-rooms
24 Bedroom ⎫ used by the elder Princesses
25 Sitting-room ⎭
26 Bedrooms ⎫ for visitors and sometimes
27 Dressing-room ⎭ the Prince of Wales
28 Clock tower
29 WCs
30 Bedrooms
31 Servants' stairs
32 Bedroom (once used as a studio)

1 A simplified plan of the first floor at Osborne House after the Durbar Wing had been added

27

dancing and games given to all the workmen and their families connected with the building of the house and the running of the estate.
Everyone enjoyed it and, as the Prince put it: '*Not the slightest irregularity*
occurred.'

Lady Lyttelton painted lively word pictures:

> Patches of children, each attended by their scarlet footmen, shining in
> the distance – Mr Anson escorting Lady Jocelyn across the park with
> her two babies. The Prince very busy with the builders. The
> equerries charging about. . . . I have been out on a pleasant stroll
> about the brick and mortar heaps, and then into the flower garden,
> and there I saw the children burst out of the house after tea in great
> joy.

She wrote of the Bishop of Oxford interesting the Queen in astronom-
ical subjects, of the Queen '*préoccupée*, but says not a syllable' when the
inevitable happened and Sir Robert Peel lost office. When the Prime
Minister came to hand over his seals of office Lady Lyttelton was down
at the beach with the children, but she felt deeply for the young Queen.
'Oh! for a woman to have such things to manage and to stand!' The
elder children accompanied their parents on a cruise to Cornwall and
the Channel Islands, Lady Lyttelton fretted for their return: 'The
children get so petted and neglected and irregular and idle . . . that it
takes long to recover.' When they did arrive safely home again, there
was the excitement of moving from old Osborne House into Thomas
Cubitt's new building.

The Pavilion was finally ready for occupation in September 1846.
The Queen wrote a description in her Journal ending:

> All is so convenient, spacious and well carried out. Mr Cubitt has
> done it admirably. He is such an honest, kind, good man. It seems to
> be like a dream to be here now in our house, of which we laid the first
> stone only 15 months ago.

The achievement did have a dream-like quality. Cubitt and the
Prince between them had thought of everything from the brass picture-
rails for the latter's considerable collection of paintings to the twin
writing-tables that stood side by side in the Queen's private sitting-
room. These were for work and the tops of the tables were exactly
level. However, to allow for the Prince's greater height, his table had
exactly three-quarters of an inch extra knee room. To the right of the
Queen's table, and a little below the edge to demonstrate that she was
the Sovereign, were three bell pulls that resembled organ stops having
porcelain ends labelled in black gothic script. The nearest read 'Wardrobe', the middle 'Page', the third to the right remained blank. With

these she could summon one of her dressers or the Page of the Presence on duty.

The house was still drying-out, though Cubitt had had the furnace working and fires burning for weeks, therefore it was not elaborately decorated; but the furnishings were complete and in the billiard-room was a table and cue-stand designed by the Prince; both made of slate enamelled in imitation of marble. In a few years this particular material, made by George Eugene Magnus of Pimlico, was to become highly fashionable. The family was happy to move in even though technically the Pavilion was still 'under builder's finish'.

There is no record of when precisely the Royal Standard was first run up on the Flag Tower. Perhaps the move was a gradual process. The Queen in her Journal dated the entry 14 September. The date inscribed on her new bed was the same. Lady Lyttelton dated her description 16 September and wrote:

> Our first night in this new house is well past. Nobody caught cold or smelt paint and it was a most amusing event coming here. Everything in the house is quite new, and the dining-room looked very handsome. The windows, lighted by the brilliant lamps in the rooms, must have been seen far out at sea.

At the conclusion of that first dinner all at the Queen's table rose to drink the royal couple's health; and the Prince responded with a house-warming psalm of Luther's. On the 17th the Prince led Lady Lyttelton outside and begged her to plant a Deodar Cedar from the Himalaya, thenceforth to be called the Lady Lyttelton Tree.

In December, when the Royal Family returned to the island, Cubitt at last produced the detailed plans of the Household and Main Wings and a specification on which he had based an estimate. His men were busy clearing the site for the Household Wing. This was sited next to the new kitchens and stable court and directly behind the old house so that only a small corner of the house had to be knocked down and it could still be used until the Household Wing was built.

Winterhalter was then painting a huge and beautiful picture of the royal family, the Queen and the Prince seated on a sofa, the children dressed formally, as the fashion was, so that it was difficult to tell the boys from the girls. Informally the princes often wore sailor-suits of the sloppy Jack Tar variety. This family portrait was to hang on the largest wall of the dining-room.

The Pavilion was drying out but there were a few defects. Lady Lyttelton found that the rising hot air of the heating apparatus lost too much heat on its way to her room. Cubitt worried and, anxious to please, got himself into a fluster. 'I will not neglect any hint of your ladyship's,' he assured her. 'I will go to the length of believing every word you say about it.'

It was a dreadful winter. The Irish endured a second and even worse famine. There was great hunger elsewhere. Tokens of the Court's willingness to share in the general suffering were badly received and unsuccessful.

Pessimistic by disposition, the Prince had seldom been so depressed. Even Osborne failed to cheer him, and he was appalled when a section of scaffolding collapsed on 10 March and four of Cubitt's men at work on the Household Wing were seriously injured, and one of them died.

The weather remained vile. That month he wrote to his stepmother that never had he seen so many ill people, and continued:

> The winter never seems coming to an end. We betook ourselves here in the hope of getting a breath of spring . . . but have found nothing but frost and a parching east wind; the day before yesterday for a change we had a foot of snow.

Possibly he had come to realize what the Queen never admitted in her long life, that Osborne was essentially a summer residence. Facing north as it did, and as yet unprotected from the prevailing wet south-westerlies, it could be a cheerless place in winter and early spring. However, April brought a change in the weather and in everyone's spirits. They celebrated Princess Alice's fourth birthday with great gusto. 'The whole family, indeed, appear to great advantage on birthdays', wrote Lady Lyttelton; though she saw trouble ahead from one of the birthday presents, a lamb named Milly all tricked out with ribbons and shells.

Thereafter the Prince still did not permit himself much freedom to enjoy Osborne, being too busy with Cubitt and his clerk of works, but his family was rapidly settling into an Osborne routine.

The Queen worked at her official despatch boxes and drove or rode out each day. Lady Lyttelton supervised the French governess, Madame Rollande, the German governess, Mademoiselle Grüner, and Miss Hildyard, the English governess who helped the children with history and geography and, her own absorbing interest, botany.

There were also diversions. The great opera singer Luigi Lablache who for years had been teaching singing to the Queen, was brought with his son by royal packet from Portsmouth for another lesson, the two speaking perfect English with the Queen, perfect Italian with Dr Meyer, the Prince's recently appointed librarian who was working on an enormous poem, and perfect Neapolitan with each other.* Then, to the

---

* In fact Lablache's father was a Frenchman, his mother an Irishwoman, and he had been born at Naples.

Prince's immense satisfaction, the well-known painter William Dyce began his large fresco on the wall of the grand staircase in the Pavilion. His subject was 'Neptune resigning his Empire to Britannia', a pretty compliment from the Prince to the Queen, but not everyone cared for the picture, and Lady Lyttelton certainly did not care for the painter: 'One of the least agreeable, and most dry and half-sneering mannered man I have ever met.'

On the following day the Queen took her first sea-bathe. The royal bathing-machine ran on rails down to the water and was already in position. The Queen entered by a door in the rear, allowed herself to be undressed and then dressed in a bathing-robe and a floppy hat, and went on to the half platform with five steps that led down into the sea. Round it were drapes of soft leather. She walked down the steps, her dresser rang a small ship's bell attached to the platform and, at this signal, the bathing attendant led the horse up the rails pulling the machine out of the water. The Sovereign of Great Britain and Ireland felt uncomfortably vulnerable. She walked about until she slipped and became thoroughly wet. Then she put her head under the water and came up gasping. After that she splashed about until she had had enough. At a signal the machine was lowered down into the water again and the dripping Queen emerged. Thereafter she never put her head underwater, nor attempted to swim, but she plunged about, as she described it in her Journal, after sponging her face with sea water.

Chapter 6

Two sides of the Cairngorms

Although so content and busy at Osborne the royal couple had not forgotten the attractions of Scotland. Early in 1847 a cruise was planned along the Welsh coast and past the Isle of Man to Scotland. On Wednesday, 11 August they left from Osborne Pier taking as their guest the Queen's half brother, Prince Charles of Leiningen, and their two elder children with Miss Hildyard to look after them. The *Victoria and Albert*, commanded by Lord Adolphus Fitzclarence, had four attending warships and the tender *Fairy*. On reaching the Clyde they transferred to the *Fairy* whilst the royal yacht made the long sea-voyage round the Mull of Kintyre. On their journey they called at Glasgow, Dumbarton, Rothsay where the Prince of Wales was cheered as their own Duke, and Inverary to be greeted by the Duke and Duchess of Argyll and their party. Amongst them was a little boy one day to be the Queen's son-in-law. In her Journal the Queen described him graphically as 'a dear, white, fat, fair little fellow with reddish hair'. They doubled back to the Crinan Canal, a waterway cut in 1801 to save the 85 mile voyage round the Mull of Kintyre, and then left the *Fairy* and boarded a decorated barge drawn by three horses ridden by postilions in scarlet. They passed through the eleven locks to reach the *Victoria and Albert* in the Sound of Jura. Visiting places of interest by barge from the royal yacht they eventually reached Fort William where they changed to carriages for the last part of their journey to Ardverikie, a house by wild Loch Laggan belonging to Lord Henry Bentinck that had been leased by Lord Abercorn.

It then began to rain.

The royal suite was not large but it proved too large for Ardverikie and there was something of a squash. It has never been made quite clear whether the Queen and her family were the guests of Lord and Lady Abercorn or they shared the house and the deer forest as sub-tenants; but, despite the terrible weather, they were determined to enjoy themselves.

The Queen commented favourably on the ubiquitous decoration of the stone shooting-lodge that some might have found overpowering. Within and without it was ornamented by scores of stags' heads and antlers, and Landseer, a frequent guest of the Abercorns, had repainted all the whitewashed walls with coloured frescoes, so that the originals of three of his most famous pictures, 'The Monarch of the Glen', 'The Challenge' and 'The Sanctuary' were ever present and unavoidable.* In her Journal the Queen noted: 'The view from the windows, as I now write, though obscured by rain, is very beautiful, and extremely wild. There is not a village, house, or cottage within four or five miles.' In any case she could not have gone out much. She was again carrying a child and in the first and most difficult three months. Doubtless she was feeling nervy and not quite herself when the youngest of the Abercorns, four-year-old Lord Claud, proved that true Highlanders wore nothing beneath the kilt by standing on his head and revealing his parts. She was cross; and, when he did it a second time, she was crosser still.

The Prince, as ever, kept himself busy. He wrote long letters and memoranda and, refusing to be weatherbound, he and George Anson escaped to visit the Caledonian Canal at Inverness that had been re-opened after five years of repairs. They stayed the night there, attended a ball, and returned having added a second Highlander to the royal establishment, an Invernesshire ghillie named John Macdonald.† Despite the appalling weather they enjoyed the sport offered by Ardverikie, deer-stalking in a well-kept forest; shooting, though they arrived on 21 August and few Highland grouse are fully grown until September–October; and fishing the loch in a variety of ways. The Prince reported to Baron Stockmar: 'Whenever we stir out we come home almost frozen and always wet to the skin . . . the grouse are wild, and the deer very hard to get at, despite all of which we are still very happy.'

Their happiness was chiefly caused by being so remote. He wrote to his mother-in-law: 'The reporters call it an "un-come-at-able place", because they are quartered on the other side of Loch Laggan, which is only to be crossed on a flying bridge, that belongs exclusively to ourselves.' Thwarted by the bridge and the weather of any proper copy one newspaperman reported: 'The Prince looked pleased with everything, and everybody, and with himself too' – a touch of malice that worried the Prince not at all for he repeated it to his mother-in-law, adding: 'Is that not a happy state?'

* The building was burnt down and the murals lost twenty-six years later.
† According to the Queen, Macdonald was already known to George Anson. That year Anson had been promoted Keeper of the Queen's Privy Purse, but he remained the Prince's treasurer and kept all his other appointments except the Private Secretaryship. This was given to Charles Phipps, a brother of Lord Normanby, who remained at the centre of affairs while Anson travelled with the Prince.

Attending the royal family was the Queen's senior and favourite Physician in Ordinary, Sir James Clark. In his sixtieth year and imprisoned by deluges in an overcrowded house and surrounded by all those trophies, he can scarcely have been comfortable. He had an unusual appearance, with craggy features and his long and plentiful backhair and whiskers swept forward as though a storm raged behind his head – an allegory of what had happened quite frequently in his life as a naval surgeon, attendant to the dying Keats, and royal physician for the past twelve years. Some of his diagnoses had been fairly disastrous,★ but he was competent enough to know that his own son, John, was far from well; so much so that he had sent him to a place in Aberdeenshire where the air was pure and the gravel soil ensured a rapid runaway of water. As a graduate of Aberdeen University and highly regarded as a climatologist, he considered the place perfect for resting and strengthening his son's lungs, and so John Clark was the guest of Lord Aberdeen's brother and sister, Sir Robert and Lady Alicia Gordon at their newly built castle of Balmoral. Evidently Sir James had been right. Enthusiastic letters reached him at drenched Ardverikie describing sunny days and fine air and splendid sport beside the Upper Dee.

The Queen, the Prince, everyone in the stone house by Loch Laggan was much interested in John Clark's letters. He was only 45 miles away as the ravens and eagles then flew, though, by road and track round Cairn Gorm and Ben Avon, Balmoral was seventy-seven, and he was dry and in sunshine. It scarcely seemed credible. Her interest in finding a holiday home re-kindled, she begged Sir James to make further inquiries about the climate and scenery, and, we must suppose thankfully, the royal party left Loch Laggan to make a rough and rainy voyage south. With them, travelling deeply into unknown territory, was John Macdonald, now formally appointed Prince Albert's Jäger.

The Balmoral estate, where John Clark was a guest, had first been owned by the Gordons, then by the Farquharsons of Inverey, then by the Duffs, Earls of Fife. The present Earl had trustees who let the estate. The present tenant, Sir Robert Gordon, had been Ambassador at Vienna from 1841 until 1846† and was one of the four younger brothers of Sir Robert Peel's Secretary of State for Foreign Affairs, called 'Athenian' Aberdeen on account of his lofty thinking and good looks. Sir

★ Notably diagnosing the stomach cancer of one of the Duchess of Kent's Ladies as pregnancy which caused fearful social repercussions and might have cost the Queen her throne.

† In the late twentieth century when the British Diplomatic and Consular Services have been mated and ambassadors have ludicrously proliferated, it is not easy to realise the distinction of a man such as Sir Robert Gordon. Then, and for a very long time afterwards, Great Britain sent out only five plenipotentiary Ambassadors: to the Porte, Vienna, St Petersburg, Paris and Berlin. Other countries were not reckoned to merit more than the importance of a resident minister.

Robert had been in possession of Balmoral for the past sixteen years improving the estate during his leaves and renovating the house to which he had added kitchens, a turreted tower and a conservatory. He had given up his post the year before and returned to Scotland to enjoy a sociable retirement with Lady Alicia frequently acting as his hostess. He would have heard of the Queen's interest in upper-Deeside from Sir James Clark who was gathering data about the climate. And James Giles, a talented Aberdeen artist, was making sketches of the countryside to be sent to Osborne.

It was the beginning of October and the Prince was busy laying out terraces in front of the Pavilion. To accord with the Italianate style of the building he planned a formal garden to meet the unbroken parkland that swept down to the sea. It was to involve a great shifting of earth, as a water-colour done that year by W. L. Leitch the Queen's drawing-master was to show, and the use of urns, statuary, solid boscage, topiary work, and the construction of fountains, pools, alcoves, decorative balustrades, stairways, a long pergola, and lawns and pathways as carefully proportioned as a parterre garden. The lack of side vistas from the terraces and an overgenerous use of colour in flower beds would prevent it from being a true Italian garden of the classical period; nevertheless the plan showed a symmetry of design and a sureness of touch on which the Prince might have congratulated himself.

Indoors there was a great unpacking after Ardverikie and re-packing ready for a move back to Windsor and a good deal of fuss. Miss Skerrett, officially dresser to the Queen from the time of her accession, though now her liaison officer with milliners and so forth, her adviser on artistic matters, and the confidential manager of her letter-copy press with a very special place in the Household, actually complained about the inconvenience of Scotch trophies. 'It would be all very well, Ma'am, if it was not for the number and length of the stags' horns to be carried away!' Then James Giles' commissioned pictures arrived. They delighted the royal couple and the Queen begged Lord Aberdeen to do his utmost to find her a suitable home there. She had not the least idea that on 8 October Sir Robert Gordon had gone down to breakfast at Balmoral and, quite unexpectedly, had died at table. Lord Aberdeen told the Queen of his loss. Being a man of sense as well as sensibility he proposed that she take up the lease of the property. At any rate, let Giles be commissioned to make further sketches of Balmoral itself and go up to London to submit a first-hand report.

After a decorous interval this was done. Giles went up to London with an account of the house and policies, and three water colours of the Castle. He renewed his acquaintance with Sir James Clark whom he had met in Rome in the 1820s and made his report on Balmoral, handing him the water-colours. Sir James then sought an audience and told the Queen and the Prince that his investigations revealed upper-Deeside to be one of the driest and best-drained areas in Scotland, and he gave them James Giles's pictures and report. They were so impressed that they decided to take up the lease sight unseen.

Lord Aberdeen was suitably thanked and the Prince's solicitor and the Fife trustees began negotiations.

James Giles was also thanked for his work and later commissioned to paint landscapes and pictures of the wild life about Balmoral. He even designed some of the Castle table-linen. But he did not enjoy it. 'I would rather not work to (*sic*) Royalty. I never made anything but a loss by it.'

Thomas Cubitt would scarcely have agreed. On completing the Pavilion he had been invited to undertake the renovation of Buckingham Palace and had accepted on condition that he would do all or nothing and refused to enter into competition with other tradesmen. So high was his standing that his conditions were accepted by the Six Commissioners for the Enlargement of Buckingham Palace and their architect, Edward Blore. He was therefore working simultaneously on the Palace and Osborne when, in December 1847, the time came for the old house to be demolished.

The Queen wrote a sad note in her Journal and, as soon as they left the Island, the Pavilion windows were temporarily sealed to keep out the dust, and Cubitt's men moved into Lady Isabella's former house, stripped it of everything useful, such as the porch, which was reconstructed as the main entrance to the old walled garden, and wooden fixtures, grates and fireplaces that could be used in the new wings, and pulverized the rest.

Chapter 7

A most determined Jacobite

So confident was the Prince of Cubitt's capacity to keep to a timetable, and his capacity for not impairing the pleasure of the Royal Family in any way during the process, that on Boxing Day in 1847 he felt able to invite his step-mama to trust herself 'to the unstable element of the sea' and pay them a visit. 'When we are in the Isle of Wight, when we are not surrounded by a Court and its formalities, our life is so quiet and simple that it would not fatigue you.'

Within two months they were enjoying anything but peace and quiet. His grandmother died, but neither he nor his brother who was visiting England, could be at her funeral. There was no semblance of reassurance in the letter he now wrote to his step-mother: 'France is in flames; Belgium is menaced. We have a Ministerial, money and tax crisis; and Victoria is on the point of being confined. My heart is heavy.'

The Queen was in fact more than two weeks from her confinement, but what an ardent rebel named 'the revolution in carpet slippers' was sweeping through Europe. Russia, under the heavy hand of abso-lutism, stood firm. So, eventually, did Belgium, but to be on the safe side Uncle Leopold had his bags packed and sent instructions that Claremont be aired just in case. It was an order that can scarcely have pleased the Queen who believed she had Claremont on permanent loan. Very soon, however, it was to be filled with the Orleans family.

France was indeed in flames. The King and Queen of the French were wandering about their former kingdom in heavy disguise. Already a trickle of royal refugees from France was arriving at Buckingham Palace, amongst them a Princess 'in real rags, her *only* clothes half torn off', and a number of children whom Lady Lyttelton described as 'puny, and *very small*'. It did not surprise her. She had very definite English prejudices about how children should be brought up and she was disgusted that the little French princes and princesses 'all ate an immense supper of white soup, beef, chickens, and loads of raspberry

jam tarts, and then were *immediately* put to bed without washing!'
Eventually the *ci-devant* King arrived. He had thrown off his wig,
shaved his whiskers, and reached Newhaven in goggles and a cap on his
pear-shaped head, calling himself 'Mr Smith'.

English republicans were encouraged to make demonstrations. A
small mob of youngsters broke the lamps outside Buckingham Palace,
its leader shouting: 'Vive la république.' On being arrested he spoilt any
image of being a true Jacobin by crying piteously.

The French Royal Family was packed off to Claremont, by permission of Uncle Leopold, where they were to remain for many a year.
Mary Anne Disraeli, whom the Tory statesman had frankly married for
her fortune, though he then came to admire her oddities and exceeding
kindness, was touched by the plight of the Orleans family. 'Such a sad
thing,' she said of the princes at Claremont, 'those four young men
thrown out of employment.' 'As if', Lady Lyttelton remarked with
asperity, 'they had been stokers! ——'

On 18 March the Queen bore her fourth daughter and sixth child,
Princess Louise. It was not an easy confinement, the worst, in fact, she
had yet endured. The Prince wrote to give the news to the King of
Prussia but on that very date, 18 March, the King was facing armed
rebellion. The barricades were up in Berlin. Bullets were whistling
about the palaces. 'We all lay flat on our bellies,' confessed the King. His
brother the Prince of Prussia was so reactionary that the Berliners called
him 'the Grapeshot Prince' and he rightly decided it was time to fly.
Like Louis Philippe he disguised himself by cutting off his whiskers,
and turned up as a refugee at Buckingham Palace nine days later. Other
countries followed suit. It was gratifying that at Heidelberg a rally
decided not to look to revolutionary France but to the 'free institutions
of England'. Nevertheless Courts were challenged in many places,
Hanover, Bavaria, Saxony, Naples, Schleswig, Holstein, even small
Leiningen belonging to the Queen's half-brother, and Coburg itself.

Suddenly the Queen herself took fright. Civil War was very near in
Ireland and at home a great Chartist meeting was called to meet outside
London on 10 April. It was only a short time since her confinement and
her nerve broke. On 3 April the Government advised that the Royal
Family leave for Osborne two days before the Chartist meeting. Vol-
unteers from all ranks flocked to defend the capital as special constables.
Keepers and grooms were there to protect their masters' London houses
from the mob.

On the 8th the Royal Family left for Osborne, and found Cubitt's
men, rebellion or no rebellion, hard at work on the terraces, and the
Main and Household Wings. The next day, appropriately enough, was
the First Sunday in Lent, and in Whippingham Church, for the first

time since her youth during the Napoleonic Wars, Lady Lyttelton heard the parson pray for deliverance from the hands of enemies. 'Abate their pride,' he prayed, 'assuage their malice, and confound their devices.'

10 April dawned – what the Queen ever after called 'our revolution'. Twenty-three thousand Chartists met at Kennington Common but half a million had been expected and the leaders were seriously disappointed. There was no march, no demonstration. Instead, thoroughly abated, assuaged and confounded, they accepted the ruling of the Police Chief Commissioner that only a handful of them might take their monster petition in three cabs to the Palace of Westminster. The rest dispersed.

The Queen still had grave doubts about the future. All she asked, she wrote to Uncle Leopold, sending him a snuff-box, was that the children should be 'fit for *whatever station* they might be placed in – *high or low*'.

Nor did Prince Albert believe their troubles were over. He wrote to Stockmar in Germany on 6 May: 'We have Chartist riots every night, which result in numbers of broken heads. The organization of these people is incredible. They have secret signals, and correspond from town to town by means of carrier pigeons.'

Suddenly, his spirits revived. His lawyer had at last come to an agreement with the agent of the Fife Trustees for a twenty-seven-year lease of the Balmoral Estate. Certain of Sir Robert's servants were to be absorbed into the Royal service, such as the major-domo François d'Albertançon who became the Queen's house steward, and John Grant the head keeper, and the gardener William Paterson who was to continue as gardener to the Queen for forty-four more years.

The Prince faced life afresh. Only a little more than a fortnight after his alarmist jeremiad to Stockmar, he wrote again to him: 'All is well with us, and the Throne has never stood higher in England than at this moment.' Nevertheless there were still some uneasy moments. The constables on duty and the officers from Division A of New Scotland Yard responsible for the safety of the Royal Family took fright when a party of Oddfellows arrived by steamer at East Cowes on a Whitmonday outing. Just in case they were disguised revolutionaries the estate was alerted. Cubitt's men, as well as all the servants and farm workers, were called to the defence of their Queen. This showed the state of everyone's nerves.★

Prince Albert had never been busier. He was desperately anxious

---

★ Officers of A or Whitehall Division of the Metropolitan Police Force always looked after the Royal Family wherever they might be in residence, and journalists who travelled from one royal residence to the other in search of copy would often see familiar faces from A Division. The protection of royalty continued to be the responsibility of A Division until 1 July, 1978.

about the resettlement of Europe, supervising the work at Osborne, planning the education of his children, organizing the summer holidays in Scotland, attending a long conference at York of the Royal Agricultural Society, besides his ordinary daily duties. So great a load of work sometimes made him fractious. One July evening during a rubber of whist in the Osborne drawing-room the Queen partnered him and managed to trump his best spade. He scolded her before her ladies. But, in the happy anticipation of getting away to Scotland, she forgave him, and wrote to her Uncle Leopold after his birthday on 26 August: 'a purer, more perfect being than my beloved Albert the Creator could not have been sent into this troubled world.' That month the Prince and Cubitt and Gruner were putting the final touches to the plans for all the terracing. Then on Tuesday, 5 September the Royal Family left for Scotland.

The voyage north had been anticipated for some time by loyal subjects along the east coast of the kingdom and at many points people gathered to greet their sovereign as she travelled past. Not one was lucky. In a great burst of speed Lord Adolphus had managed to lose the escorting steamers, go off course, and the Queen and the Prince were virtually lost at sea. The mistake corrected, the *Victoria and Albert* surged on and arrived at Aberdeen twelve hours early.

The city fathers had determined to make the Sovereign's arrival a great day in the history of the city, and their plans had to be hurriedly re-adjusted. They could scarcely be faulted. The *Illustrated London News* covered every detail of welcome from the time the Queen stepped ashore to the time she reached Balmoral Castle at a quarter to three. It was a triumphant progress through elaborately constructed arches of flowers, evergreens, heather, moss; one of oats, barley and wheat, and one 'composed entirely of stags' heads with splendid antlers'. There were loyal addresses and brief replies, breakfast at Cults, luncheon at Aboyne, cannon firing from a mountain summit to announce their arrival at Ballater. The last arch at Crathie bore the legend 'Welcome to your Highland Home, Victoria and Albert'. The enthusiasm was immense, and the welcome extraordinarily warm considering the length of memories and the fact that the 1715 rebellion had begun in the same parish at Braemar only 10 miles upriver.

Balmoral, derived from a Celtic word, that in the course of time was to give its name to so many thousands of places and houses in the most unlikely places, even to a suburb of the Belgian town Spa where, exactly seventy years later, the Queen's eldest grandson the Kaiser was to sign his abdication, was almost unheard of in 1848. The Castle, which for a time the local people now insisted on calling 'the Palace', was a pretty house with mullioned windows with flamboyant tracery, and stepped and fancy gable-ends, and embattlements, and projecting turrets at angles with lancet windows, and round towers topped by cone-shaped roofs like magicians' hats. It had soft French touches not found south of the border, but was by no means old having been largely rebuilt by Sir Robert Gordon and completed only nine years before.

Neither the Prince nor the Queen regretted taking the lease sight unseen. Their best hopes were realized and they were charmed by the house.

That same day the Queen noted down the rooms they had at their disposal. Downstairs was a hall, a dining-room, and a billiard-room cum library, the shelves loaded with books and a small collection of local rocks, and the table lighted by overhead triple lamps but no downward reflectors. Upstairs the old drawing-room had been altered to make a private sitting-room. It was 'a fine large room' according to the Queen, though James Giles's watercolour stored at Windsor made it seem rather small and, uncharacteristically, not overcluttered with furniture. Naturally it was decorated with stags' heads, but only four of them, and a Landseer, together with a portrait of the Prince's favourite greyhound, Eos, and above the mantelshelf, a copy of the Winterhalter painting of the Royal Family in the Osborne dining-room. Next door was their bedroom and the Prince's dressing-room and, not far away, three rooms for Miss Hildyard and the two elder children. The Queen added: 'The ladies live below, and the gentlemen upstairs.'

She was not being thoughtless; merely concise. Doubtless some members of the Household felt rather as if they were camping-out; for example, one Lady-in-Waiting was billeted in a detached cottage and had her breakfast sent over in a wheelbarrow. But another observer noted that the house 'possessed much comfort but no splendour . . . The house was nearly all bedrooms', which suggests more agreeable quarters than those provided the year before at Ardverikie. Evidently, however, there was no luxury. 'The bedrooms discovered no more costly hanging than the now discarded white dimity.' The French-style conglomeration of a castle was interesting, small, cosy, entirely *Gemüt-lichkeit*. Nevertheless the Prince was a realist. He and the Queen might have wished to live the simple life of a laird and his lady but it was impossible. Each had a Household and there was a retinue of travelling servants in addition to those engaged locally.

Lord Aberdeen had asked the Balmoral doctor to make arrangements for their reception and the Prince immediately took to him as an enterprising, energetic man not frightened of responsibility. In fact, it was not long before Dr Robertson had added to his work as a general practitioner – and his practice stretched for 30 miles – the general supervision of the royal demesne, and ultimately he was to become

Commissioner to the Queen, to the Prince, and to the Prince of Wales.

For advice on immediate minor enlargements and alterations, the Prince sent for the late Sir Robert Gordon's architect, and five days after the royal arrival the *Aberdeen Journal* informed its readers: 'We understand that John Smith, Esq, architect, has received Her Majesty's command to attend at Balmoral today.'

Mr Smith's firm had been responsible for the finest of all the triumphal arches made to welcome the royal family to Aberdeen and we may be sure that George Anson would have brought this to the Queen's notice. But John Smith's time at Balmoral was mostly taken by the Prince who walked with him around the castle and asked him to make plans for a number of additions that he had in mind.

After building Osborne without an architect the Prince showed tact in consulting Sir Robert Gordon's architect. He also showed an understanding of the Scots who, like the Germans, so valued qualifications that they even, on occasions, had the initials of their degrees and diplomas incised into tombstones. Allegedly John Smith was also sweetened by vague talk of the possibility of other and larger buildings being planned. Otherwise he might have felt some chagrin at being summoned for such a small commission.

Smith was highly thought of in Scotland where he had done an impressive amount of work, much of it in the tudor style, thus earning himself the nickname of 'Tudor Johnnie'. His father, a master-builder of great character, was also known by a nickname and called 'Sink'em' Smith because, like an angry old sea-dog, that expletive was so often on his lips. 'Sink'em' had had the wisdom to send his son to London to be trained as an architect, and was at Aberdeen harbour to welcome him home when the ship almost foundered in a storm. He was in a great state lest John would 'gae doun wi' all his plannies'. Fortunately the ship made the quayside and the 'plannies' were well used throughout the north-east of Scotland; so much so, that, after the death of old 'Sink'em', 'Tudor Johnnie' had the largest architectural, building and cabinet-making business in the area, and was City Architect of Aberdeen. Now his largely rebuilt Castle at Balmoral was being lived in by the sovereign and her family and he had a royal commission. There can be no reason to suppose that 'Tudor Johnnie' did not go home content.

Pictures of modern Balmoral have appeared on so many greetings' cards, calendars, box covers and in books and magazines all over the world that its environs, once glowingly described as 'the scenic sublimities of upper-Deeside and the Cairngorms', have become very familiar; but they do not, in fact, correspond exactly to what the Queen and her consort saw from their windows in 1848. The essential contours of the land remain, but, little by little, the wildness has lessened, tamed by time and prosperity. Some of the heather and wild furze gave way to plantations, grazing and other farmlands; the two-roomed hovels, as crude as the Irishmen's cabins, made of stone and sods and thatched with heather, their floors beaten earth, their windows permanently shut, and with a surrounding croft, were gradually replaced by cottages in brick or granite, roofed by slate, and with a neat vegetable-patch; farmsteads changed as succeeding generations farmed with new ideas and new methods; even the Dee altered with time and when floods and storms scooped at the bed and banks and shifted pools and boulders.

Dr Robertson had a daughter Patricia, who became a Mrs Lindsay, and in a book she published the year after the Queen's death, she underlined the difference between the old and the new Balmoral. When the Queen first took up residence beside the Dee, her people hardly spoke any Gaelic. This was because the Gordons had never been considered to be true highlanders and so, on their policies, south of the Dee the Gaelic language had largely died out, while north of the Dee, owned by the Celtic Farquharsons, the people spoke hardly anything else. This would not have pleased the Queen who, already, was the most determined Jacobite of all the house of Brunswick. The Stuart blood may have flowed very thinly indeed in her veins and arteries, but it seemed to thicken considerably north of Berwick. Could she have rewritten history, doubtless she would have done, and given plausible explanations for the fact that Culloden was lost chiefly because so many of the chieftains held back; that there were highlanders actually fighting for 'Butcher' Cumberland, and that quite soon after the battle they were ready to enlist in the British Army. And Mrs Lindsay underlined another fact that the Queen could scarcely have found to her liking. In 1848 in the parish of Crathie and Braemar there were 378 Roman Catholics, doubtless loyal subjects but still owing some obedience to a foreign sovereign, as the Queen considered the Pope. On the other hand, the ministers and elders of the Church of Scotland and, since the Disruption of 1843, of the Free Kirk too, were somewhat austere with strong views on dancing, idle strolling, music, and profanation of the Sabbath, and the Queen was particularly fond of the first three and by no means a Sabbatarian.

However, there was so much of beauty and romance and she had such a feeling of well-being during their short holiday, that the Queen was exceptionally happy. They ate strawberries and raspberries from the garden long after these fruits had finished in England. Taking their eldest son, they drove through the great wood of Ballochbuie, and, sighting stags, concealed themselves in a hide of heather and hurdles, from which the Prince had one shot and got his stag, a 'royal'. On another occasion he also shot two more red deer and a roebuck. They explored the River Muick and the loch above it, a place famous for trout and midges, and, very significantly, they inspected a shiel or hut of Alt-na-Giuthasach not far from the loch and decided to improve and alter it. They scrambled up the great mountain of Loch-na-Gar to the south, partly by pony and partly on foot, and, near the summit, had a picnic luncheon.

Loch-na-Gar was the mountain that had so impressed Byron, who as a boy was taken by his mother to drink and bathe in the iron waters of Pannanich Wells near to Ballater in the hope of strengthening the enfeebled muscles of his leg, and he recalled it in one of his less happy quatrains.

'England! Thy beauties are tame and domestic
  To me who has roved o'er the mountains afar:
Oh! for the crags that are wild and majestic
  The steep, frowning glories of dark Loch-na-Garr!'

This absolutely reflected the Queen's mood when they left Balmoral, travelling by carriage all the way to Montrose where there was a railway. There was no royal train and their special had no particular comforts save that it stopped at Perth and Crewe so that they could sleep. The second stop was rather forced on them as travelling on a Sunday would have excited the Sabbatarians.

Shortly after arriving home at Osborne the melancholy Queen had her nerves exacerbated by a calamitous voyage aboard the *Fairy* from Osborne Pier to Gosport. The royal tender was not quite shipshape, 'some trifling bolt or screw wrong', but she was quite seaworthy enough for the passage under ordinary circumstances. However, when they were approaching a line of battleships of the Channel Fleet, a squall sprang up that put the *Fairy* at hazard, and, just ahead, a boatful of people suddenly turned turtle. Lord Adolphus at once let down a boat as other ships did, but, correctly considering his first duty was the Queen's safety, he would not heave to in the squall, and the Queen and the Prince and their children all saw the men drown.

Everyone was greatly distressed, but even when the shock was over the Queen continued abject. She was also upset by news from Vienna. In this dreadful year of revolution the illustrious Metternich was driven into exile, a less fortunate colleague, the Minister of War, hung from a streetlamp, and now Vienna was being bombarded by Imperial troops and the epileptic Emperor Ferdinand forced to abdicate in favour of his eighteen-year-old nephew Franz Joseph. Such changes invariably made the Queen nervous. But it was not this either that so depressed her.

Lady Lyttelton put her finger on it: 'The Queen has returned in her usual devoted, passionate admiration for the Highlands. Leaving them is always a case of actual *red eyes.*'

It must have seemed an answered prayer when, very soon afterwards, the Prince told the Queen that Mr Anson had been pressing his solicitor, Mr White, and Mr White had been pressing the Fife Trustees and the Gordon brothers and the Farquharsons to sell, or let on a long lease, not only the Balmoral estate but also the neighbouring estates of Abergeldie and Birkhall and the forest of Ballochbuie. And Mr White had met with some success. The Farquharsons were not to be moved for many years to part with Ballochbuie, even on a lease, but the Gordons leased Abergeldie, and did so until the 1970s. A price had been agreed for Birkhall that was to be bought at once in the name of the Prince of Wales, and the Fife Trustees were willing and ready to negotiate for a long lease or an outright sale for Balmoral.

Possibly the Queen felt that to lose her heart so spontaneously to Balmoral was in some sense a betrayal of Osborne, for she was at pains to show how much she loved her island home.

After business at Windsor and in London she and the Prince travelled a second time that autumn to the island. On this occasion they were accompanied by Thomas Cubitt who was to give a detailed report on the progress of the building. The magazine *Builder* had already published an article on the work as the new part appeared to be almost completed. In fact, as Cubitt explained, a good deal yet remained to be done.

The unfinished house was spacious and symmetrically designed. To match the Flag Tower on the Pavilion was a Clock Tower at the east end of the main front. The enclosed loggia with the open loggia above constituted two floors. Therefore the extension towards the Clock Tower also had two, the Duchess of Kent's apartments being at ground level. Elsewhere the Main and Household Wings had three floors above the basement, both wings amply provided with staircases, baths and water-closets. Many of the suites and single rooms were for visitors, and for the children as they grew up and left the schoolroom, and for the ladies of the Household. Certain others were set apart for intimate servants: the Queen's dressers and the Prince's valet and personal attendant.

The long, spacious entrance-hall that joined wing to wing and met the original loggia at right angles was named the Marble Corridor because Gruner had extravagant plans for its decoration with marble statues and marbled pilasters. Its main entrance was halfway along and opened onto the carriage-ring. There was another entrance for the Household at the south-west end of the Marble Corridor.

It had always been intended that the gentlemen should continue to sleep at Barton Manor and walk, ride or drive to the main building where on the ground-floor of the Household Wing there was the library, a writing-room and a billiard-room, and a large Household dining-room for those not attending the Queen's dinner. The Main Wing had at its centre an imposing Council Room with three large windows, the centre one opening to a flight of steps to the first terrace. To the east were rooms for royal visitors; to the west an Audience Chamber, and a room for the Privy Purse.

It was an impressive piece of work even at that unfinished stage, and nothing had been forgotten from ice-house to a shell-alcove and what was called the Pier Landing House on the beach and propagating houses in the walled garden.

The Prince made a few other plans; for extensive stables and coach-houses and tackrooms to be built beyond the walled garden, and for gardens for the children, and that month he marked the site for a fairly large building not far from the kitchens. This was to have two floors; the ground-floor to house upper servants and a sick-room, and the first floor for livery servants. It was to be named the Servants' Barracks.

For a supervisor and improver as the Prince was, the creation and embellishment of Osborne would never cease; nevertheless he was aware that these were his last major plans. Cubitt had indicated that within a year the house would be sufficiently finished for him to leave it in the competent hands of a clerk of works who would enter the royal service. Within two years the proposed neo-classical decoration of the Marble Corridor should be completed, and once the plasterwork was bone dry, Gruner would go on to make sumptuous designs for the Council Chamber and Audience Room as well as re-design the temporary ceilings of the drawing-room and the billiard-room. The terrace work would take longer because it involved the shifting of tons of earth, the construction of massive concrete retaining walls 25 feet deep, and laying hundreds of yards of paths, first with French rock-asphalt then with a mixture of curry-coloured tufa and coloured beach-pebbles.

But the landscaping was virtually done and the Prince had the imagination to visualize that in time the plantations and coverts and avenues of trees and single plantings would grow to blur the clear view of the house from the other side of the river Medina. Gradually the mass of Cubitt's work would appear to sink into its surroundings, and harmonize perfectly with the tilled and fallow farmlands, green parks and woods, and the ever-changing colour of the sea.

Chapter 8

A second private home

Lord John Russell was a bantam-sized man with the nickname 'Finality Jack'. His long parliamentary career in both houses, which began in 1813 even before he came of age, was studded with some great triumphs and some great humiliations. In private and political life he was dogged with ill fortune. Even at the peak of his career, when he first received the seals of office as the Queen's Prime Minister, the day was entirely spoilt by the death of his favourite brother. Therefore he was a sorely tried man, so accustomed to adversity that he must, surely, have become a little cynical. How this affected his reaction when, in November 1848, the Queen announced she intended to spend a part of each year more than 600 miles from the seat of Government is not quite clear but, like every subsequent First Minister, he could scarcely have approved.

The Sovereign's regular withdrawals to the Isle of Wight were already vexatious to her ministers; and the year before, Lord John had considered it his duty to accompany the Royal Family to Balmoral, partly as a guest, but partly so that the business of government could go on. This, as the Queen well knew, did not cease at the Prorogation of Parliament in the summer, and autumn sessions had not yet been found necessary – but was a continuous process. He had trusted, ineffectually it seemed, that the Queen's love for the highlands would diminish. Reason argued that it would be quietly killed by the loneliness of upper-Deeside, the lack of society, the sheer discomfort of roughing it in one of the most primitive parts of the realm where, despite its reputation as one of the driest areas in Scotland, it still had an over-generous ration of mist, damp and rain. The boredom of being cooped up in a small house would surely teach her that no-one could live solely on scenery, however sublime, and that bad communications made Balmoral monstrously inconvenient. Reason, he now realized, was not to enter into the matter. The Queen and the Prince had made their will known, a regal gesture that a Russell and a Whig must have found particularly distasteful. An undertaking had been entered into with the owners of the property and the Prime Minister was faced with a *fait accompli*. A second private home for the royal family was to be established in the wilds of Aberdeenshire.

All Lord John could do was warn the Prince that no public monies could be provided either for the leasing or purchase of the property or for any improvements to it, and if he and the Queen were set on this regular exile so far from Westminster, a Minister in Attendance would always need to be present. The expense of this, and for estafettes, would have to be met by the Privy Purse. In other words Lord John laid the onus entirely on the Prince, and turned to the vexed question of how to deal with his Foreign Secretary, Lord Palmerston, who, on his own initiative, had madly supplied Sicilian rebels with arms to fight against their own king.

Prince Albert accepted the Prime Minister's view and presumably from a position of strength. He was not the sort of person to make negotiations without a clear knowledge of what was at his disposal and that he would not have to go begging to the Whigs. That year he was thirty, by the standard of the time approaching middle-age; with a suggestion of a second chin and inclined to portliness and baldness, but an air of authority and that *gravitas* so admired by noble Romans, though rather less by noble Britons. Doubtless his head was already buzzing with ideas for the improvement of Balmoral, and there must have been long colloquies with the Queen and George Anson, and his solicitor Mr Edward White, on that very subject, but *gravitas* enabled him to hold his hand until matters had been formally arranged with the Fife Trustees and the Gordon family.

Fortuitously he was more than usually busy. In addition to daily work on despatch boxes, he and Anson and Phipps and the authorities planned the details of a royal visit to Ireland at the beginning of August; he drafted speeches for ceremonies there and for visits to Grimsby, Winchester and Weymouth; interested himself in a large variety of subjects from the necessity of teaching Gaelic and Welsh in their national schools, to the public provision of vegetable allotments, and Savings' Banks; chaired meetings; wrote scores of letters about the crisis of the previous year and the control of foreign policy. Above all, he was becoming heavily committed to the idea of an exhibition to be held in London sponsored by the Society of Arts of which he was president. He wrote to his brother from Osborne: 'I am working out a plan for a large industrial exhibition in London for the whole civilized world.'

There were many visitors to Osborne in the summer of 1849. The

Duchess of Kent was there to make certain arrangements with Thomas Cubitt about her apartments. The Prussian Ambassador, the Chevalier Bunsen, paid an informal visit and noted that the royal family habitually spoke German.★ Sir Robert and Lady Peel and their daughter were there for a time and even the addition of three made 'a good squeeze at Church, and a most indecent, scrambling, extra-parochial congregation, overflowing into the churchyard'.

This was a clear indication to the Prince that the church built by Nash in 1804 was inadequate. Even allowing for a small number of royalty-gapers who, in Scotland, were to become offensive, the large additional congregation from Osborne House to the normal worshippers at Whippingham Church created a serious problem. The Prince set his mind to it. Enlargements to the chancel would have to be made.

Then Sir William Hooker arrived from Kew Gardens with the flower of what the botanical world terms 'a vegetable wonder'. It came from the Amazon where its leaves grew to the size of tea-trays and could bear great spread weights upon them because of the structure of the under-surface. The flower was in a japanned black box and, when fully opened, was the most magnificent water-lily smelling slightly of melon. It was shown round the family at tea on the lawn and the Queen expressed herself delighted and asked Sir William to dine. She was unaware, and the secret was kept until after her death, that in the process of naming the plant, when the claims of its various discoverers had to be respected, it had ended as *Victoria amazonica*, a name so suggestive of insult to the Queen that botanists had agreed to a temporary compromise and in her lifetime it was called *Victoria regia*.

After Sir William's visit there was a summer *fête champêtre* for everyone at the house. Lady Lyttelton admitted honestly that it was 'noisy, merry and intensely boring as usual'. She was wearied by the heavy dinner in a tent, then hornpipes done by the crews of the royal yachts and country dances, and 'footmen and housemaids pounding away their ale'.

A week later Lady Lyttelton said goodbye to four of the royal children. The Prince of Wales had long left her province and, at the age of six, had a suite of his own at Buckingham Palace, a tutor and a small household, and Prince Alfred had also left the schoolroom, but both were especially dear to her. So were the precocious Princess Royal and

---

★ It was then customary for all members of all royal families to be tri-lingual, and Queen Victoria and her eldest daughter also had a working knowledge of Italian. It was required of the Queen's Maids of Honour that they should speak, read and write faultless French and German, and have some understanding of Latin. The Prince had a German Secretary in his household, and, after 1861 the Queen felt the need of a German Librarian and Secretary to deal with official letters and to file archives. She herself wrote all personal letters in German and French.

Princess Alice who were still in her charge. She worried for them all in Ireland, as she worried for the Queen and the Prince.

Only three months before an abortive attempt had been made on the Queen's life by a mad Irishman, and Ireland was so unsettled that Habeas Corpus had been suspended. Strong doubts as to the wisdom of the visit had been aired by A Division of the Metropolitan Police, but, on ministerial advice, the Queen and the Prince had decided it was worth some risk. The visit was not to be ostentatious because of the general distress, and the Royal Family was largely based on the royal yacht moving north from Cork to Belfast, though there was a short stay at Phoenix Park Viceregal Lodge which the Queen thought charming. They wished to show that, far from being indifferent to the Irish troubles, they had a personal interest in the welfare of the people, and on leaving Dublin, the Queen paid her subjects a unique compliment by standing on the paddle-box of the *Victoria and Albert* to wave goodbye and ordered the Royal Standard to be lowered three times as a salute to the nation. To some extent it was a successful diplomatic visit though not to the extent that Lord John Russell had hoped. As tokens of their goodwill the Prince of Wales was created Earl of Dublin, and the Queen's third son, born nine months after the visit, had Patrick amongst his Christian names, and later was created Duke of Connaught.

The royal party went on to Glasgow where, predictably, the Prince found that a view of two quays reminded him of Paris; took a train to Perth; and thence travelled 57 miles by carriage through the Spittal of Glenshee and the Devil's Elbow, to be received at Balmoral by MacKay playing his pipes and John Macdonald in full dress.

Apparently Sir Robert Peel had also taken a house in Scotland for, on 21 August, the Prince wrote to his friend: 'I hope you like your highland home as much as we do ours.' And to Stockmar he emphasized his and the Queen's great pleasure in being at Balmoral for the second time. 'The highlands are glorious and the sport plentiful.'

The sport was not then what it was to become. The Prince was accustomed to the battues of continental Europe when game of all kinds, from bear and wolves to wild pig and hares, were driven to carefully-placed guns, and seven years before he had taken part in one at Taymouth. But that had been one of the very last ancient drives that formerly played so large a part in the social and economic life of the highlands when the roebuck and red deer and feathered game had been driven chiefly for the larder. Since the taking of game had become a serious sport the larger proprietors had begun a system of managing the mountain moor and valley that constituted a deer-forest. The sheep were kept away from the deer-pastures. Because heather took ten years to mature, one tenth of the whole forest was burnt off each year to provide continuous feeding grounds. A few proprietors had begun to make sanctuaries in the heart of the forests where the deer could breed and rest, free from disturbance save the depredations of poachers.

The deer were taken in a variety of ways. There was coursing or running deer with rough deerhounds in pairs, the larger going for the beast's shoulder and then his neck, the other for the haunch. Occasionally smooth greyhounds were used that were game to seize on the shoulder of a running deer and kill it swiftly, but they lacked the weight of the deerhounds to bring the prey down. Then there was the almost casual walking-up of deer that depended chiefly on a combination of chance, a good dog, and an expert knowledge of the territory. The naturalist-sportsman Charles St John who lived at Nairn when the Royal Family were first at Balmoral, was just such an expert and very adaptable. One day, out for woodcock, he saw signs of deer, drew the shot from one barrel, replaced it with ball, and within a few minutes had bagged a fine hind. Then, in woody country, it was possible for a few ghillies to 'move' a deer towards a gun in a hide. But stalking was the most usual method and ultimately became the only method of taking deer in Scotland. It required great knowledge of the forest, and great patience and endurance.

In those very early days the Prince probably used a John Manton double-barrelled muzzle-loader with a detonating system, firing conical half-inch lead bullets, or a Greener-type rifle. Neither had much of a range, no more than 200 yards, and the chance of a second shot was remote. He would go out with John Grant, the ghillie he had taken on with the house, and Macdonald the Jäger he had engaged at Fort Augustus the year before; or he would direct the ghillies to beat towards him in the hope of seeing a stag; or, being seldom without a gun or rifle, he took every opportunity he could, even on drives and walks with the Queen, to take a shot. She was very keen that he should enjoy his sport and quite unsqueamish about carcasses. For this sort of informal shooting the Prince wore the ordinary country topcoat and strapped trousers of the period. For formal stalking, though it was by no means obligatory, he might have worn some sort of waterproof jacket with many pockets, and trousers that could be buttoned tightly round the boots. The important thing, as he said himself after his first experience of stalking, was to be 'dressed entirely in grey'. Only the highlanders wore the kilt, but this was grey as well.

At that period there were far less esoteric rules and lore about sport and there were fewer prejudices. Fox-hunting in the highlands was very different from the chase with horse and hounds the Prince had enjoyed with the Belvoir in the shires; very different even from the fell hunting in the lake district where John Peel of Troutbeck hunted fox on foot. Foxes in the highlands were bigger and stronger and, as killers of sheep, grouse and deer, as well as salmon, they were the princes of vermin and mostly too clever to be trapped or snared. Highland fox-hunting was a matter of using firearms and several couple of slow-hounds, strong and with excellent noses, and an assortment of lurchers, greyhounds and terriers, and the chase demanded even more stamina than stalking, following a fresh scent at a jog trot through ravines and morasses and over mountain screes until the fox was within range of a rifle or a long-barrelled fowling piece. Then, slowed down by a ball or a dusting of heavy shot, he would be finished off by hounds.

There were also less fine distinctions about angling and fishing and the sport was far less exclusive. On the lochs fish could be and were taken in a variety of ways; with draw-nets and hang-nets, floating lines baited with worms, frogs and trout; trolling with a parr; or what was called swimming an 'otter', a device made of wood and weights and lines and barbed flies that worked rather like a fluttering underwater kite. Because an 'otter' gashed as many fish as it caught, it was ulti-mately outlawed, but it was in common use in 1849 as the quickest way of filling a basket. Fly-fishing on the Dee was not the norm, though artificial flies were tied and each water in the highlands had its speciali-ties. Minnows were also used. The most common way of taking salmon was by netting where the bottom was regular and not too deep, or by spearing as the fish struggled upriver or leapt up a fall. Spearing could be done alone but only by the very skilled or the very adventur-ous because, once the salmon was thrashing on the end of the 16 foot pole, it needed considerable balance and strength to hold him and twist him through half an arc to drop him in a dry place before clubbing him to death with a priest. More wisely, the spearing or leistering was done by a cheerful company. A year after this second stay at Balmoral the Queen and the Prince went leistering with all their own people and a neighbour and their friends, using spears as well as nets, but between the hundred of them they only managed to spear one salmon. Leistering was better done by torchlight at night but, because this encouraged poaching, it had already been declared illegal. The royal party much enjoyed it, the Queen describing it as 'picturesque in the extreme. I wished for Landseer's pencil.' But there was a moment of horror as two over-enthusiastic ghillies dropped in a deep pool and one could not swim. However, he was saved by Dr Robertson who jumped in and pulled him out.

How different much of this was from sport as it was to develop and become, one day, almost a major industry in the highlands.

But though in 1849 the Prince rejoiced in the fact that sport was plentiful, there was a great deal to do besides. Birkhall had to be looked over and alterations planned. The Prince also put in hand some other estate matters. He ordered plantations to be made and wrote to his Private Secretary, Colonel Phipps: 'I am just considering what can be done here, where the cottage accommodation borders on the Irish. The price allowed for a cottage is £15!!' He was determined on the improvement of the housing and workshops, stables, and cottages were built on the estate, and a pre-fabricated ballroom of corrugated-iron plates on a timber frame attached to the Castle, even before negotiations were completed with the Fife trustees.

On that same holiday the Prince and George Anson were frequently busy with an English guest to the Castle. Henry Cole was something of a polymath: one of the powers behind the founding of the Public Record Office and the setting up of Hill's penny post, the first to publish a Christmas card, editor of the *Journal of Design*, author of children's books, musical and artistic, fascinated by engines and gadgets, and also a superb organizer who at present was absorbed in his vision of a great international exhibition. For some time he had been in regular communication with the Prince's Private Secretary about the project, and had had audiences with the Prince. The three men constituted the driving force that gained the all-important support of industrialists and commercial managers both at home and abroad and made the Great Exhibition possible.

But, as well as sport and work, there were several expeditions into the wild countryside. Only half a century before travellers had drawn their coach blinds to shut out the 'horrid crags' and savagery of Scotland. Now the Queen and the Prince exulted in the desolate peaks and mountainsides, the great peat mosses tufted with cottongrass, and the stark landscapes close to their second home. Writing about one family expedition to the isolated, topmost loch on the River Muick that lay on the further side of Loch-na-Gar, the Queen noted that, amongst the ghillies, was John Brown. It was her first mention of a name that, in the years to come, was to cause sensations.

It demonstrates the Prince's exceptional capacity for doing half a dozen things at once that, busy as he was at Balmoral, and with plans for the Great Exhibition maturing at the back of his mind, he decided to learn Gaelic. He had a huge dictionary and took lessons from John Macdonald. But it is doubtful if even so determined a man mastered very much of that very difficult language. As the Queen noted: 'It is a very difficult language, for it is pronounced in a totally different way from that in which it is written.'

The Queen made no attempt to master Gaelic, but she was fully occupied; learning more reels with the children; hearing them recite

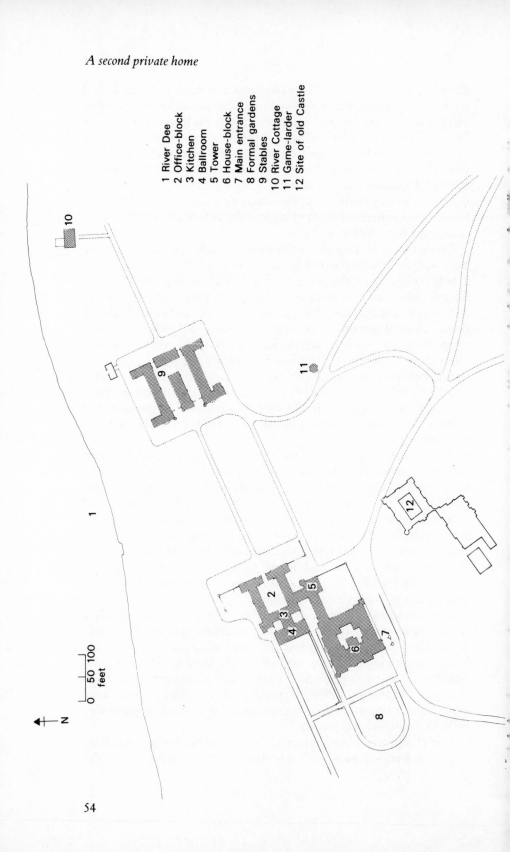

A second private home

1 River Dee
2 Office-block
3 Kitchen
4 Ballroom
5 Tower
6 House-block
7 Main entrance
8 Formal gardens
9 Stables
10 River Cottage
11 Game-larder
12 Site of old Castle

N

0 50 100
feet

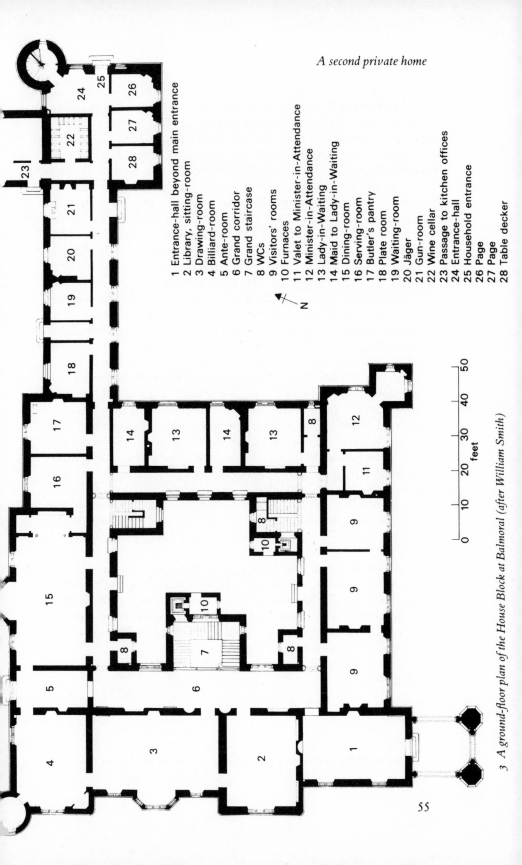

1 Entrance-hall beyond main entrance
2 Library, sitting-room
3 Drawing-room
4 Billiard-room
5 Ante-room
6 Grand corridor
7 Grand staircase
8 WCs
9 Visitors' rooms
10 Furnaces
11 Valet to Minister-in-Attendance
12 Minister-in-Attendance
13 Lady-in-Waiting
14 Maid to Lady-in-Waiting
15 Dining-room
16 Serving-room
17 Butler's pantry
18 Plate room
19 Waiting-room
20 Jäger
21 Gun-room
22 Wine cellar
23 Passage to kitchen offices
24 Entrance-hall
25 Household entrance
26 Page
27 Page
28 Table decker

N

3 A ground-floor plan of the House Block at Balmoral (after William Smith)

0   10   20   30   40   50
              feet

55

German poetry; visiting the estate tenants; discussing business with Lord John Russell who again had made himself Minister in Attendance and who was embarrassed to be informally visited by his sovereign in the bed sitting-room put at his disposal and not received formally in audience; even holding a Council Meeting in the little Castle, for which the presence of the Clerk was required. Mr Charles Greville therefore had to take the long drive from Perth over the mountains and was surprised to find he enjoyed his short visit. He attended the Braemar Gathering and Games, a small enough affair then; and, for so carping a critic of royalty, he expressed no small admiration for the Queen and the Prince living privately in a small establishment. 'There are no soldiers and the whole guard of the sovereign and of the whole Royal Family is a single policeman who walks about the grounds to keep off impertinent intruders or improper characters.' Neither he nor Lord John joined in the dancing of reels; they played billiards instead.

What Lord John made of this cementing of the Queen's devotion to North Britain can be imagined. So can his feelings when, as though they were not far enough from Westminster, the royal couple left him and George Anson to look after things, and retreated still further from civilization to Alt-na-Giuthasach, the cottage they had had renovated during the year. In fact two cottages had been joined by a corridor. One had been slightly enlarged by a wooden addition, re-arranged and furnished, and the ceilings as well as walls re-papered. This was for the Queen, the Prince, and a Maid of Honour, and their two lady's maids. The other cottage, permanently lived in by a ghillie called John Gordon and his wife, was for everyone else. The sovereign and her consort were entirely cut off from affairs of state with one Maid of Honour, two maids, a cook, a footman, the Prince's personal attendant, Rudolf Löhlein, his Jäger, John Macdonald, and a handful of snuff-taking ghillies.

The Queen noted in her Journal that they took a twenty minutes' walk to Loch Muick, which meant the lake of sorrow,* took out two boats, explored the lochside at various points, enjoying the wildness and desolation, and fished with a net. They took seventy trout. 'In going back, Albert rowed and Macdonald steered; and the lights were beautiful.' After dinner there was whist.

Five miles from the last tenuous thread with affairs they were exceptionally content.

---

* Elsewhere she gave a different translation, that it meant '*pigs, not* a pretty name'.

Chapter 9

Great changes

When the Court returned to Osborne in October, 1849, Lady Lyttelton was pleased with Miss Hildyard's report on the royal children, and especially that they were beginning to develop what was then described as a proper sense of charity and later as a social conscience. Their energy was prodigious. Even in bad weather they did not stay still. Lady Lyttelton told her daughter:

> The royalties, grown up and growing, spend much time during the heaviest gales and rain racing up and down my pet gallery (the open one)* in a way that would kill down most families speedily . . . This morning is lovely, blue sky and fleecy clouds and sparkling sea . . . enough to counteract my professional business in which I am now quite embarked again – accounts, tradesmen's letters, maids' quarrels, bad fitting of frocks, desirableness of rhubarb and magnesia, and, by way of intellectual pursuits, false French genders and elements of the multiplication table.

Their Governess admitted that the children had been much impressed by Scotland though she herself was not enamoured of the country or its products, and certainly not of Inverness tweed which she compared with 'second-best horse cloth'.

The Queen's persistent lament at having left Balmoral greatly irritated her. On 5 October she complained that the Queen was still extolling the highlands, certain 'that Scotch air, Scotch people, Scotch hill, Scotch rivers, Scotch woods are all far preferable to those of any other nation in or out of this world; that deer-stalking is the most charming of amusements, etc. etc.' Lady Lyttelton added with unaccustomed asperity: 'The chief support to my spirits is that I shall never see, hear or witness these various charms.'

* This useful open loggia above the Marble Corridor and the connecting wing to the Pavilion was improved, or spoilt according to one's view, by a temporary glass and iron screen in 1877, and, later still, by a permanent structure in a Betjemanesque conservatory-cum-railway-station style.

As might be expected in such a closed community, the Court was not the scene of perpetual cordiality; yet only three days after Lady Lyttelton's grumble, it was united by common mourning.

George Anson had left Balmoral with the royal party on 27 September, and, because his wife was carrying a child and was not at all well, he had sought the Prince's permission to stop in Derby and go to visit her at her parents' home in Staffordshire. There, at New Lodge in Neewood Forest, at one in the afternoon on Monday 8 October he was seized with some sort of paralysis or fit and in just under three hours he was dead.★

Anson had been popular at Court and with ministers. Everyone grieved at Osborne. The Queen was frantic with concern for Mrs Anson who was one of her eight Bedchamber Women. As it turned out, she need not have been for Mrs Anson successfully bore her child and, by strange chance, of all the children born to them this was the only one to thrive; and six years later she made a second happy marriage.

The Queen was also frantic with worry about Prince Albert who was in floods of tears. Tears, then as now, were not regarded as a sign of unmanliness by the aristocracy and working people. The stiff upper lip was very much the mark of all grades of the middle class.

But after the initial shock and burst of weeping, the loss of so close a friend as well as an invaluable adviser made the Prince desolate. He did not attend the funeral at Sudbury in Derbyshire but appointed no one as his Treasurer, and, strangely, the office of Keeper of the Queen's Privy Purse remained vacant for a considerable time, an assistant doing the necessary work. Many months passed before Colonel Charles Phipps was given both George Anson's chief appointments and the Prince took on as his Private Secretary, Colonel Grey, son of Earl Grey, a former Prime Minister.

Had Stockmar been in his tower at Windsor when George Anson died it would have been a solace to the Prince but some time before the Baron had taken himself off to assist with the re-constitution of Germany. Prince Albert wrote to him: 'The blow is painful, and the loss immense. If you could come to me now, I should regard it as a great act of friendship.'

Unfortunately Stockmar was feeling his age and beginning to imagine things about his health. He felt he was in no condition to travel. And so the Prince turned to the monotony of strenuous work to dull his misery.

But some hard blows still lay ahead. During the month they spent away from Osborne playing their official part in the London season, the

★ By a strange coincidence one of the Prince's Grooms of the Bedchamber was General Sir George Anson, and he died only a month after the Treasurer. They were not related.

Queen was subjected to a brutal attack by an ex-officer who leapt into her open carriage and, before the eyes of her children, commenced to beat her with a knobbed cane. The Prince excused the man as 'manifestly deranged', but he was greatly shaken by the viciousness of the attack.

Then, two days later, Sir Robert Peel was thrown from his horse in Rotten Row. He was a big, heavy man and smashed his collar-bone and shoulder-bone. Under ordinary circumstances he had an acute sensibility to pain, finding even the prick of a needle unbearable. It was inconceivable to imagine what he suffered under those compound fractures. For three days he lay in agony, and then died.

The Prince had lost his second and only friend in Britain. 'He has felt, and feels, Sir Robert's loss *dreadfully*,' wrote the Queen. Once more Stockmar was asked to return to England. 'If you can come, pray do so, for we have need of you,' pleaded the Prince. But even now Stockmar was not able to come, and Lear-like misfortunes heaped upon the Prince's head.

His mourning was exacerbated by an attack on the Great Exhibition that Anson and Peel had done so much to support. It came from the press, and, in Parliament, from the very protectionists who had toppled Peel from office. They saw the Exhibition as an encouragement to free trade, and attempted to trounce it by censuring the choice of the site in Hyde Park. Unwisely they chose as their spokesman Colonel Sibthorpe who was so reactionary that, if he lost control, he really could not be taken seriously by anyone. He loathed all change, all progress, declaring 'he would rather meet a highwayman or see a burglar on his premises than a (railway) engineer', and the Prince had no cause to thank him for it was Sibthorpe who had moved the amendment before he came to England that the consort's customary income of £50,000 be reduced to £30,000. Fortunately, the Colonel became frenzied in the House of Commons. He prayed that hail or lightning be sent from heaven to destroy the Exhibition, and his hysteria lost the protectionists their vote of censure.

As much as anything to the memory of his two great friends, the Prince threw himself passionately into organizing the exhibition hall, soon called the Crystal Palace because it was constructed of iron and glass and built in cruciform fashion enclosed two fine elms at the end of each transept.*

Work became the Prince's anodyne. Lord John Russell was again quarrelling with the Foreign Secretary about his reckless management

---

* The Crystal Palace was designed by Sir Joseph Paxton, gardener to the Duke of Devonshire, who conceived the idea of examining the leaf of the giant water-lily *Victoria amazonica*. 'Nature', he said, 'has provided the leaf with longitudinal and transverse girders and supports that I, borrowing from it, have adopted in this building.'

of affairs. He took his troubles down to Osborne to consult the Prince, and an immense memorandum was the result plus a sharp note from the Queen to show to Lord Palmerston 'to explain *what it is she expects from her Foreign Secretary*'. The Prince interested himself in the smallest details of the arrangements for the Great Exhibition.

But he tried to make some time for his children. Lady Lyttelton described a pretty picture of him joining in the Princes' play.

> Such merry voices sounding from all over the lawn in at my window, and a pretty sight to see and think of. Old Count Mensdorff★ recovering from his gout in a wheeling-chair drawn by a tiny pony, the Queen standing by, most attentively taking care of him. The Prince and his two boys noisily and easily managing Prince Alfred's new kite which is unrivalled in soaring ambition, and really gets almost out of ken. Then plenty of red coats dotted about, all waiting.

Misfortunes continued to pour upon him. 'Germany appears to me to be going utterly to the dogs,' he wrote to Stockmar. 'Are there no longer men of heart and head, who might avert the disaster? It is altogether too sad.' Even sadder was the death of poor old Louis Philippe at Claremont and then that of his daughter Queen Louise of the Belgians. Uncle Leopold was a widower for the second time.

It was but another weight to further Prince Albert's *schwermut* when Lady Lyttelton came to the conclusion she should retire and leave the younger children to the care of someone else. No one wished her to go, and she was pressed to postpone her departure for a little. But ultimately she did leave the royal nurseries in January, 1851, at the beginning of Exhibition Year. At the same time Thomas Cubitt submitted his final account and formally gave up the works at Osborne.

These great changes, like the loss of the Prince's two great friends, marked the start of a new era for the Royal Family. This was prominently marked first by the success of the Exhibition that was so resounding that it confounded all the Prince's critics, and then, in 1852, by the formal acquisition of Balmoral.

A price was at last agreed between Mr White and the Fife Trustees and the 17,400-acre estate that marched to the summit of Loch-na-Gar became the property of Prince Albert for the sum of 30,000 guineas.

★ Uncle by marriage to both the Queen and Prince Albert.

Chapter 10

Accommodation for at least a hundred

After first visiting Uncle Leopold in Belgium the Queen and the Prince went to upper-Deeside to take formal possession of the property.

A delighted step-son wrote to the Duchess Marie of Saxe-Coburg-Gotha on 3 September:

> Balmoral is in full splendour, and the people there are very glad that it is now entirely our own. The deer were so very polite as to show themselves yesterday close to the house in the sacred number of three. Whether from a reverential feeling on our part, or from excessive lack of skill, I know not, but three of us, to wit, Lord Malmesbury, Col Phipps, and myself shot . . . and missed them, each of the others twice, and I, as became my rank and station, four times.

It was an exceedingly happy holiday marred by only one melancholy event, the death of the old Duke of Wellington who had been a private counsellor to the Queen all her adult life, a close friend of all the Royal Family, and godfather to Prince Arthur who was named after him. The Queen was deeply conscious of her own loss and the loss to the nation and she ordered that the Army should mourn for the Duke as long as for a member of the Royal Family, but the intoxication of actually possessing Balmoral helped to put her grief on one side for renewal at the time of the Duke's splendid heraldic funeral nine weeks later.

All the great estate houses were in occupation. At Birkhall Sir James and Lady Clark were enjoying a family holiday and, at the same time, caring for a Miss Parthenope Nightingale who was highly neurotic and had been born, as her name suggested, in Naples, and whose more famous sister was born, as her name also suggested, in Florence. The Duchess of Kent and her son Charles of Leiningen were installed at Abergeldie Castle, a place she used regularly each summer from 1850, despite the supposed hauntings of a witch, constant manifestations of bad luck, and a rickety aerial cableway over the Dee, which was a dangerous contraption that once drowned a newly married couple.

There were organized and spontaneous drives and rides and explorations. There was plenty of excellent sport. There was a ball on a boarded lawn given by Duff neighbours; the ladies wearing the plaid scarf, the gentlemen the kilt with doublet and black neckcloth,* diced hose and pumps, and armed with a dirk beside the tasselled dress sporran and a skean-dhu stuck in the right stocking; a joyous evening when the royal party was greeted by seven pipers at full skirl, and highlanders shouting 'Nis! nis! nis!' – the Gaelic equivalent of 'Hip-hip-hurray' – and reels were danced to the light of resinous torches; and all without a word of stricture from the local Kirk Session. There was the building of a cairn on Craig Gowan to the south of the house, a heap of rocks laid individually by members of the Royal Family, the Household, and all the servants and local neighbours, to the playing of the pipes and the absorption of a good deal of whisky. There were as ever, raspberries and strawberries to enjoy in the late northern season. We may be sure, too, that between them the Prince and Miss Hildyard kept the children fully occupied with their natural history collections. Balmoral had flowers that did not grow at Osborne, the greatest treasure being an orchid called Creeping Ladies' Tresses that rambled through the moss and pineneedles of the woods. And there were butterflies to catch never seen on the Isle of Wight such as the Scotch Argus and the Large Heath for which the Prince had a special affection because it also bred in Thüringia where it was called *Mohrenfalter*. Then there were birds to observe and identify: Goosanders and Corncrakes, Merlins, Oyster Catchers, Whimbrels, Siskins and Twites.

Inevitably there were some unpleasantnesses. The Queen, Landseer-fashion, was sketching the carcass of a stag shot by her husband when 'poor Vicky, unfortunately, seated herself on a wasp's nest and was much stung'.

Lord Malmesbury, who had twice missed his stag on the Balmoral lawn, and Foreign Secretary in the new Tory Administration of Lord Derby, was Minister in Attendance. Whether or not he enjoyed himself was not recorded, but he did say that the Queen and the Prince were perfectly happy together, and was supposed to have made rude remarks about Sir Robert's house as 'totally unfit for royal personages'. Another Minister-in-Attendance, Lord Clarendon, was to refer to it, not unkindly, as 'the scramble of rural royalty'. Now that the Prince had become owner there was no need for him to hold his hand any longer

---

* Prince Rupert of the Rhine invented the froth of lace called a jabot worn by western highland gentlemen, but it was not usually worn in the east.

and in his head and on paper he made extensive plans to do something about the scramble.

Fortuituously in August, only a month before, the Queen had been given a present. All her life she was given presents that ranged in value and variety from furs, diamonds and carriages to a bicycle and a pumpkin that weighed 140 pounds, but the gift of John Camden Neild was the most valuable and perhaps the strangest of all. He was a miserly bachelor, nominally a barrister, who at his death, after legacies to his two executors, bequeathed the whole of his fortune to the Queen. It amounted to half a million pounds. As the old man had no known relations, and Uncle Leopold thoroughly approved of her accepting, the Queen did so, increasing the legacies to the executors, restoring the chancel of the church where her benefactor was buried and putting up a memorial window.

The Balmoral estate was nominally Prince Albert's but his own fortune was not great. Mr Neild's bequest permitted him to enlarge his vision for what was really needed, a new house built at a small distance from the old.

To those born during or after the disintegration of the order that, with some upheavals, existed in England from 1381, and in Scotland for far longer, it might seem extraordinary that the Prince envisaged his new Castle would have to provide accommodation for at least a hundred people. Therefore it would be of value to assess, as far as possible, who needed to be accommodated.

The outdoor staff on the estate under the head-gardener, head-keeper and head-groom, largely lived in lodges or at the stables, but the indoor staff under the steward and housekeeper, could not have been sufficient for a royal visit. They would need supplementing and this was not simply a question of a pair of extra footmen and a few maid servants. In the travelling suite there were cooks, the Queen's coachman, and outriders, her piper, attendants on the royal children old enough to travel, and selected pages and grooms of the presence, an officer from A Division of New Scotland Yard, her personal servants and her husband's.

Beyond this, part of the Queen's Household then in waiting would have had to accompany her, and, although in her old age and as a widow the Queen was content to have less of her ladies in attendance, it is unlikely that in Prince Albert's lifetime she much diminished her usual Household when she was in Scotland. This must have included two Ladies of the Bedchamber, or two Bedchamber Women, and two Maids of Honour, each with a lady's maid. Amongst her Gentlemen were a Minister in Attendance, the Keeper of the Privy Purse, the Master of the Household, a Lord in Waiting and a Groom in Waiting, and two equerries, with possibly a Gentleman Usher, each with a manservant. She would not have taken a Domestic Chaplain because either the Church of England Service was read in the Castle drawing-room or, more usually, the Queen and the Prince walked over the Dee by the chain-bridge to take their seats in the Balmoral part of the gallery of Crathie Church.* The Prince found the preaching and doctrines of the Church of Scotland much to his taste and the Queen truly believed she was Head of the Established Church of Scotland as well as that of the Church of England. It later fell to Disraeli to enlighten her that she was 'Head' of neither; but 'Supreme Governor' of the Church of England and that 'the connection of the Sovereign with the Kirk is purely civil'. However, this unwelcome disclosure was not to come for several years and in 1853 she was still in her happy state of illusion. She also regarded Dr Robertson as the Commissioner of Balmoral and a Kirk elder rather than as a general practitioner, therefore a Physician in Ordinary would have been in the suite.

The Prince's household was smaller and Colonel Phipps doubled up as his Treasurer and Treasurer to the Prince of Wales as well as the Queen's Privy Purse, and Colonel Grey was left in England as Private Secretary.† There were only his two Equerries and Dr Becker, the librarian, with their valets.

Providing accommodation for so many besides the members of the royal family and the private visitors, demanded skilful planning. In addition there were the functional rooms that were necessary for the maintenance of such an establishment at that time; pantries for plate and glass and napery, larders, stores for oil, candles, linen, coal, and wood; kitchens and bakehouses.

It was plain to the Prince that Sir Robert's castle, however much enlarged, would never be really satisfactory. He had the land, he had the schemes in his head, at last he had the resources to talk what Stendhal called 'the noble language of architecture'.

On 8 September, 1852 he sent to Aberdeen for his architect.

---

* Members of the Free Kirk met in Dr Robertson's barn, which, so soon after the Disruption, shows a surprising breadth of understanding from a man who was an elder of the parish Kirk.

† The Queen did not have an official Private Secretary until some time after the Prince's death and even then she had to beg for one. Presumably this was because, in theory at any rate, her First Minister was reckoned her confidential Private Secretary; but the lack of one caused a lamentable amount of extra work for the Prince.

Chapter 11

The elusive Mr Smith

It was not 'Tudor Johnny' who answered the Prince's summons to Balmoral. Like old 'Sink'em' he was dead. He had been ailing for some time and had died in July that year. His business and offices fell upon his partner and son William Smith who found himself City Architect and Superintendent of Work that, besides the supervision of public buildings, also involved keeping the streets cleaned and lighted and running up a scaffold for executions.

Unlike his father and grandfather, William Smith was rather a shadowy figure in Aberdeen Society. He had no nickname. But because he left so few traces and so slight an impression of his personality, he might fittingly have been called 'Elusive Smith'. It was not that he had a weak character, though some members of his profession have scorned his acceptance of the Prince's ideas in the planning of the new Balmoral, inferring he was a toady and insufficiently aware of the dignity of his position. Here they were wrong, William Smith's position as an architect was already assured. He had no need to be sensitive about relationships with his client. He swiftly recognized what Thomas Cubitt had recognized, that the Prince had modern and interesting ideas and was a gifted designer not simply an architect *manqué*, and that he was the true creator of the building. As a professional architect he conceived it was his duty to have overall supervision of the construction, put the Prince's ideas on paper, offer suggestions, make any necessary modifications, and ensure that the craftsmanship was accurate, beautiful and absolutely up to the high standard of Messrs Smith. Moreover a twelve-year-old grandson was once moved to describe him as an 'aul' de'il', and that suggested a certain force of character.

Smith's career was straightforward enough. Educated in Aberdeen, he went to London to work for eighteen months under the eye of the founder of the Royal Institute of British Architects. Then, before returning to work with his father, he spent two years in Italy and Greece painting and sketching and making notes. At the age of twenty-nine he married the daughter of a Naval Surgeon, the ceremony taking place in the drawing-room of his father's house as was the custom in Kirk circles at that time. He was fond of music and painting in water-colours, and was a devout Presbyterian. His obituary notice mentioned his 'highly sensitive nature' and how he shrank from publicity. The panegyric preached after his death mentioned his courtesy and integrity, and his great reticence. Shyness made him the natural friend of animals and children, which was just as well because his house was full of both. He and his wife were blessed with the Psalmist's quiverful, and had sixteen children. Possibly the Family Bible, that recorded all the children's births and marriages and deaths, suggested a reason for his withdrawal from the world. Those of the children who died young, at the ages of 2 and 3, and 10, and 20, all died of tuberculosis, as did his son John, the only architect in the family, at the age of 40, and another son who predeceased his father by nine months. In William Smith's home there could be no excitement; there was a perpetual hush, and everyone trod lightly; it was a house of invalidism and sustained sorrow.

But all this lay ahead when Prince Albert summoned him to Balmoral. Smith had been married for five years, and his only regret was that, as yet, he and his wife had had no children. He was young, only two years older than the Prince. And at once they got on.

Considering how many people recorded their disapproval of Prince Albert, his capacity for getting on with the people who knew him well and mattered to him most suggested that, though a natural shyness sometimes made him appear proud and stiff, he did have an amiable side.

The Queen noted that the two men spent the whole morning together, choosing a new site a little more than a hundred yards from the old house, aligned so that it had fine views. A glance at a small-scale map could suggest that Balmoral was in a hole surrounded claustrophobically by huge mountains, but in fact the riverlands at that point were wide enough to permit the enjoyment of a variety of prospects rare even amongst the many beautiful places then existing in Great Britain.

The Prince was determined to take the maximum advantage of the complete break from Sir Robert Gordon's castle. The soil was right, the site was right. Together he and William Smith pored over rough sketches, paced out rough measurements, and made notes. Because of its closeness to the Dee that frequently flooded there was no question of having a large basement of offices such as Cubitt had built at Osborne. A carefully sited coal-cellar and a boiler-house were all that Smith advised below ground level. Therefore, in his overall plan, the Prince separated the living-quarters from the working-quarters. In fact his block plan bore some resemblance to Tudor Johnnie's original work for

Sir Robert Gordon, and to the plans he made for the Prince in 1848 that were never executed. Though, ultimately, seen at eye-level the buildings would seem to be a conglomeration and the details lost, the Prince's plan, looked at from above, was of two rectangular blocks, each enclosing a court and connected not end to end or side to side but corner to corner. At this meeting point, and joined to the two blocks with wings, was to be that common feature of all Scottish baronial castles, a square tower. This was to have five floors, the fifth given over to a four-dialled clock, and projecting turrets topped by pepper-pots at three of the corners with a long circular staircase at the fourth corner that gave access to each floor and, above the leaded and parapeted roof, provided an ornate flag tower for running up the Royal Standard. In addition to all this were to be stables even larger than the office block and venison★ larders. There were also to be a pair of buildings near the river, presumably for housing water bailiffs and storing fishing gear.

Considering the world-wide fame of the Castle, its first plans and elevations were extraordinarily difficult to trace. There were no copies at the Balmoral Estate Office, none in the Royal Archives at Windsor, and no official at either place was able to give a lead. The Aberdeen city and university libraries and archives were equally bare. So were Grampian Regional Archives. After months of inquiry copies were located held by the Royal Commission on the Ancient and Historical Monuments of Scotland, and the Commission kindly provided photographs on which the plans on page 54 and on page 55 were based. The originals had been stored in the files of an eminent firm of Edinburgh architects, Rowand Anderson, Kininmonth & Paul, that had been responsible at some time for later alterations or repairs to the Castle. On dissolution of the partnership and renaming of the firm in 1976, the Smith originals were handed, with other collections of drawings, to Edinburgh University on permanent loan. The hunt for that particular slipper was lengthy and painstaking but was rewarded with success. The hunt for Prince Albert's sketches and roughed-out plans was blocked by the discovery that, in the opinion of William Smith's great-niece they were kept for a time in Aberdeen then taken to London where they were blown to pieces in an air raid during the Second World War. At their first meeting, however, the Prince's rough plans were handed to William Smith for his draughtsmen to work on, and both were in accord about the main principles of the design.

The architect was invited to share the Queen's table at luncheon, an unusual distinction because unlike most parents at that time, the Queen

★ In his natural history notes Charles St John observed that at that period the generality of highlanders 'call every eatable animal, fish, flesh or fowl, venison, or as they pronounce it "vennison" . . . they tell you that the snipes are "good vennison", or that trout are not good "vennison" in the winter.'

and the Prince sometimes allowed their elder children to be at luncheon
and it was a true family meal. William Smith found himself being
questioned on the Disruption between the Church of Scotland and the
Free Kirk that had taken place nine years before over the question of
church patronage. He himself belonged to the Church of Scotland but
he spoke admiringly of the sacrifices made by the Free Kirk ministers
who had given up their livings for conscience sake. It was at this point,
when taking a second generous helping of pudding from his father, that
the future Edward VII, evidently impressed, made what must surely
have been one of the most remarkable public statements of his life.
'Papa,' he said, 'I think I should like to be a Free Church minister.'

The architect left that afternoon, much impressed by his contact with
the Royal Family, his head and note books full of the Prince's ideas. The
aim was a piece of scenic architecture so that the new house in the Scottish baronial style and the new gardens should be in exact conformity
with the ranges of foothills rising to the summit of Loch-na-Gar.

Because the Prince could not often be in Scotland to supervise the
landscaping himself, it was arranged that James Giles be called in to
interpret and draw up the Prince's rough designs, and, with the help of a
surveyor, James Beattie, oversee all the work out of doors. William
Smith was responsible for taking on contractors and subcontractors,
sanctioning their work, and all else. The buildings were to be of local
stone, and the labour-force also local.

Articles in newspapers and periodicals, entries in guides, even works
concerned with the architectural and historical heritage of Scotland,
have perpetuated the idea that 'the Prince's "Deeside Thüringia" . . .
was entirely a local product'.* It was true that the main contractor was a
Mr Stuart from the prison town of Peterhead, the head mason and all
his assistants were north-easterners as well as the clerk of works, but,
added to the list of sub-contractors who were responsible for joinery,
plumbing, the slating, bell-hanging and iron-work – all of whom were
from Aberdeen – was an exception: 'Mr Cubitt, of London, the hot
and cold baths.' It was not only a testimony of the Prince's loyalty to a
man he much admired, but also a just exchange for the many giant
granite urns and fountains constructed in Aberdeen by Messrs
McDonald and Leslie to decorate the Osborne terraces. And there were
two other exceptions. Most of the furniture was to be supplied by the
London firm of Holland; and the London sculptor John Thomas,
whose work was admired by the Prince, was to be commissioned not
only to supply carved reliefs for the outside of the building, but also to
design a raised flower garden to the south of the tower and the connecting wing. England did pay its small contribution to the Prince's castle.

* The *Scotsman* of 12 September, 1953.

Chapter 12

'The work is terribly hard'

On arriving at Osborne for the autumn of 1852 the Royal Family found the Marble Corridor entirely completed.

Mr Moxon and Mr Muller, men employed to paint the elaborate designs of Ludwig Gruner, had marbled the pilasters that divided the corridor into bays and painted the coved ceilings in classical motifs using the classical colours of black and red, umber and blue-green. The floor was tiled with Minton ware from the Potteries fired in the same colours and, at regular intervals along the corridor were marble statues on marbled plinths. One was a life-size statue of the Queen by John Gibson sculpted in the late 1840s. Some were animals. Many were heroes and divinities from classical legends. A number were on pivots so that, theoretically, they could be revolved.

More than forty years later two young Equerries to the Queen were to discover that some of the statues were massive. In an idle moment they swivelled a figure of Psyche, that beautiful wretch condemned by jealous Venus to do superhuman tasks, and to their dismay she slowly toppled into their arms. It required all their strength to lower her without accident to the tiled floor. Footmen were summoned to assist. But the marble beauty defied all their efforts. The next day a crane was employed to replace her on her pedestal and the Queen sent a direction to all members of the Household that they were not to play with the statues.

To welcome visitors to this neo-classical hallway, the word 'SALVE' coloured gold was let into the pavement, and that December it greeted Lord Derby who had crossed the Solent to hand in his seals of office, and then it greeted Lord Aberdeen who had come to be asked to form a government. As he professed to be neither Whig nor Tory, Conservative nor Liberal, forming a Ministry took a good deal of time, but at last, to the Queen's relief, he managed it. Understandably, her grasp of the two-party system at that period when it was undergoing such Laocoon-like struggles to sort itself out was not profound. The Prince was there as her 'permanent minister', and, if there had to be change, it was better to have someone she knew in command. 'Dear Lord Aberdeen', was a personal friend and neighbour in Scotland.

In April 1853 the Queen's fourth son and eighth child was born. At her special request, Sir James Clark gave his permission for chloroform to be judiciously applied by an expert anaesthetist from Edinburgh, and she found it made a great difference. Thus she allied herself to the cause of 'Aetherial' Simpson, the pioneer of chloroform, who held that pain was not a decree of Providence, and she made both it and him respectable.

By this time she was feeling so thoroughly Scotch herself that not only did she give the infant Prince Leopold a third Christian name of Duncan, but she also determined that he should have a wet nurse from the highlands. It was a frustrating experiment. The nurse turned out to be one of the very few people on the Balmoral estate who had no English. She could only converse with the piper and John Macdonald and was unintelligible in the nursery. Furthermore the baby did not thrive and Sir James Clark declared that his compatriot's milk was unsuitable. Despite the fact that she herself, in her father's expression, had been 'nourished at nature's founts', the Queen abhorred the thought of nursing her own babies. Once more she looked at the appositely named Cowes where a shipwright's wife was found with abundant milk for the infant prince.

Although her confinement had been less painful and exhausting, the Queen suffered her usual depression afterwards and, when it was discovered that the baby had haemophilia, her depression deepened. Hysteria alternated with sulks. Not for the first time, there were emotional scenes between the royal couple that greatly disturbed the tranquillity of Osborne.

If the Prince tried to escape his wife she followed him, still wrangling. If he pretended that nothing had happened, she accused him of not caring. If he did manage to get away, he made the mistake of writing a rational account of her failings and begged her to argue on paper rather than with her mouth. Rather naturally this provoked her further. Thereafter he simply tried to keep out of his wife's way at Osborne until they left the island for London and a short part of the season. After that the Prince went to military exercises under canvas in wet weather, caught a chill and contracted measles. The disease passed relentlessly through the family and the Household at Osborne. Everyone was well enough for a review off Spithead, the first of its kind to show the superiority of men-of-war with screw propellors and, at the end of August, the Queen and her consort paid a visit to an Irish great exhibition held in Dublin. In September, they all went north to Balmoral.

Elusive Smith had not been idle since the previous October. Building materials, with horses and their leaders and farriers, wagons, barrows, scaffolding, ladders, tools and other essentials had been gradually assembled. A work force had been gathered and housed in long wooden shacks, but neither the craftsmen nor labourers had been entirely co-operative and occasionally had struck for higher wages. Strikes were becoming more common. The Prince was of the opinion they sprang from the labour shortage resulting from the popular emigration to Australia, China and California. This had resulted in a rise in the cost of necessaries and of wages. Understanding the reason, he was not averse from paying the men more.

He was fortunate in that the estate contained some of the best building granite. Sir Charles Lyell, a leading geologist, was an old acquaintance, and had twice paid visits to Balmoral. He had examined this granite in Glen Gelder south of the Castle towards Loch Muick and analysed it as of pure quartz, felspar and mica, without any chalk; in other words, top-quality stone of an uncommon whiteness with a fine grain.

Even before the long winter broke labourers had begun to win it from the quarry at Invercalder by blasting or breaking it out with rockdrills and steel wedges. There are no records of powered saws being used there, though hand saws and steam saws had been in existence for some time. Granite being an intractable, adamantine stone, not easily cleaved by wedges or dressed to rectangle, meant a great deal of very hard hand-work. The blocks were hauled to the site on wagons and worked on there. Masons handwrought the detailed work such as the cornices and lintels by pointing, clawing, chiselling and smoothing. Slate could not be obtained locally. It was brought over the northern hills by pack mule from the Gordon country of Strath-bogie. As soon as the ground allowed, drains and foundations had been dug and the building begun. By the time of the royal arrival the ground-floor of part of the house was almost up.

It was no new thing for the Queen to open or lay foundations for structures already founded, open and even in use. A ceremony was arranged so that the new Balmoral Castle should be properly founded and blessed.

The Queen was less lyrical than usual in her published account of the event. She merely noted that it poured with rain from ten until two, that her mother brought a party over from Abergeldie for the occasion, and she copied out the printed programme that read like any Army Order. It 'was strictly adhered to.'

The reporter of the *Aberdeen Journal*, one of the more than a hundred newspapers extant in Scotland at that time, was more effusive in his description of what happened after the Parish Minister had prayed for a blessing, and the royal party had signed a dated parchment and placed it in a bottle, with current coins of the realm, for sealing in a cavity. That done –

> her Majesty was handed a silver trowel, and being supplied with mortar, laid it on in the most precise and workmanlike manner. The upper stone was now lowered to its bed and adjusted. The Queen next applied the square and plummet, and the builder having pronounced the work perfect, her Majesty struck the stone three times with a golden mallet. The Cornucopia was then offered. A quantity of corn, as cut from the field, over which the Queen poured wine and oil as a symbol of peace and plenty.

With rising excitement the reporter went on to say that at 4 o'clock the workmen, preceded by the architect, the contractors, the carpenter, and the mason, proceeded to the Iron Ballroom where covers had been laid for 140 guests. There was a most sumptuous dinner with many toasts. Athletic exercises on the lawn followed. Then there was a ball, Willie Blair, the Royal fiddler, putting life and mettle into the heels of the dancers. Apparently the royal party were not a little surprised at the vigour of the reels. A plentiful supper sustained the dancers until the ball ended.

Doubtless the ample supplies of whisky provided were supplemented. Certainly the mason had a private supplier of smuggled and illegally distilled whisky. Being named Charles Stewart he was known locally as 'The Princie'.

Once more the Kirk Session was silent. It even remained so when presented with evidence that the sixty-foot long ballroom put together by iron pilasters, plates, bolts and nuts, was eventually to be replaced by an even more spacious and more permanent granite ballroom built to run the length of the west side of the new office-block.

Beyond her brief description of the stone-laying the Queen published little in *Leaves* about their stay at Balmoral in 1853. She failed to mention that, only a few days after the ceremony a fire swept through the workmen's living quarters. No lives were lost but the men's property was destroyed. New huts were quickly built and an account rendered to the Prince for private belongings lost that amounted to £3 18 11s. 7½d. It was immediately paid.

Three Ministers in Attendance followed each other. The Prime Minister, 'Athenian' Aberdeen, was there in full highland dress, elegantly dancing reels with his royal mistress. Lord Clarendon was also there with his sharp but genial references to Joseph and Eliza as he called the Prince and the Queen to the very small coterie of society in London that corresponded to the exclusive *crème de la crème* of Viennese society. The third, less welcome Minister was Lord Palmerston who never troubled himself to get on with either the Queen or the Prince. Before he left England his wife, Lord Melbourne's sister, had begged: 'Make yourself agreable (*sic*) and to appear to enjoy the Society.' There was not much pretence about Palmerston. He refused to discuss affairs of state beyond the broadest hinting. He would not dance reels. Instead he played billiards with the Prince. It was as well, perhaps, that he was in attendance for only one week.

The Prince enjoyed himself. He shot well so that there were four carcasses in the new game larder. He busied himself with making plans and overseeing the building. He wrote to Stockmar on 12 September full of news about the new house: 'The work is terribly hard, and for cheapness' sake the walls will have to be carried up several feet thick.' At the beginning of next month he wrote again. This time there was a chill note: 'Come soon if you can. Your counsel and support will be of extraordinary value to us! The Turks have declared war.'

Chapter 13

Topsy-turveydom

The Turkish débâcle heralded a period of great trouble for the Prince. His part in the events that led up to the declaration of the Crimean War were as widely published as they were misinterpreted. Members of the Royal Family were accustomed to being held up to opprobrium. Indeed the lampoons, street ballads, and cartoons they suffered were vastly more wounding than anything published about the British Royal Family in the twentieth century. But this attack on the Prince was ferocious. Amongst other charges he was accused of treachery to England. Londoners crowded to the Tower expecting to see him arrive at Traitor's Gate.

Stockmar conceived it his duty to be a Job's comforter and sent a large memorandum on why the English Court was unpopular. The Prince wrote to thank him for his 'wise words at a time when we might fancy we were living in a madhouse'. He continued: 'The state of affairs is precisely what you indicate. Only here and there I am able to fill up details which may have escaped you at a distance', and went on to write an even larger memorandum than the Baron's.

The Queen became so upset by the 'atrocious calumnies' smearing her husband that, at the beginning of the Parliamentary session at the end of January 1854, she obliged both parties to clear his name publicly in the House of Commons. Then her piper, MacKay, went out of his mind; old Lord Anglesea, who had lost a leg at Waterloo but who still sailed at Cowes and was the last Captain of Cowes Castle, died of a stroke at the age of eighty-six; the Crimean War began; and cholera spread not only amongst the troops, but everywhere and killed at a frightening speed. A guest of Lady Palmerston's was taken ill in her drawing-room and died in two hours.

The Queen was heartened by the arrival at Court as a Lady of the Bedchamber of Jane, Lady Churchill, with whom she at once established a close rapport and who was to be the longest-standing friend of her life. And she fended off news of humiliations and privations suffered by her Army at the front either by refusing to believe the despatches or by aggressively insisting that no inquiry could be made into Army affairs until the war was over and done with.

The Prince, no longer in danger of the Tower, devoted himself passionately to the re-organization of the Army Commissariat.

At Osborne they both took some solace in the placing of a locally-made swimming bath between the tea- and boat-house at the beach hut with a mosaic floor and domed ceiling dignified by the name of the exedra. There was a difference of about 14 feet between the highest spring tide and the lowest ebb so the bath was moored 200 yards from the shore and served by a small boat manned by a pair of sailors from the royal yacht. It was made of wooden battens that kept bathers safely in and went up and down with the tide. At the centre was a movable grating that could be raised or lowered at pleasure. The same sort of collapsible baths had been used on the reaches of the Thames, though not with much success on account of the foul water. Off Osborne beach the bath was a great success and many of the royal children learnt to swim there as, eventually, did many of their own children. Another attraction at Osborne in the summer of 1854 was the final assembly of a pre-fabricated Swiss cottage. It had been arriving piecemeal for months and at last could be constructed near the children's garden plots. It was a complete chalet containing miniature furniture, a miniature kitchen and dining-room, space for the children's natural history collections, and even had the miniature shop of a grocer named Spratt. The Prince had an idea that the ordinary accomplishments were not enough. His children dug their plots with tools and barrows made by Mr Cubitt's men, and the produce of his sons' work was sold to the kitchens at market price to teach them the value of money. His daughters cooked cakes, and they sold and bought at the tiny counter of Spratt's 'Grocer to her Majesty' to learn the same. Some of the nine children might have learnt from these exercises to be practical and count their change and know what money was about, but none of them made it very evident in their grown-up lives. A sizeable fort was also built where the princes might play soldiers, now generally called Prince Arthur's fort because he was the only one of the four to exercise the profession of arms.

Occasionally suitable boys were invited to stay to play with the young princes and that summer young Lord Edward Percy St Maur was a visitor and was given, as a parting gift, a picture of Osborne House made entirely of closely packed coloured sands from Alum Bay. It was, and still is an art form peculiar to the Isle of Wight, and the reproduction of Lord Edward's picture shown in plate 7 indicates how fascinating the medium was considering the limitations imposed on it.

Seen through a glass, even the details of the lightning conductor on the clock tower, and the colours of the Royal Standard flying from the flagstaff can be made out. The Prince, who appreciated craftsmanship and knew what young boys liked, might conceivably have had a hand in choosing the gift, but it is unlikely they saw much of him during the Crimean War when he was so exceptionally busy.

As well as his investigation into Army supplies, dictating memoranda, writing letters, and consulting experts, he supervised the trials of a new royal yacht – strangely another paddle *Victoria and Albert*, not a screw-driven ship – designed a Royal Pavilion at Aldershot with an interior that suggested the tent of an eastern potentate; and, when work on despatch boxes permitted, he supervised improvements to the estate at Osborne, and, from a distance, because their visit to Scotland in 1854 was short, he tried to keep in touch with the work at Balmoral.

The Queen was too wrapped up in the war to enjoy Scotland in her usual way, though she did find great comfort in a sermon preached at the Kirk by a minister who was to become her intimate adviser, Dr McLeod of Glasgow. The comfort was not sustained for long, because in some ways, 1855 was even worse than 1854.

There was yet more frenetic topsy-turveydom: Lord Palmerston, whom she could not abide, was forced on her as First Minister; the death of Britain's enemy, the Emperor of Russia; a State Visit by the Emperor and Empress of the French, Britain's hereditary foes but now her allies; all the children stricken with scarlet fever and the second floor of the Osborne Pavilion like a hospital; and a return State Visit to France, landing at 'the very anchorage where Napoleon had proposed to invade England' to the strains of 'Rule Britannia' played by a French band. Finally, a little before Christmas, came the expected but sad news that Thomas Cubitt had died at his country house. In her Journal on Christmas Eve the Queen recalled his excellence: 'A better, kinder hearted or more simple, unassuming man never breathed and Osborne must ever be bound up for us with the memory of this excellent man . . . We feel we owe much to him.'

1 Brighton Pavilion, 1845. A water-colour by C. R. Stanley

2 Old Osborne House in October 1844. Water-colour by C. R. Stanley

3 New kitchens at Osborne designed by Thomas Cubitt

4 Part of Prince Albert's dressing-room at Osborne

5 The Queen's sitting-room in the completed Pavilion

6 Osborne in August 1847, during construction. Water-colour by W. L. Leitch

7 Contemporary picture in coloured sands of the completed Osborne House

8 Tools, barrows and cart used by the Royal children in their gardens at Osborne, c. 1854

9 The shore at Osborne

10 Thomas Cubitt, builder of Osborne. By an unknown artist

11 William Smith, architect of Balmoral, 1861

12 Old Balmoral Castle. A study in pioneer photography by George Washington Wilson

13 Prince Albert's dressing-room at Alt-na-Giuthasach, 1849. A water-colour by an unknown painter

14 New Balmoral under construction, 1854. A photograph taken by William Brookes, an enthusiastic English amateur

15 The drawing-room at Balmoral. A water-colour by J. Roberts

16 The Queen's dressing-room in the new Castle. A water-colour by J. Roberts, September 1857

17 A photographic portrait of the Royal Family at Osborne, 1857 (in an *Early Album belonging to Albert Edward, Prince of Wales*)

18 Queen Victoria's Birthday Table at Osborne, 1861. A water-colour by J. Roberts

19 Rudolf Löhlein. A contemporary study

20 John Brown in 1860

21 The first Garden Cottage at Balmoral. A water-colour showing the Queen working at her despatch boxes

22 The Glassalt Shiel. A water-colour by W. Simpson, 1882

23 Benjamin Disraeli,
Earl of Beaconsfield.
A photograph by Messrs
W. & D. Downey

24 Jane, Lady Churchill in
1862

25 A Ghillies' Ball at Balmoral. A water-colour by W. Simpson

26 Balmoral Castle seen from the north side of the Dee. A picture drawn by
Victor Prout and etched by Swain

27 The Queen in old age. Photograph by Milne of Ballater

28 The Munshi and nephew.
Photograph by Milne of
Ballater

29 Osborne House from the air

Chapter 14

An old shoe for luck

War was then a matter for sovereigns, statesmen, armies and navies. Beyond reports in the newspapers it did not obtrude upon the lives of the generality of people. Save for the fact that it distracted the overall designer from paying Balmoral the amount of attention he might have wished, the building of the new Castle continued as though the struggles against Russia in distant parts were of no account at all.

It was the dawn of photography but a few professionals and many amateurs were making studies. These were mostly of still-life subjects because human beings did not find it easy to freeze for the time required for an exposure.

One amateur with considerable talent in the composition of a picture was William Brookes the squire of Croft near Leicester, who in 1854 was on one of Mr Thomas Cook's conducted tours to and through Scotland from his headquarters at Leicester and, happily, he had with him his photographic apparatus. This could have been no lightweight, but, then, though already inclined to portliness, he was only thirty-two and had the enthusiasm of all pioneers. He took four photographs in Scotland or, in contemporary jargon, he photographized four compositions. One was the excellent picture of Balmoral under construction which is reproduced as plate 14.

The absence of workmen was essential or their inevitable movement would have spoilt the picture. Therefore it was either taken on a Sunday or, more likely, as the shadows show the sun was fairly high, it was taken during a dinner hour. William Smith's plans pinpoint the subject: the south-west corner of the house block where the *porte cochère* was to be.

The building was carefully designed so that only where imposingly lofty rooms were required did it have two floors as shown on the left-hand side. The rooms on the left are easily identified. At ground level the two windows with a trestle against them are of the entrance-hall; beyond are the single window of the library and the bay-window of the state drawing-room. Above the drawing-room is the Queen's private sitting-room; above the library her bedroom; then, in the turret set in the angle of the wall with a neatly-carved cone-base, what Queen Victoria always called 'the little room', from which she would have had a perfect view of Loch-na-Gar. Finally above the entrance-hall, and still open to the sky, is her bath- and dressing-room. The right-hand door to the rear of the room leads to a corridor and stairs up to her wardrobe. The door at the centre leads to her bedroom. The lens did not quite catch the billiard-room beyond the state drawing-room with the Prince's bath- and dressing-room above, that completed the west front.

The photograph has additional interest in that to some extent it shows the methods of building construction with granite. The walls of the interior of the Queen's dressing-room are only roughly dressed in readiness for the plasterers' work. Outside it was different. The rough-hewn blocks that litter the foreground of the photograph had yet to be hand-worked to achieve the polished whiteness of the outside walls. And how very finished the masons' work looks compared with the hoists and the primitive-looking ladders and standing platforms that they used. There appears to be a fence of wire near the two upended carts. Conceivably at this stage sheep were grazing where soon there would be a wide carriage way.

The plate of this frozen moment of history in his bags, Squire Brookes returned to Leicestershire to live an equable life, photo-graphize more compositions, sit on the bench, bring up eight children, and enjoy his golden wedding.

It scarcely seems credible that the subject of this photograph taken halfway through 1854 should have been ready for occupation by September the following year. Of course the whole Castle was not yet complete. The office-block was scarcely begun and the tower and the wing that connected it to the house-block were only half-finished; but the massive house-block was up.

Thomas Cubitt's speed in building Osborne was matched equally by William Smith. The masons must have worked prodigiously consider-ing the amount of stone used. Stone and labour had been saved, and the maximum sunshine in a cold climate ensured, by inserting many windows in the building, some of a considerable size. There were to be 180 in the house-block and the tower. There was a heating system as at Osborne; hot air arising from two furnaces and a boiler-room up wall-flues and beneath fire-proofed floors. To supplement this heating there were no less than sixty-seven fireplaces in the sixty-eight public rooms and private apartments. There were also four bathrooms and fourteen water-closets.

Again as at Osborne, the building scheme had been planned so that the old house could be used in the interim period while the tower was finished and the office-block built. This ensured continuity of enjoyment for the Royal Family, and it is doubtful if any other arrangement could have been afforded by the Privy Purse, but it condemned the old house to demolition. Had funds allowed it, the new Castle might have been sited at some distance up-river, the carriage-ways and plantations made to conform, and the prospects would have been as pleasing if not quite as fine as they were from the site chosen by the Prince and William Smith. Then, fittingly screened by woods, the old Castle could have been kept *in situ* as an extra house on the estate, a type of dower-house; and a worthwhile building not destroyed. But the decision had been taken and a temporary wooden corridor had been put up between the offices of the old house to the new house-block, not only for general use as a promenade in wet weather, but also for carrying food in hot-water containers on wheeled trolleys from the old kitchens. For the present the gentlemen of the Household and most of the servants still lived in the old house. Everyone else moved into the new.

As the Queen and the Prince entered from under the *porte cochère* François d'Albertançon hurled an old shoe after them for luck and both were delighted with the largely finished work; furnished, papered, tapestries and curtains and pictures hanging, carpets down, books and ornaments arranged, doubtless some of the moulded plasterwork still awaiting paint or gilding when thoroughly dry, but otherwise complete.

It has often been stated that the interior of the Castle has been much altered since the reign of Queen Victoria. The state and royal private apartments on the west front have already been listed from Squire Brookes' photograph. The rest of the house-block in 1855 can best be described as follows. The entrance-hall led to the ground corridor and this led to an ante-room, all on the west side, and all with an elaborately designed floor in encaustic tiles and wall-niches for statuary. The south of the ground floor provided apartments for distinguished visitors and, with its own small entrance-hall, a suite of three rooms for the Minister in Attendance and his valet.★ Above the Minister's suite was the second, much smaller, tower of the Castle, unusual in that it was square for three floors up, then octagonal, with lancet windows and a parapet

★ As both the Queen and the Prince considered the dignity of the Privy Council deserved a most splendid Council Room with an Audience Room at Osborne, it is surprising that neither was provided at Balmoral where there were frequent meetings of the Council. Nor, at first, was any special room set aside for use as an office by the Keeper of the Privy Purse. The apartments for the Minister in Attendance was the Prince's sole concession to officialdom at Balmoral. Possibly it emphasized that Balmoral was a private holiday home owned by the Prince while Osborne was a semi-official residence because it was the private property of the Sovereign.

above, and was capped not with a cone but with a cupola shaped like a sugar-castor and topped with a weather-cock. There was accommodation for two of the Queen's Ladies with their maids on the east side. On the north side was a butler's pantry, a serving-room, and a large dining-room that led into the ante-room. Halfway along the grand corridor on the west side was the grand staircase with wide and shallow stairs carpeted in red, the whole lighted by a single hanging lamp. This led directly to a corridor that stretched the whole length of the west side where the Queen and the Prince had their private apartments. As they liked to have their children close at hand, the princesses were accommodated along the south side of this first floor, and the princes and their tutor along the north side. There were spare rooms on the east side. Above the less lofty south and east sides was a second floor chiefly for the accommodation of valets, dressers, lady's maids, and the Queen's wardrobe.

There were four baths for the Queen, the Prince, and their children. Everyone else did without. But this was no hardship at a time when service was plentiful and ungrudgingly given and a hip-bath could be taken before a fire in a bedroom. Houses were so spare in plumbing that what is properly a lavatory, that is, a washing-basin with taps and a drain, was almost unknown, and all dressing-rooms and many bed-rooms were provided with matching sets of hand-basins and ewers of cold water on a wash-stand with a slop pail and a chamberpot. There were also towels on 'horses' and bells to ring for hip-baths and hot water. The new Balmoral Castle, with its fourteen water-closets in the houseblock – even more than there were at Osborne – might then have held the British record for a large establishment.

William Smith's drainage plan was simple but adequate. All roof-water and effluent met at a junction 55 yards from the Dee and ran through a pipe of glazed tiles straight into the river.

By the middle of the century it had not yet become customary to cram rooms with furniture, pictures, potted palms and knick-knacks. The mode, however, was coming in, and there was only just sufficient room for comfort especially as there were no particularly large rooms at Balmoral. The Queen noted in *Leaves*: 'We looked at all that has been done, and considered all that had to be done; and afterwards we went over to the poor dear old house . . . and settled about things being brought over.'

The completed decorating and furnishing seemed to show the mid-Victorians had a taste for bright colouring. The dining-room, with its bay window looking towards the Dee, had one large table, covered, when not in use, by a strawberry-coloured cloth. The carpets were polychrome, the curtains red, the walls green. The drawing-room was lighted by four-branched candelabras held by highlanders carved in Parian marble, and there were plenty of tartans. It was the same through most of the building. Evidently the Queen's wish was for an extensive use of tartan in the furnishings and decorations. There were tartan wallpapers, tablecloths, rugs, carpets, upholstery and curtains; so many that even a Scot amongst them, Lady Augusta Bruce, Lady-in-Waiting to the Duchess of Kent at Abergeldie, was quite taken aback. She said the medley was not quite 'flatteuse' to the eye. Eventually the word 'tartanitis' was coined to describe the prevailing decor. And almost half a century afterwards it was still the same. One of the Queen's grandchildren, a daughter of Prince Alfred, described the decoration as 'more patriotic than artistic and had a way of flickering before your eyes and confusing your brain'. The thistle motif was equally ubiquitous, and, on the walls, were sporting trophies that grew in number as the years passed, and dozens of pictures of stags alive and dead. Most of the paintwork was said to be marmalade-coloured but as marmalade could vary from chrome-yellow to liver-brown it was not particularly descriptive.

The holiday on Deeside in 1855, when the Royal Family moved into the house block, was one of the most memorable. There does not appear to have been any form of house-warming, no German hymn by Luther, nor any toasts; but only three days after their arrival, the stationmaster of Banchory, the end of the new Deeside Railway line from Aberdeen, galloped up the valley with telegrams for the Queen and for Lord Granville, the Foreign Secretary, who was Minister in Attendance.

Sebastopol had fallen.

The year before a huge bonfire had been prepared on Craig Gowan, a hill to the south of the house in the vain hope of having something to celebrate. This had suffered in the winter, but not a great deal, and it was quickly pulled together and added to and set alight. It attracted people from all over the estate.

Such was the Queen's euphoria that she commanded her boys be awakened so that they could see the bonfire.* They at once wanted to go up there where the Queen's new piper was skirling a pibroch, John Macdonald and John Grant were discharging shot in the air, and there was much cheering, shouting and consuming of whisky. Down by the house the steward, old François d'Albertançon, tried to contribute by letting off squibs but most failed to go off.

---

* These were Prince Alfred, aged ten, and Prince Arthur, aged five. For the first time the Prince of Wales was not with the family in Scotland. He had been sent on a walking tour in Dorset with his tutor, which was not a success as he disliked both walking and his tutor.

The Queen, who always had either a naïve view of or a blind eye to the effects of whisky, described in *Leaves* how the Prince came down from the bonfire to tell her: 'the scene had been wild and exciting beyond everything. The people had been drinking healths in whiskey, and were wild with excitement.' Indeed they were. Some time after, when the Queen was undressing, they streamed down the hillside singing under her windows, pipes playing, and still firing off guns. To Stockmar the Prince shortly described it as 'a veritable Witches' dance, supported by whiskey'.

The next excitement was of a more private nature. Prince Albert was convinced that the future of his beloved Fatherland depended on the Germanizing of Prussia rather than the other way about, and he and the Queen and Stockmar had long planned that the intelligent and highly gifted Princess Royal should marry Prince Frederick William of Prussia, and thereby inject a little liberalism into reactionary Berlin. He had an understanding with the heir to the Prussian throne, the Prince of Prussia who had fled to England in the year of revolutions, that their children should marry, and Prince Frederick William, or Fritz as he was known in the family, was not disposed to disagree. He had an 'establishment' in Berlin and was said to have two children,* but he knew his duty. The 'establishment' should be closed and he would marry the Princess Royal. They had met only once before, at the Great Exhibition, when she was ten and he nineteen. She had much admired him. He would have been rather peculiar if he had returned her feeling, but even then he had guessed his destiny. The Prince Consort had written in his autograph album none of the usual sentiments or puzzles; simply 'May Prussia be merged in Germany, and not Germany in Prussia. Albert.' Now they were twenty-four and fourteen, and though the idea of child marriages was abhorrent to Prince Albert, he realized that Prince Fritz might be snapped up in the marriage market unless he could be tied down by at least an unofficial declaration and betrothal. Therefore the young Prussian was invited to end his summer holiday after a cure at Ostend with some stalking at Balmoral. He arrived on 14 September with Colonel von Moltke who later was to become the Prussian Chief of Staff.

The Prince and his A.D.C. were the first distinguished visitors to occupy the special apartments in the house block. Prince Fritz bagged a stag on his first day and five days later pressed the Princess's hand when 'accidentally' they had been left unchaperoned. He then made a formal

---

* According to an American periodical, *Science*, one of the Prince's natural grandsons was the prominent scholar, Professor Oskar Morgenstern, of New York University, co-author of *Theory of Games and Economic Behaviour*, and once considered a likely Nobel prizewinner. He died at the age of seventy-five on 26 July 1978.

offer to the Queen who said that no marriage could take place until Vicky was at least seventeen. Some days afterwards he was given permission to give Vicky a bracelet. It seems she was much taken, greatly in love and, besides Moltke, the only person fully in charge of the situation. Prince Fritz was nervous. Prince Albert had neuralgia and rheumatism and was agitated. The Queen was also tense. Stockmar was informed of the 'bonne bouche' but continued to be unhelpful, refusing no less than four pleas that he cross the Channel to give of his wisdom.

On 29 September the young couple became privately engaged to be married and a sprig of heather changed hands. On 1 October the Prussians left to be followed by a forty-page letter written by the love-sick princess. Moltke in his dry way remarked on the sudden accumulation of news.

The Prince took time off from stalking to instruct Dr Robertson about the ordinary estate work due to be done in the next twelve months and the making of new plantations. There were already avenues of white poplars from slips sent from Rosenau because the Prince persisted in comparing upper-Deeside with Thüringia, although his fly-by-night brother Ernest, who was permitted to visit Balmoral that autumn, said they were not in the least alike. He was also establishing large larch plantations. They reminded him of the German forests and were being strongly recommended by the Royal Society of Arts for producing timber that was almost immune to immersion in water, but, though larch cultivation in Scotland was no new thing,* it was one of the few of the Prince's improvements disliked by the local people. He also consulted with William Smith and Giles and Beattie about avenues and paths and the laying-out of gardens with glasshouses at some distance to the south of the house. To make the approach more even and yet seem natural, a large piece of ground had to be scooped out from the front of the house, and as the office-block and the ballroom were to be built at a lower level than the house-block, a terrace had to be made running the length of the north side outside the dining-room windows. The ground to the west was to be levelled, contained by a balustrade, and made into a formal garden of rose beds and a pool with a fountain set in lawns. The roses were selected from species and varieties that would be in flower during the time of the royal visits. And there was other work to be completed: the stables and kennels, game-larders in addition to the venison-larder, an ice-house, lodges, cottages and gateways.

Views and ideas exchanged, and orders given, the Royal Family left

* Before 1826 the 4th Duke of Atholl had improved the poor Dunkeld land by planting over 14 million larches.

for England. The Prince wrote to Stockmar: 'We miss the fine mountains and the pure air of Balmoral, but are on the other hand indemnified for these by a superabundance of business. I have worked out a scheme for the Reorganization of our Army in the Crimea.'

All things considered, it was a feat that when the Queen and the Prince returned to Scotland at the end of August the next year the old house had entirely disappeared and only a commemoration plaque marked its site, the tall tower was finished, the terrace work done, the ballroom built, and the office block in working order.

The last was not as large as it was to become because two wings beyond the main entrance or Pend Door were added at a much later stage. Nevertheless besides the corridors, staircases, lobbies and a covered way on the kitchen side of the yard, it contained more than fifty rooms that varied in size from the huge kitchen that ran to the full height of both floors to rooms subdivided into cubicles. Besides the kitchen there was a bakehouse, and an oven six feet by six and a half feet surrounded by three and a half feet of walling, an office for the clerk of the kitchen, pantries, sculleries, storerooms, linen-rooms, lodges for the gate-keeper and night-watchman, a coffee-room with its own larder, a steward's room for the upper servants, a servants' hall for the lower servants, and accommodation at varying degrees of comfort from the rooms of the housekeeper, master cook, and the royal piper to the kitchen maids' quarters. Not only were all these buildings up but they were complete with furnishings and decoration; and certain embellishments had been added to the exterior of the house block.

A little more than a month before the royal visit the sculptor's work had arrived by steam packet at Aberdeen and been transported to the Castle where scaffolding had been specially erected for the placing of certain bas reliefs, shields and coats of arms, and a three-dimensional figure of the Scotch lion couchant. Mr Thomas had sent his foreman to supervise the work, and the sculptor himself had arrived by way of Windermere to see it in place. The Scotch lion was like a huge chessman, made of white metal and gilded, and weighed about an hundredweight. This had been fixed on the summit of the octagonal roof that topped the bay-window of the princes' dormitory and the dining-room on the north front. On the west front were the royal crests of England and Scotland and the crest of the Prince of Wales, and bas reliefs showing St Hubert, of great importance to the Germans as the patron saint of huntsmen, with St George on one side and St Andrew on the other. On the new ballroom was yet another relief showing King Malcolm Canmore presiding at the first Braemar Gathering. The Royal Arms of Scotland were on the south face of the tower. Significantly there were also symbols of the ownership of the Castle by Prince

Albert. His personal arms in marble were on the most prominent part of the main entrance and above the window-gables along the wing joining the house-block to the tower were seven gilded crests of Saxe-Coburg-Gotha: Jülich, Cleve, La Marck, Thüringen, Meissen, Berg and Saxony.

The insistence on the German connection might have been made at the Queen's suggestion, but she was sufficiently a realist to know her beloved husband was unpopular in her kingdom and unlikely to have proposed anything that emphasized his foreignness. Besides this she was enamoured of Scotland, had the romantic but totally erroneous notion that she was the Queen of the Scots, and would surely have preferred local emblems and decorations to alien crests. Almost certainly it was the Prince's own idea, a manifestation of the fact that he belonged to a royal house of ancient lineage and he resented the condescension of the British and their total indifference to his position. Being branded as a traitor in the press only two and a half years before had bitten deeply. At the time he wrote confidentially to Stockmar that when he first arrived in England:

> Peel cut down my income, Wellington refused me my rank, the Royal Family cried out against the foreign interloper, the Whigs in office were only inclined to concede to me just as much space as I could stand upon.

The arms of 'the foreign interloper' first welcome visitors to Balmoral Castle to this day.

It was the same within the house. The Prince made his personal mark. He had already made certain innovations to Great Britain, notably the introduction of hot luncheons instead of the cold collations of former times, and the frock-coat as an article of day-dress, though not, as tradition had it, the Christmas-tree which was introduced years before his arrival either by Queen Charlotte or her daughter-in-law Queen Adelaide. But, on the whole, he believed in subscribing to the customs of the people amongst whom he lived. In Scotland before and during his lifetime there were less esoteric rules about highland-dress that purists have since endeavoured to impose. In ancient days the highland chieftains wore skins as well as weaves, and either the kilt or breeches or, more frequently, both, and were always armed to the teeth and got up with feathers and Celtic jewellery. Their following, being generally poverty-stricken, wore what they could get and were thankful for it. At the time of the Jacobite risings most highland gentlemen wore tartan trews and jackets or doublets. Then, when the Industrial Revolution speeded up the process of weaving, new tartans and dices appeared and they were widely used throughout Europe. Indeed when

Wellington and the allies were trying to settle Europe after Waterloo, tartans were highly fashionable amongst the ladies in Paris. It has already been noted that Lord Aberdeen, though not reckoned a high-lander, nevertheless wore full highland dress at Balmoral. And the Queen herself had no sooner attached herself emotionally to Scotland than she plunged all her male children into what she called their 'high-land things' and they often wore them in England. John Macdonald and the royal piper were required to wear highland dress everywhere, and the only person ever known to object to doing so was a Danish manservant of the future Princess of Wales.

To begin with, Prince Albert wore hodden grey or the Royal Stewart tartan but, when he built Balmoral, he devised his own tartan, more restrained than the Royal Stewart, a pleasing design of lilac, red and black on a grey background. This was called the Balmoral tartan and was worn at Balmoral by privileged people. The Prince also assisted the Queen to create a Victoria tartan.

So he had made his individual mark both inside and outside the Castle when, with the Queen on his arm, they went into the house on 30 August 1856.

William Smith's work was done. He returned to Aberdeen to find that royal patronage had added to his already thriving business. As a man, his life grew sadder, and gradually he became more lonely. At a good age, thirty-five years later, he died a widower outliving ten of his sixteen children and leaving what was then not an inconsider-able fortune of £30,000. This was because as an architect he had gone from strength to strength, designing, amongst other things, banks, churches, schools, an extra floor to a prison, fever-wards, hospital-buildings, and an annexe to the city lunatic-asylum. He made no public remark about Balmoral Castle at any time, quietly accepting the judg-ment of his peers. Some did not hesitate to put his work in 'pepper-pot and gingerbread' class. Others emphasized the superb craftsmanship for which he was responsible but were lukewarm in their praise of the overall design. Others have pronounced it fitting. Amongst laymen there has been the same diversity of view. The very latest royal opinion on William Smith's ability was given as recently as September 1978 when Queen Elizabeth, the Queen Mother, declared firmly to Smith's great-granddaughter: 'He was a good architect.' Queen Victoria would have agreed, though naturally and correctly she saw the principal inspirer of the work as her beloved Prince Albert. At the Prince's command a cartouche surrounded by stags and hounds was affixed to the Castle that showed the Queen's name and his own as the builders of Balmoral, and William Smith as architect.

Chapter 15

A slow permeation of presence

Because the greater part of their time was spent on the Isle of Wight or in Aberdeenshire, the rooms and corridors and grounds of Osborne and Balmoral slowly became permeated with the Queen's presence, and, to a lesser extent, with that of her husband.*

Reciprocally the two houses had a considerable emollient effect upon their feelings, Balmoral the more powerful because it was so cut off from the centre of affairs. Prince Albert almost always found it a place of peace. It was a sedative to the Queen's temperamental jolts up and down, and seldom was this so clearly shown than at Balmoral in 1856.

It rained and it blew for the first part of their holiday, and everyone had colds or influenza, but the Queen was a new woman in what she now called 'this dear Paradise'. She was delighted to see her Standard flying high above the tower. She was delighted with the levelling that had so improved the policies. She was delighted that there were already flowerbeds below the north terrace-wall and roses in the garden beneath the windows of her private apartments. At the centre of this garden was an eagle-fountain, a gift from the King of Prussia that had formerly decorated a greenhouse at Windsor.† She rhapsodized about her 'dear Albert's own creation'.

This was the same person who, at Osborne, had been a bundle of nerves. There were many contributory causes, the most prominent

---

* Since 1901 Balmoral has had other influences to banish Queen Victoria's, varying in effect from Edward VIII's calamitous visit in 1936 when Mrs Simpson acted as hostess and deeply offended his family, to the affectionate care that his brother, George VI, showed for the estate. Osborne House, on the other hand, is a veritable fly in amber, despite the fact that thousands go through the turnstiles each year. The 'Queen' means only one person at Osborne. Out of season especially, Queen Victoria's presence is very real.

† It is no longer there having been replaced by a sculpted chamois. Possibly the fountain was tucked out of sight, suffering the same fate of unpopularity as innumerable public houses called 'The King of Prussia' that, in the First World War, were hurriedly renamed.

being that, strongly against the advice of Sir James Clark, she was again carrying a child and finding it lowering, irksome, and, according to an authoritative source, for the first time somehow degrading. Nor at Osborne could she cope with the problems posed by the growing-up of her elder children. While undergoing the moods and fancies of her own condition it was beyond her to sympathize with the moods and fancies of adolescence. On top of all this her pride received a jolt when she asked her ministers to give her husband the formal title of Prince Consort by Act of Parliament and they had advised against putting up a bill because it would almost certainly be defeated.

Balmoral raised her from this despondency as nothing else could. To her great delight Mr Nightingale and his daughter Florence whose work at Scutari she much respected, were staying at Birkhall with Sir James Clark and there were formal and informal meetings both at Balmoral and Birkhall. Possibly, at that moment, at the height of her fame and in full vigour of her womanhood, Miss Nightingale was the epitome of all that the Queen longed to be herself. At the beginning of the year she had written to express her admiration and the assurance of her prayers, and sent Miss Nightingale a unique personal decoration that consisted of a St George's Cross in red enamel, the inscriptions 'Blessed are the Merciful' and 'Crimea', and was surmounted by the royal cypher in diamonds. Meeting her heroine in person would have consolidated her Balmoral-induced euphoria but, though on 14 September she wrote to Uncle Leopold that they were enjoying the most beautiful weather and the trophies from stalking were piling high, the Queen's depression returned when they left Balmoral for Windsor. She was temperamental to the point of sobbing and wailing. She felt and said she was neglected. Then her half-brother, Charles of Leiningen, died and she was distraught. The Prince, made more melancholy than usual by the lowering atmosphere, wrote to his stepmother: 'The autumn wind has wrenched away another leaf from our family tree.'

The King of the Belgians warned his niece not to dwell on death in her present state. She replied that grief never seemed to affect her health. But this was wishful thinking. Autumn at Osborne brought no relief. She vexed the Prince so much that he was sharp with her. The ceilings of the billiard-room and drawing-room gleamed under the paint and gilding of Gruner's new design that had just been executed, and upstairs the Queen was begging her husband not to scold her in front of the children. As had become his odd and irritating custom, he wrote rather than spoke his reply: 'My love and sympathy are limitless and inexhaustible.'

At long last Baron Stockmar and his son came to England, the old gentleman a great reconciler and full of advice as to how to get the best dowry for Vicky from the British Parliament. But it was not a happy winter and the Queen disliked moving to London for her confinement. When it took place she had a very bad time. The Prince, announcing the birth of his last daughter, Beatrice, wrote: 'She kept us waiting at the door for 13 hours before she would come in.' This was on 14 April. Guns in the Park and from the Tower fired a salute for the birth of a Princess of the Blood. On 30 April the bells were tolling for the death of another, Princess Mary, Duchess of Gloucester, last surviving child of George III.

The Queen, whose spirits had momentarily gone up, felt them drop again. They plummeted further when Stockmar announced that he was leaving for Coburg and he doubted if his health would ever permit him to return.

Sir James Clark was anxious about the severity of the Queen's post-natal depression and urged that the family move as soon as possible to the peace of Osborne. But bad news followed them there. The sepoys in the Indian Army had mutinied.

Prince Albert was much affected by the Queen's misery. A visit to dirty Manchester to open an Arts Treasure Exhibition fatigued him greatly. Returning, exhausted, to the Isle of Wight he even managed to complain: 'Osborne is not looking as green as it should.' Nevertheless he was cheered by a decision of the Queen to bypass Parliament and give him a title. By Letters Patent she created him Prince Consort and a meeting of the Privy Council at Osborne on 25 June authorized the creation and ordered the necessary alterations to be made in the Book of Common Prayer. He told his step-mother that now he had legal status in the English hierarchy, a point that constitutional lawyers might have debated, but, though it roused no enthusiasm in Great Britain, it was a help when travelling abroad where precedence mattered.★

It was as the Prince Consort that he represented the Queen at the marriage of Uncle Leopold's daughter to the Archduke Ferdinand Maximilian at Brussels.

In late July the Queen's depression was sporadically banished by regattas, drives round the Island, bathing and boating, picnics, natural-history expeditions, cooking and gardening at the Swiss Cottage, fruit collecting in the walled garden, kite-flying, fishing and sketching parties.

★ Parliament in 1840 had refused the Prince precedence 'next after her Majesty in Parliament or elsewhere', but the leaders of both parties and the Lord Chancellor agreed that he might be given precedence next to the Queen by Letters Patent. This was done but abroad the procedure did not have the force of an Act of Parliament and the Prince was frequently refused precedence and placed apart from his wife.

There were also quasi-state visits in perfect Osborne weather. A Russian grand-duke proposed himself; then Prince 'Plon Plon' Napoleon; and a week later the Emperor and the Empress of the French.

Though he did not himself trust the Emperor, the Prince was glad for the Queen's sake that this visit took place. She had an obvious penchant for Louis Napoleon. He mystified her, and she was fascinated by the aura of adventurer which he possessed more than any of his family. He had presumed to flirt with her on her State Visit to Paris. She also admired the beautiful Empress Eugénie who had been so amiable as to send a present on the birth of Princess Beatrice. Pleased that the visit raised the Queen's spirits, the Prince Consort was flattered by the Emperor's congratulations on his new rank, and showed interest in his preoccupation with the occult. Spiritualism was the fad of the day. There had been table-turning in the Osborne drawing-room before. Now after dinner in the white and gold state drawing-room, imperial and royal hands touched over an occasional table in an endeavour to peer into another world. The Queen did not mention this in her gleeful report to Uncle Leopold, which incidentally provided conclusive proof that she held no brief for Sabbatarianism:

> Good Osborne in no way changed its unpretending privacy and simplicity, and with the exception of a little dance in a tent on Sunday (which was very successful) and additional carriages and ponies, our usual life remained unchanged.

In the royal collections at Windsor are two faded sepia photographs of the departure of the Emperor and Empress from the Osborne pier. Considering the infancy of photography and that the seamen in the admiral's barge were 'at oars', that is, with their heavy oars pointed skywards, they are amazing successes. There are blurs and smears, but the main figures can just be made out. A posed, and therefore better photograph of the whole of the Royal Family was taken outside the Osborne drawing-room the same month which is reproduced as plate 17. The fashions of the day did not favour the children except the two elder boys with their loose, Byronic clothes. The Princess Royal showed by her dress that she had been emancipated by Confirmation and betrothal. Her sisters Alice, Helena and Louise appeared to be in the uniform of a religious community. Little Prince Leopold was dressed like a girl, and his elder brother, Prince Arthur, swathed in his 'highland things'. The baby was scarcely visible, but, after long practice the Queen certainly showed she knew how to handle one. Her own face was drawn, the downward lines at the corners of her mouth pronounced. She looked rather more than her age. The Prince, no thinner on top than many men of almost thirty-eight, showed imposing *gravitas*.

Not long after the Imperial visit the Queen of Holland arrived to stay and proved a breezy guest. Her activity, the Queen reported, was astounding. 'She sees everything and everybody and goes everywhere.' After that, the Queen and the Prince took Cousin George, the Duke of Cambridge, and six of their children on a cross-Channel voyage to Cherbourg. There they found fortifications under construction which gave rise to much speculation. Against whom, they all wondered, was the Emperor with his imposing waxed moustaches and air of gallantry, preparing such extensive defences?

The Foreign Secretary travelled with the Royal Family to Balmoral. The Prince wrote to the Baron: 'We have brought the exhausted Clarendon with us, and the air will do him good.' But how much rest Lord Clarendon, or the Prince for that matter, could enjoy was doubtful. The news from India was grave. 'The horrors committed on the poor ladies . . . makes one's blood run cold.' So was the news from Berlin that the King had gone off his head. The Queen wrote at once to Leopold, '*What* have you heard?'

India and Berlin soon called back Lord Clarendon to London but not before he had had the opportunity to admire and use the new iron bridge that the Prince had built over the Dee.

There had been a public right of way along the south bank of the river as far as the bridge at Invercauld where the Farquharsons lived. It was an ancient road along which great herds of cattle had once been driven south to market, the cattle welcomed for the dung, the drovers less welcome as they were a thieving lot always on the look-out for game and poultry. To ensure privacy the Prince had had recourse to a Highway Act of 1835 that allowed, for good reasons, the diversion of a road and the cancellation of a right of way. A capacious iron bridge had been built near Crathie Kirk to divert all traffic from Birkhall and Abergeldie to the road on the northside of the Dee. It was opened in what the Queen termed 'highland state'; that is, there was a triumphal arch, through which the royal carriage drove, the road lined with Lord Fife's men, and there was plenty of pipe music, and plenty of whisky. There was even a tent for royalty and the gentry to take tea, and a band to play outside. And, inevitably, there was a shower of rain.

In the main, showers and cold meant nothing to the Queen. It was at about this time that she begged the use of a gardener's cottage that had been built across the levelled lawns beyond the site of the old castle. It stood in trees and was only 200 yards from the main entrance. It was there that she liked to work at her despatch boxes, partly in the open air; and she would take tea there, even on occasions, breakfast. The Prince was happy to indulge her and the gardener was located in another of the well-built granite cottages that had begun to pepper the royal estate.

When not working at her boxes the Queen filled a good deal of her time taking the Princess Royal and Princess Alice and Lady Churchill to see the village people, taking small gifts to the needy and chatting to the others, even peeping into the cottage of the whisky-loving Willie Blair, the so-called Royal Fiddler who had a habit of calling on the parish minister on his way home from any festivity to prove, often fruitlessly, that he was sober, an exercise that must have sorely tried that reverend gentleman. The Queen remarked in her Journal that the people seemed so pleased to see them. She was touched and gratified by their reception.

The Princess Royal enjoyed herself less because on many occasions until they left the local people kept reminding her that this was the last visit before her marriage and, with Celtic gloom they invariably said: 'I suppose we shall never see you again!'

The Prince was as busy as ever, in fact, busier, because for the first time he had no confidant in England. The Prince of Wales was causing him anxiety. His letters were jejune. He girded against the regimen approved by Baron Stockmar. He had an ungovernable temper, was greedy, and was singularly lacking in consideration for other people. It was not simply high spirits that had moved him to drive a flock of sheep into Lake Windermere on a walking-tour, but thoughtlessness about the consequences of such an action. As an experiment, and to give him still more companionship with other selected companions, the Prince Consort had sent them off for a four-month tour of the Rhine valley and Switzerland with a tutor, and with General Grey, and Grey's nephew-by-marriage, Colonel Ponsonby, one of his own Equerries, in charge of the party.* The Prince of Wales, therefore, missed the Balmoral holiday for the second time; but his thirteen-year-old brother Prince Alfred was there and often in his father's company.

The Prince had plans for this second son who, except in the unlikely event of Duke Ernest producing an heir, would inherit Coburg. He should be trained for the Royal Navy. Meanwhile they went shooting and stalking together, and the young prince was introduced to the methodical management of a large estate, noting that nothing was too small for the supervision of his father, from the ordering of a tea service marked with the Balmoral cypher from Thomas Goode with a scalloped edge and two designs on each piece, to the re-designing of the

---

* The experiment was not a great success. Mr Gladstone's eldest son was one of the party and news of 'a little squalid debauch' on the Rhine scandalized his father. Very probably this was not much more than a kiss and a brief scuffle with a chambermaid, but it is significant that, so far as is known, it did not reach the Prince Consort's ears.

home farm at Invergelder. There was so much to do that it must be done gradually; replacing the crude bothies with stone-built cottages, making new tracks and keeping old ones in repair; putting up fencing; and reclaiming waste and marshland.

Chapter 16

'Our cheerful and unpalace-like rooms'

The Reverend Mr John Middleton, Minister for thirty years of the vast parish of Glenmuick, Tullich and Glengarin, that included part of the royal estate, kept a sporadic record of events that vividly show the hard and humdrum life on upper-Deeside. Occasionally he took time off to visit Aberdeen or Stirling, or even Edinburgh, but mostly he farmed his glebe, shot rabbits and fished for the pot, and travelled miles to see his scattered flock. Admonishment seemed a regular part of his vocation for, as in many country communities, a first child was often born before the parents married. His diary-entries for the beginning of 1858 were short and infrequent, but of particular interest.

> January 1st   Present at Plough Match
>   3rd   Collection for the Jewish Mission £2. 4s. 1d.
>   23rd   Corn winnowed. 5 qurs. 5½ bush.
>   24th   Absolved Jane Bowan and in the afternoon baptised her illegitimate child, the father, James Carson, being in Edinburgh.
>   25th   Attended the Dinner at Balmoral in honour of the marriage of HRH the Princess Royal with HRH Prince Frederick William of Prussia. Came home about 3 a.m.
>   28th   Adam Hay found dead (from the effects of intemperance) at the Inn Door.

Whilst their people in Scotland and on the Isle of Wight feasted, the Queen and the Prince Consort went through understandable agonies at seeing their first child sail away. Possibly the Prince suffered more as he was particularly attached to his daughter and he was only too aware that her liberal spirit would chafe against the restrictions of the Prussian Court after the considerable freedom she had enjoyed at home. But once the Queen had recovered from the shock of seeing her daughter leave England for ever, she could scarcely have failed to feel a certain degree of relief. She was a possessive wife and her husband had given a great deal of his time to her daughter. Now she had time to herself again. Then, suddenly, she realized that in her married daughter she at last had a confidante to whom she could write about everything from the imperfections of her husband to the use of opening medicines. Possibly she overdid it. Certainly the Prince Consort and the Baron thought so, and the Prussian Court accused her of overpressing her daughter and interference, but if letting off steam is good for an over-heated boiler, the opportunity to be frank, even to the point of rude-ness, did no harm to the Queen who ordinarily was obliged to keep her emotions under some sort of control.

She wrote to her daughter on 1 March 1858 and made an extraordi-nary admission from someone who stubbornly refused to think Osborne as anything other than perfect, who loathed heat and never openly confessed to feeling chilly: 'Here all is white and the wind sets so strongly on the windows that we can't get the rooms above 50-52 and so on, and it is bitterly cold.' Five days later she had been visited by Prince Albrecht of Prussia and she wrote: 'I am so glad Abbat liked our dear Paradise here.' Then, very much down to earth, she went on, 'Bertie had a sick head-ache yesterday from imprudence.'

The Prince of Wales continued to be a great anxiety to his parents. 'The systematic idleness, laziness – disregard of everything is enough to break one's heart and fills me with indignation.' Prince Alfred, on the other hand, had begun his preparation for entry to the Royal Navy at Alverbank, not far from Osborne, and was often over for luncheon, even dinner.

The Queen in her letters gave some delightful descriptions of life at Osborne at that period: sending Isle of Wight ivy to Berlin so that her daughter could wear it in her hair. She recommended the adjunct of red ribbons and a few diamonds as she herself wore at dinner one evening after which she read *Jane Eyre* aloud to the Prince until it was time for their evening duet at the pianoforte. Complaints of exceptional heat were to be expected, though not perhaps as early as 24 March: 'It is completely a hot summer's day – quite incredible and really very try-ing.' Suddenly, out of the blue, comes the startling statement: 'I think people really marry far too much; it is such a lottery after all, and for a poor woman a very doubtful happiness.' Then, with a better sense of proportion: 'We must none of us complain when one has such cause for thankfulness as we all have . . . those poor ladies at Lucknow.'

From 1848 the Queen had almost always kept her birthday on 24 May at Osborne and the arrangement of the Birthday Table, as it was called, was often a work of art. A painting of the Table and the decorations made for her birthday three years later in 1861 is shown in plate 18 and indicates the trouble that was taken. On her birthday in 1858 the Queen reported to her daughter that it had rained at Osborne. After a family luncheon the children gave a musical concert in her honour. The only backslider was the Prince of Wales. He contributed nothing. In the same letter the Queen commented rather eccentrically on the fact her daughter was already carrying a child: 'The horrid news contained in Fritz's letter to Papa upset us dreadfully. The more so as I feel certain almost it will all end in nothing.' Her Olympian prophecy proved false. It all ended in Kaiser William II.

In May the anxious Prince went personally to see his daughter in Potsdam and while he was there the Queen wrote to describe home life at Osborne:

> Yesterday there was a grand tea at the Swiss Cottage – and imagine good Affie by way of amusement exhibiting his air pump and steam engine (puffing and blowing all the time – in the tool house) to Grandmama . . . He dined with us last night and sat next to me. He is a dear, good, clever promising child – whom God may bless!

Prince Alfred was the great favourite at that time. It did not augur for a happy summer because, as she well knew, the Prince Consort was determined that the boy should leave home and go to sea, which she did not want at all. Her eldest had been sacrificed at the altar of marriage. The Prince of Wales was to live with his own Household at White Lodge in Richmond Park and later travel abroad. She could sustain the loss of these two children from her home, but the thought of losing her second and very dear son to the Royal Navy was insupportable.

There was a plan for both the Queen and the Prince to visit Potsdam in August. In her most challenging mood – she had been quarrelling with Miss Hildyard – the Queen told her daughter she had not the least enthusiasm for the journey but it would give her the opportunity to see if Vicky had improved in various respects: 'The standing on one leg, the violent laughing – the cramming in eating, the waddling in walking.'

In fact the visit turned out to be more of a success than anyone could have expected, though the Prince Consort was deeply upset when Cart, his Swiss valet for twenty-nine years, died at Morges on Lake Geneva while they were away from home. 'I cannot think of my dear husband without Cart,' wrote the Queen in her Journal, 'we had to choke down our grief all day.' On their return the Prince Consort wrote feelingly from Osborne to his daughter at an early hour on 1 September. He had taken to wearing a wig in the mornings when it was chilly. 'Osborne is green and beautiful, but the weather cold and stormy. Mama will be much hurt when she gets up and finds I have had a fire lit.'

But as foreseen it was their second son, rather than early-morning fires that was to be the cause of much quarrelling at Balmoral during that month. Prince Alfred passed his three days' entry examination on 3 September and his father was delighted. His mother was not. Nothing pleased her. Neither of her private paradises soothed her. Beside both the Solent and the Dee she was aflame with vexation and, while doubtless her husband bore the brunt of it, a good deal was vented on her daughter in letter after letter. A proposal from Berlin that the family should visit Balmoral the following autumn provoked a typical outburst of contrariness. The Prussian family would be welcome at Osborne in May and at Windsor for Ascot, but not at Balmoral in the autumn. 'I don't want that at all . . . I won't have you then; God knows if we shall be here then!' She was so worked up about her son going to sea that she went so far as to declare: 'Altogether I don't like being here this year at all. I enjoy the scenery and being out very much but I hate the life here.' Unable to restrain herself any longer, she burst out in an impassioned letter: 'I have been shamefully deceived about Affie . . . Papa is most cruel on the subject.'

The touch of hysteria evidently worried her daughter, her son-in-law, Baron Stockmar and his son, and, ultimately, through Lord Clarendon, the Prince Consort. He did his best to control the flow of letters. His efforts invoked more jeremiads. 'If you knew how Papa scolds me for (as he says) making you write! . . . Papa has snubbed me several times very sharply.' The private apartments of the royal couple must have been distinctly uncongenial to both that autumn. The Courts of Europe had it that the Queen was going the way of her grandfather. This was far-fetched but she certainly showed a childish petulance at being crossed.

Prince Alfred's future was not the only cause for her tantrums. It has been averred she had a bad conscience about letting her daughter marry so young; she was still only seventeen and carrying her first child: and that she was furious because circumstances made it impossible for her to be at the confinement. 'I ought to be there and can't – it makes me sick and frantic.' Then, peevishly: 'Why in the world did you manage to choose a time when we could not be with you?'

All this seethed in her mind and made her spar with her husband who had other troubles besides a tearful wife. His dear Cart had been replaced by a German, Kohler, but though the young man was intelligent he had never been in service and breaking-in a new valet to one's personal ways was tedious. Evidently Kohler was not a successful appointment for, in the following year, a Swiss, Gustav Mayet, replaced him. Then his equally dear John Macdonald was failing. He had married an Inverness-shire Macdonald, Anne, and they had four sons and three daughters, but neither their care nor that of the royal physicians made any difference. He was obviously going into a decline and had little strength though he insisted on leaving his family in the south as was customary and travelling with his master to Balmoral. But there were no more lessons in Gaelic and he became so breathless out of doors that he rarely left the bed-sitting room next to the gunroom that had been his from the beginning. It was on the ground-floor of the connecting wing and from his window he had a view of the Dee and the hill plantations beyond. Then the Prince's former garderobier, King, was in the grip of drink, and appeared to be incapable of holding any post he was given, and his successor, Bray, showed signs of tippling. Drink being so easy to lay hands on, and John Begg, the distiller of Easter Balmoral providing such a quantity of his special blend in bottles with an attractive blue and black label, or, more generally, by the gallon in casks, tippling was almost an occupational hazard in the royal service. It would not be long, the Prince knew, before Bray would have to be replaced. Destitute of friends in England after the deaths of Anson and Peel, his close servants mattered greatly to him and they were not plentiful. In fact only his personal attendant, Rudolf Löhlein, remained. He too left his wife and family each year to travel to Balmoral. It was a sacrifice that some of the upper servants and members of the Household made with varying degrees of willingness.

The Prince would take refuge in work with his Treasurer, who had been knighted and was now Sir Charles Phipps, and Dr Becker, or discuss the estate with Dr Robertson, and there was stalking and all the other sport offered by Balmoral, but the Queen's sullens and her explosions that autumn must have been very uncongenial. Then faced with returning to England, she suddenly became a different woman. Possibly the presence of guests also helped. Uncle Leopold's second son, their young cousin of twenty-one, Philip of Flanders was there for a time. So were the Count and Countess de Persigny. Persigny was a romantic man, the Emperor's greatest friend, one of the original conspirators of his restoration, and once sentenced to a prison-sentence of twenty years for his sake. Described as 'the incarnation of Napoleonic fanatacism . . . undoubtedly the Loyola of the Empire' with his waxed moustaches and gallantry, he should have fascinated the Queen, and very probably did. At any rate, the prospect of uprooting made her write in *Leaves* in the only entry for that year: 'Oh! how I gazed and gazed on God's glorious works with a sad heart, from its being the last time.' And her daughter at Potsdam must have been astounded at the *volte face*: 'I feel so sad, as you know and feel for me, at the bitter thought of going from this blessed place . . . and returning to tame, dull, formal England.'

When they reached England Prince Alfred left for service at sea. The Queen was upset but rational about his departure: 'it is nothing to parting with a daughter.' She said she found Windsor after Balmoral 'like jumping from day into night – fine as it is!' and confessed: 'I long for our cheerful and unpalace-like rooms at Osborne and Balmoral.' She did not have to wait long. There was typhoid, or a fever like it, at Windsor and across the river. A royal footman died. Three hundred of the boys at Eton were ill and the school closed down. The Royal Family went to Osborne where Countess Blücher was appointed the Queen's representative at her daughter's lying-in – 'and do what providence has (I think so cruelly!) denied me'.

Evidently there were reconciliations at Osborne. The sculptor, William Theed, was at work on a portrait bust of the Prince Consort. The Queen recorded 'a beautiful bust of dear Papa – the best done yet; and his beautiful little ear was cast'.

Chapter 17

Fledglings from the nest

The birth of Prince William of Prussia in January 1859 was badly managed and his left arm was dislocated, though this was not revealed for some time. The Queen and the Prince Consort were at Windsor, grandparents at thirty-nine.

Doubtless celebrations were ordered for the tenants at Osborne and doubtless they were less rumbustious than the ball at Balmoral. Dr Robertson sent a report through Sir Charles Phipps of a great 7 o'clock tea party for mothers and daughters in the servants' hall presided over by Mrs François d'Albertançon, Mrs John Grant, and Mrs Paterson and the head-gardener's wife; the men and the boys meeting in the iron ball-room. An address of congratulation was voted for, 'a little drop of Begg's best administered', and the party began in earnest. There was an abundance of roast beef, bread, ale, and whisky toddy, and much singing and dancing. The doctor left at two in the morning and said: 'they were going on at it "fast and furious". I hear that at 5 it knew no stop or diminution.'

Ignorant of her grandchild's deformity but aware that her daughter had had a very bad time the Queen wrote tenderly, sent sensible little presents, interesting news, and sound motherly advice; though, as frank as ever, she admitted from Osborne in March 1859 that she had no adoration herself for very little babies and particularly not in their baths.

'Air,' she urged her daughter, 'air is what you want . . . or you will become sickly and old before you are 20,' and she recommended the Prince Consort's custom of having a thermometer in every room, the opening of windows thrice a day, and the absolute necessity of installing water-closets.

It was to Osborne that Vicky travelled alone to tell her parents about the baby's dislocated arm. She called the visit 'a hurried scramble' for she could not stay long; but she achieved her object. Neither of her parents loaded her with pity or disgust or were anything other than ordinary. Sir James Clark was consulted and he said vaguely that these things sometimes righted themselves. No one fussed, which was the important thing, and in her correspondence thereafter the Queen made nothing special of the deformity. They both looked forward to seeing the child, an arrangement that was planned for a summer visit to Coburg in the following year.

That summer there was war between the French and the Austrians. The British Ministry was bound to neutrality by the fact that the cabinet was divided into three distinct camps; the anti-French, the anti-Austrian, and the anti-Italian. Because of their policy, the Queen called Palmerston and Russell 'the old Italian Masters', and she worried about her husband: 'Papa works too hard, wears himself quite out by all he does. It makes me often miserable. If it were not for Osborne and Balmoral and then again Easter at Windsor – I don't know what we should do.'

Peace was proclaimed in less than two months and all was tranquil at Osborne. Happily for everyone the Queen had become more accustomed to the loss of the fledglings from the nest. If three were gone, six still remained. She indulged her fondness for fresh air by sitting outside and writing under the trees, or in the lower alcove of the terrace-garden where there was the sound of fountains, or in the exedra close by the sea.

The seventy-three-year-old Prince Esterházy, former Austrian ambassador to St James's, who had appeared at the Queen's coronation his uniform 'dripping with diamonds', and whose son and heir had married one of her own bridesmaids, was invited to Osborne. The Queen wore the Garter ribbon to honour him and ordered the covers to be removed from the drawing-room chairs and crystal lustres, but he put everyone out and spoilt dinner by arriving at eleven at night. He declared he was desolated to have missed the train and expressed his apology to the Queen by slipping his hand up her sleeve and tickling her chubby forearm. She was charmed. The Prince Consort was less pleased when the old gentleman suddenly hugged him in greeting. He quickly retreated, but the grand piano was behind him and prevented his escape, and Esterházy continued holding him tightly by the waist while he gave elaborate explanations of the recent Austrian reverses. When at last he was able to extricate himself from his guest's embraces the Prince Consort showed him the Council Room and the Audience Room that had finally been finished by Gruner. The former was decorated by a mass of gilding and two almost life-size portraits of the Queen and the Prince painted on Sèvres porcelain after originals by Winterhalter. The small Audience Room was made enchanting by a large central chandelier showing the Prince Consort's favourite flower, the convolvulus, its green leaves and shoots vigorously alive.* The old Hungarian nodded and approved, and continued his non-stop apology for mistaking trains and arriving late.

Osborne was peaceful and the family's central home, but it was too near London for complete seclusion. At the beginning of September they travelled north for the first time by night; not in anything so lavish as a continental sleeping compartment but with mattresses on the floor of the Queen's special saloon. It seemed to answer, for they slept well, but they found the difference in temperature unsettling – from 70 degrees in sultry weather at Osborne down to 40 degrees in a violent gale at Edinburgh.

They went briefly to Holyrood House – only one water-closet in the whole dank building – and the Prince Consort had a conference with those who were supervising the Prince of Wales's studies in the city. They then went on to Balmoral.

The Duchess of Kent was not well enough to be at Abergeldie. Even Osborne for the Queen's birthday had been too much for her. She had been packing to go there when she was suddenly stricken with what was at first diagnosed as erysipelas. In fact it was the beginnings of cancer that kept her to Frogmore House. To the Queen's displeasure the sub-tenancy of Abergeldie Castle was taken by one of 'the old Italian Masters', Lord John Russell. Lady John, his second wife, had advanced opinions that did not endear her to the Court.

By now the Queen had become accustomed to Prince Alfred's absence and she had discovered her real favourite was Prince Arthur. He was to remain so all her life and no small credit for the undoubted popularity and cordiality of the future Duke of Connaught was due to the training and care of his Governor. Each of the princes had a Governor. General Bruce, brother to Lady Augusta Bruce, the Duchess of Kent's Lady-in-Waiting, had responsibility for the Prince of Wales. Major Cowell looked after Prince Alfred, even accompanying him to sea. Prince Arthur's Governor was chosen with the greatest care by the Prince Consort and the Queen and at once taken to him. Major Howard Elphinstone had been wounded and decorated with the VC for valour at the siege of Sebastopol; he spoke English, French and German with equal ease, largely because although his name made him seem to be a Scot, he was in fact three-quarters Russian. Steady and reliable, a talented painter and musician, the Major's only obvious failing was an inability to spell English very well. He was young but very firm, and he had the patience of Job in his relationship with the Queen. She accepted

* This is either the work of Carl Hackert or of Spinn, both of whom made chandeliers of a similar kind in Berlin. The maker's name has not been traced on the chandelier or in any Osborne records.

that, having been put in charge of her son, the Major had full responsibility for him; yet she did not hesitate to send probing letters at any hour of the day, not folded and sealed but enclosed in narrow envelopes; and nothing was too insignificant in the young prince's life to miss her notice. She would ask about the length of time necessary for dressing, about drill-instruction, what underclothes the boy should wear, the names of other boys, such as the son of General Grey, with whom he might like to play; but they were generally couched in the form of a suggestion or a request never a command. The Major ruled a small household within the greater Household: a tutor, inappositely named Mr Jolley, a sergeant footman and a number of personal servants, but all the gentlemen of the Household were a generation older than he and doubtless he sometimes wondered if he was right in the head to give up active service to look after one small boy and on such a whole time basis.* Moreover he had inherited from his mother her nose for comfort, a habit of neatness, and a sorrowing disposition. He found the protocol, the tartanitis, and the piercing draughts of Balmoral very trying. But, despite initial doubts, he stuck to his post, and remained as the Duke of Connaught's Comptroller even after they both had married. That summer the Major was only twenty-eight, and he had so little time to himself that the Prince Consort told him he must get out and about more. It was good advice and welcome, but not all that practical. Prince Alfred had spent a short leave at Osborne and gone back to sea, and Prince Leopold had been left at Osborne as had the baby. But only the Prince of Wales and his unmarried sisters were able to enjoy family excursions – Prince Arthur was too young.

Mount Morven, 2,862 feet high, and more than 10 miles to the north-east was climbed by a small party, the Queen on a little pony so fat that it 'panted dreadfully'. The British Association met at Aberdeen and the Prince Consort presided at a meeting. Later a *fête champêtre* was given to 'huge omnibuses and carriages laden with "philosophers"'. There were highland games, piping and reels. They entertained other guests, the Duke of Richmond and, once again, cousin Philip of Flanders. They made expeditions into the wilds on foot and on pony, one of them of 35 miles, and they all climbed Ben Muich Dhui, eating a picnic-luncheon on the mist-shrouded summit.

Most of this was not for the nine-year-old Prince Arthur and therefore not for Major Elphinstone. They enjoyed fishing-expeditions, long walks, initiation into stalking; there was even talk of making a dam

---

* Members of the Household mostly went into waiting for only part of each year. Even those, like Lady Churchill, who were more or less permanently at Court, had regular leaves. Governors were less fortunate. After almost four years of continuous service Elphinstone was given his first leave of a fortnight.

and asking help from the ubiquitous John Brown. Apparently this was not to be thought of. Elphinstone wrote in his journal that, on putting the idea to the Queen, she had quickly replied: 'Impossible, why, what should I do without him! He is my particular ghilley!' The Brown legend of later years seldom mentioned how often and how insistently the Queen made this claim long before the death of her husband.

For his patience and care of Arthur at Balmoral, the Major received his first gift from the Queen: a set of waistcoat-studs in granite.

Chapter 18

'So overwhelming a calamity'

There was something about the Victorians, their marathon walks, their powers of endurance, and their capacity for work, that put their grand-children and great-grandchildren into the class of the effete.

Five days before a great fall of snow at Osborne that had the Prince Consort, members of the Household, and the royal children out of doors building a snowman, tobogganing and sliding, a Lady of the Bedchamber came into waiting having travelled by ship, open cart, carriage and train, over snow-blocked highland passes all the way from the Isle of Skye. She had only just recovered from the grippe, and was due to be confined in mid-February, but nothing prevented her from doing her duty as she saw it.

The Prince Consort had once had the same endurance, and an amaz-ing talent for packing so much work into a day; but, from the winter of 1859–60, to those who knew him best, he showed signs of increasing strain and a corresponding inability to bear the weight.

The Queen noticed it, of course. At the same time, in her robust way, she obviously thought he ought to pull himself together. After his death she admitted that he had 'lacked pluck'. She was sure that his priorities needed re-ordering. He was always 'overfond of business'. Her own spirits were soaring. She was seeing plays, reading novels, fidgetting because her eldest daughter was already carrying a second child, but, while still of the opinion 'it is an awful moment to have to give one's innocent child up to a man', she was very much on the look out for a suitable *parti* for Alice.

The royal couple had their squabbles, but the Queen was quick to defend her husband when the memoirs of the scientist Humboldt were published in which he averred the Prince had said the Irish like the Poles deserved to be thrown overboard. The fact was that Humboldt, a brilliant man, but frustrated by homosexual passion and thus made sour, mistranslated the Prince's perfectly correct assessment that the awful condition of the Irish was as bad as that of the Poles. The Queen and her daughter were furious. The Prince Consort was merely annoyed that he had been misreported. He rather shrugged off the smear.

Returning to Osborne from London she remarked in March that he had 'forgotten his annoyances in looking at his plants and listening to the birds, etc.' Then in April she wrote to her daughter to disclose that her husband's old garderobier had died of delirium tremens and he had rid himself of his present one and appointed Archie Macdonald in his place. Archie was very young, only eighteen, so doubtless he was given the post to please his old father who died only a month afterwards.★

At last Princess Alice was satisfactorily provided for. Prince Louis of Hesse-Darmstadt had proposed himself for Ascot and then asked for her hand. He was told to return in six months, but this was a mere formality.

Lord and Lady Clarendon and their daughter Constance were at Osborne soon after Ascot and Princess Alice chattered about Prince Louis and her excessive love for him for two whole hours – causing Lord Clarendon to say of the Princess to a discreet friend: 'She is just like a bird in a cage beating its wings against the bars and if she could get out *wouldn't she go it!*' He also had something sharp to say about the Queen playing at 'the royal game of summer' at Osborne, for in chilly weather all the windows were open, everyone's nose was blue, guests shivered through dinner, and the Queen expressed the doubt if it was not too hot to drive out. Apparently a long talk with the Prince elicited nothing new for Lord Clarendon. The Prince had so little energy. Indeed he had recently written to Berlin comparing his treadmill existence to that of the donkey circling to raise water from the well in Carisbrooke Castle.

The Princess Royal, having as efficiently prepared for her confinement as if she was going to be executed, was safely delivered of a healthy girl. The news was received just before the Osborne annual *fête champêtre*. The family celebrated with cooking at the Swiss Cottage, and 'To dear Alice it was a very eventful day, as Papa told her all.'

On the way to Balmoral there was a stop at Edinburgh to visit the Duchess of Kent. She was staying at Cramond and was so unwell that the journey to Abergeldie was too long. From Holyrood House the Queen wrote to say her daughter's choice of the name Charlotte was

---

★ Three of John Macdonald's sons did well for themselves; the eldest entering the diplomatic service and becoming an expert on Japan and Japanese, an unusual distinction so soon after the United States had forcibly opened up the Land of the Chrysanthemum at the point of Commodore Perry's guns; the second, Ewen, becoming the Queen's Agent at Claremont; and the third, Archie, looked after the Prince Consort until his death when he was appointed first garderobier and afterwards, Jäger to the Prince of Wales.

not to her liking. From Balmoral she wrote to say they had made the experiment of travelling by rail to Aboyne and two hours' posting in sociables, tactfully omitting to mention that the horses had bolted and they had had a few anxious moments; sent a sprig of bell heather and a sprig of French heather; and, on the day of the christening in Berlin, noted the baby's health had been drunk 'but her name astonishes people here very much'.

In contrast to her vigorous letters, there was a detectable weariness in those from the Prince Consort. His birthday was on a Sunday and therefore not celebrated until the following Thursday: 'The 26th fell on a quiet day in Scotland, but to me the quiet was the very thing, and accords best with my mood.' He had done little at Osborne that year except lay the first stone of the new Whippingham parish church and alter the line of the road between Barton and the Barton Cottages. There was equally little now to do at Balmoral because all his improvements to the estate had been completed the year before and the new buildings of the Invergelder home farm well under way. He thought of installing a dairy on the most modern lines.

Possibly he personally supervised the arrangements for what the Queen called in *Leaves* 'The First Great Expedition', Certainly it would have been his idea; an adventure to the other side of the Cairngorms made incognito, as far as such a thing might be possible. The police inspector from A Division was sent ahead to look over the ground. Maids and extra luggage, including wine, were sent by carriage along a different route; and the Prince and the Queen, travelling as 'Lord and Lady Churchill', with Lady Churchill as 'Miss Spencer' and General Grey as 'Dr Grey', and accompanied only by John Grant and John Brown, made the long journey to Grantown-on-Spey by sociables, ponies, on foot, and by ferry and barouche. There they spent a night at the inn, dining on 'soup, "hodge-podge", fowl with white sauce, good roast lamb, very good potatoes, besides one or two other dishes . . . ending with a good tart of cranberries'. Grant and Brown with the two maids apparently 'were very merry in the "commercial room"'. The next day, in mist and rain and somewhat tired, they toiled back to Balmoral; the Queen quite exhilarated by the adventure.

In September there was a family reunion at Coburg. It began in a melancholy fashion with the Prince arriving too late for his step-mother's funeral. It was a delight to see the Princess Royal and, for the first time, their grandson William. The Queen was far more sensible about his deformity than many women would have been. The Prince, though, already saddened by the death of his step-mother and by the realization that this was almost certainly the last time they would see old Baron Stockmar, was not himself. He wanted, above all things, to

enjoy the company of his favourite daughter, to talk about the problems of her life at the Prussian Court with its different customs and,
perhaps, help her solve them; but he was so utterly down that he
managed much less than he had hoped. Then he was shaken by a
carriage accident in which the coachman was badly hurt and one of the
horses was killed. He himself was cut and bruised. Initially the Queen
was worried, but he talked merrily through dinner, and she was reassured. Old Baron Stockmar was a doctor and he was not at all reassured. Indeed he came to the conclusion that the Prince was in such a
state of nervous debility that a really severe illness could carry him off.

With the helpless feeling that things were slipping between his
fingers, the Prince made nostalgic pilgrimages to the places he had
loved as a child. It merely increased his depression; and, walking with
his brother, he burst into tears on seeing a favourite view. 'I shall never
see it again,' he said.

Like Lady Macbeth and her husband, when one was weak the other
was strong. The Queen had been level-headed, calm and purposeful all
through the year. Not even a severe chill and attack of colic on the
journey back to England put her down. She wrote to the Princess Royal
from Brussels giving her the bare details of her illness, and continued:
'But let us not think of that – but of the blessed, happy time we all spent
together at dear old Coburg – that delightful fortnight, except the
dreadful episode of Papa's accident, which we could enjoy so peaceably
and which was so gemütlich and quiet.' Her nerves were far stronger
than the Prince Consort's at this stage; consulting Sir James Clark and a
new favourite physician, Dr Baly 'about darling William's arm', and
sending his mother their encouraging opinions in writing; being practical and ordering the *Victoria and Albert* to take the Empress of Austria to
Madeira, for the Empress was in the grip of a nervous breakdown and,
being a Wittelsbach, everyone feared for the permanent loss of her
reason; trying to help the Empress Eugénie who, infuriated by the
Emperor's infidelities, had promptly left France and gone to Scotland at
the worst possible time of the year. On her way back she called on the
Queen at Windsor and the Queen and the Prince Consort returned the
compliment by visiting her at Claridge's after the Smithfield Show.
When she returned to France the Emperor was at Boulogne to receive
her and make what amends he could.

It was an extraordinary time. Walker, who had united Nicaragua,
was shot. Garibaldi, who was trying to do the same to Italy, was fêted.
The Summer Palace at Peking was burnt and looted by Europeans in
the name of progress. Lincoln became President of the United States,
and the southern states began to secede, which was followed by civil
war. The Prince of Wales returned from six months in Canada and the

United States where he had been treated so well that the Queen begged her eldest daughter: 'Don't therefore abuse the "Yankees" for their national defects – on this occasion at least.'

Princess Alice and Prince Louis of Hesse-Darmstadt became officially engaged; and the latter at once found himself in the hands of the Queen's dentist and 'good Sir James' for the correction of his teeth.

January brought deaths. The mad King of Prussia died and Princess Frederick William, Princess Royal, became Crown Princess of Prussia. Dr Baly, the Queen's new doctor, was the sole victim of a curious railway accident at Wimbledon. He fell through the broken carriage floor and was run over. 'Sehr traurig,' wrote the Prince in his Journal. Another physician, Dr William Jenner, was sought out by Sir James Clark, who in theory had retired.

Then, though it was not without warning, the Duchess of Kent died at Frogmore House, her hand in the Queen's, but not aware whose hand it was.

The Prince Consort had had a wretched winter; ill, melancholy, for ever busy with his paper-work, even carrying out his full programme though racked with pain; and, according to the Queen, he had been 'very trying'.

Now, suddenly, the Macbeth roles were reversed. No matter what it cost him he had to look after the Queen for she fell headlong into a nervous breakdown. This was partly caused by the discovery that, on paper at any rate, her mother had really loved her; and remorse for her conduct towards her when she first came to the throne. Whether or not the Duchess of Kent had been a good mother was beside the point. In recent years she had proved herself brave, considerate and a good grandmother.

The Queen went through her mother's papers but was persuaded to refrain because they excited her so. Impulsively she made Lady Augusta Bruce a resident Extra Woman of the Bedchamber. It turned out to be an excellent appointment for Lady Augusta became a close friend. But the past, the present, regrets, and a feeling of being abandoned, were all too much for the Queen. She wept copiously. It was, literally, a case of heels drumming on the floor. She could not stand the sight or sound of any save a chosen few. Her daughter came at once from Berlin to comfort her. She found her father also in need of consolation. The Duchess of Kent's Comptroller had died not long before and her affairs were in disorder. She had appointed her son-in-law as sole executor and so, in addition to his many commitments, he now had an extra load to bear. Though her visit was so short, and most of it she necessarily spent with her mother; she found time to calm her father by reading aloud to him from *Idylls of the King*.

The Prince Consort and his three elder sons went to the funeral, and afterwards got the Queen back to London. 'Albert is so good', she wrote to Uncle Leopold, 'and does all with such tenderness and feeling. Vicky goes on Tuesday, and we on Wednesday, to Osborne, where I think the air and quiet will do me good.'

To this her uncle replied with a solemn warning that the pleasantness of spring might excite grief because the dead could not share it.

As the Prince believed that Osborne was the very best place for his wife he cannot have been pleased by such extraordinary tactlessness. He admitted to Stockmar:

> You may conceive it was and is no easy task for me to comfort and support her . . . I am well-nigh overwhelmed by business, as I do my utmost to save Victoria all trouble, while at the same time I am Mama's sole executor . . . to add to which, Lady Phipps had a nervous seizure the day after Mama's death, and Sir Charles . . . is powerless to help me.

Meanwhile his eldest daughter arrived back in Germany to find Berlin buzzing with the rumour that the Queen had had to be restrained in a padded cell. The same dreary rumour was circulating round Europe. She at once informed her father. He kept it from the Queen and did his best to soothe her agitation.

Osborne was not yet quite finished. The new stable-block beyond the walled garden had come into use that January but there were still things to be done and all work had to be suspended. The Queen was abnormally sensitive to sound. On a perfect day of good weather, the spring flowers all out, the birds singing, she could not stand the noise of carriage wheels on the made-up road. With infinite patience she was indulged. 'Alice has driven me every morning in the little Sardinian pony-carriage which, with india-rubber wheels, makes no noise.'

But the most worrying thing for the Prince was the Queen's listlessness and her incapacity to take pleasure in anything. She broke down after a Council Meeting in London and, half-way through dinner, she fled the room. She tried a change of scene and stayed at White Lodge in Richmond Park for a time; said she felt better; then 'dreadfully nervous'; and returned to Osborne for a visit from Uncle Leopold on her birthday. 'How I dread it! We shall make it as little like one as possible. No music (that would kill me) – no change of mourning – and dine merely *en famille*.'

A few days after their arrival on the island the Prince was almost thrust into eternity. The Chancel of Whippingham Church was being enlarged and the Prince made a formal visit to the work, rather oddly dressed in a shepherd's plaid trousers and a white stovepipe hat with a mourning band attached. He climbed up the scaffolding with the rector and the estate foreman; the latter an enemy of the rector's son who lay in wait behind a gravestone armed with a catapult. The boy missed the foreman but caught the Prince who cried out, leapt into the air, and was only just prevented from falling by his companions.

The task of looking after the Queen was made easier by Uncle Leopold's visit, then by a lengthy visit of the family from Berlin when the swimming bath was in constant use, and finally by a visit of the King of Sweden.

The Queen began to find life and Osborne more tolerable; but her grief was recharged on 17 August when they went to Frogmore with myrtles and immortelles to visit the mausoleum built at the Prince Consort's order for the remains of his mother-in-law. She was the first occupant of a royal graveyard that Lord Clarendon declared unique because it lay in marshland.

A visit to Ireland on the way to Balmoral was not a success. The Prince of Wales was there with his regiment. The Queen wrote to Uncle Leopold on her husband's birthday that 'Bertie marched past with his company, and did not look at all so very small.' A strange maternal remark. She also mentioned that the regimental music had included a march composed by her dead mother which was most upsetting. She did not mention that the Irish, who had heard the Humboldt story, showed what they thought of the Prince Consort in no uncertain manner.

It was in Scotland that, by the careful planning of three more one-day excursions, and two more two-day 'Great Expeditions', the Prince finally brought healing to his wife's torn nervous system. She re-discovered her sense of pleasure. On the very last expedition to the valley of Cairn Lochan, they ate an elaborate luncheon in the rarefied air of the Cairngorm heights 'on a precipitous place, which made one dread any one's moving backwards.' Afterwards 'Albert wrote on a bit of paper that we had lunched there, put it into a Seltzer-water bottle, and buried it there, or rather stuck it in the ground.'*

Balmoral was at its best again. The buildings at the home farm were all completed. Only the Prince Consort's modern dairy needed finishing. After a very exhaustive search a most beautiful princess had been found for the Prince of Wales and he had gone to Germany, ostensibly to observe army manoeuvres but also to meet Princess Alexandra of Denmark; and he arrived at Balmoral to say he was much pleased with her. Prince Louis of Hesse-Darmstadt paid a visit and, as a chosen son-in-law, was initiated to the exhausting sport of stalking.

* Quite naturally the consideration arises: has it ever been found? If so, by whom, and where is it now?

On 21 October the Queen wrote with deep feeling: 'Oh! those beloved hills – that pure air – those dear people – all must be left to-morrow. But I am truly grateful for what I have enjoyed.'

At Windsor *rôles* were once again reversed.

It was the Prince's decision that his delicate son Leopold should be sent to the French Riviera for the winter. On 4 November he left in the care of Sir Edward Bowater, a veteran of Waterloo, and Lady Bowater.

But after 12 November, when news came that the Portuguese Royal Family had been stricken with typhoid and the King and the Prince were dead, it was the Queen whose energies were most noticeable. Her husband was ill himself with some unspecified *malaise* – the aches and pains of toothache, headache, neuralgia, rheumatism – and he was deeply distressed about his Portuguese relations. Then he heard from Stockmar that, in the summer while serving with his regiment in the Curragh, the Prince of Wales's fellow officers had slipped an actress, Nellie Clifden, into his bed. It was an inevitability that, in the Prince Consort's low state, and with the example of the Queen's father and uncles and his own father and brother before him, he magnified out of all proportion. He told the Queen. They agreed it would be easier if the Prince of Wales was not aware that she knew of the escapade and the Prince Consort wrote to his son then spending a period at Cambridge. Against advice and in foul weather he inspected Sandhurst cadets. He dragged himself out to shoot with the Queen's half-nephew, Prince Ernest Leiningen, and he went up to Cambridge to see his son. Within three days he was unable to go out shooting or eat any luncheon but did his duty by attending, partially, a review of the Eton volunteers. Sleepless, racked with pain, unable to eat, utterly miserable, the Prince worked at a despatch to the British Minister in Washington. It concerned the high-handedness of the Federal Government in taking confederate officers from a British steamer; but was expressed so belligerently that it was tantamount to a declaration of war.

Scarcely able to hold a pen, the Prince Consort re-drafted the note. On the same date the Queen wrote to her daughter: 'We shall go to Osborne on the 13th and truly thankful I shall be.' By the 7th Lord Palmerston had discovered what was happening and insisted that action be taken. Sir James Clark's wife was mortally ill and the poor man was hurrying backwards and forwards between his home and Windsor. The Prince Consort's other Physician in Ordinary was old and long past the height of his powers. Dr Brown of Windsor, Apothecary to the House-hold, who had attended on the Duchess of Kent in her last illness, was invited to assist in case he should feel hurt. Dr Jenner, who had taken the unfortunate Dr Baly's place as Physician Extraordinary, was new to the post and felt his junior position. Even so, considering that he had recently distinguished himself by discovering the difference between the germs of typhus and typhoid, it was remarkable that he was so sanguine. It was also extraordinary that, after the typhoid epidemic of two years before, nothing had yet been done to improve the pestiferous sanitary arrangements at the Castle, the barracks, or in Windsor or Eton.

Warned exactly of the way things were going, old Lord Palmerston, the Prime Minister, wrote to Colonel Phipps: 'One can only hope that Providence may yet spare us so overwhelmingly a calamity.' He demanded yet another opinion, that of Dr Watson, a specialist. Sir James Clark called him in, and Dr Watson saw the Prince Consort twice a day, but only muttered the words 'some improvement'. Dr Jenner said there was 'a positive gain'. Old Clark, knowing the Prince's debility and his dread of fever chose to keep the truth supressed.

Eventually the Queen was told he had a low fever, a synonym for typhoid. Courageously she accepted the separation from her husband, and took into her own hands again work on the despatch-boxes that for so long had been his. She wrote to her daughter, who was carrying her third child: 'Don't be alarmed about adored Papa . . . But you will imagine easily that I am much worried. Sir James writes to you himself. Don't alarm others pray. You shall hear daily.' She ended on a practical, encouraging note: 'He doesn't suffer the least pain of any kind. We shall not be able to get to Osborne when we wished, but that we can't help.' This was putting a brave face on things.

In an agony the Queen watched her husband wandering in delirium from room to room. He could only sleep with the aid of ether. He worried incessantly, particularly about young Prince Leopold in Cannes, for his Governor had been taken ill and it was feared he was dying. His mind rambled, but always, always he complained of rheumatic pains. She could do little for him. He was nursed by his Equerries and his closest servants; Rudolf Löhlein, Archie Macdonald and the young Swiss, Gustav Mayet. They were devoted and infinitely patient but they were not trained to nurse a sick man. Eventually their master settled in the Blue Room where both George IV and William IV had died.

There was sinking and rallying until, on 14 December, Dr Watson ordered that his bed should be moved out a little from the wall. Dean Wellesley read the prayer for the dying.

Surrounded by his family, his servants and the members of his Household, at a quarter to eleven in the evening the Prince Consort died.

Chapter 19

The greatest depth of grief

Not permitted to touch her husband's body for fear of infection; hating her eldest son for, as she believed, worrying him into his grave; unable to endure the thought of the burial; the Queen rushed to Osborne, arriving there in the deep mourning that she never afterwards relinquished.

Her family and courtiers gave what help they could. The King of the Belgians was there. Duke Ernest arrived from Coburg, grey with sea sickness and soaked through by a gale that raged in the Solent, to be clasped in the widow's arms. Her eldest daughter was in the early stages of pregnancy and was forbidden to travel, but the Crown Prince reached Osborne as soon as he could. All her other daughters were with the Queen, Princess Alice having at once moved in to sleep in her bedroom. Prince Alfred was at sea; Prince Leopold at Cannes where it was decided he should remain through the winter although Sir Edward Bowater had died; and Prince Arthur had been left at Windsor with Major Elphinstone. He and the Prince of Wales would be principal mourners. The Queen's uncle, her brother-in-law, and son-in-law left for the furneral at Windsor, and returned afterwards to the Island. Princess Feodore, the Queen's half-sister, was there; as were her half-nephew and his wife, the Prince and Princess of Leiningen.

Seldom had Osborne House been so crowded. Sir James Clark and Dr Jenner, all the members of the dead Prince Consort's Household and many of the Queen's, braved the Solent in winter weather to give condolences.

Miss Nightingale, herself a prey to the most morbid fancies, wrote of the Queen at this time: 'She always reminds me of the woman in the Greek chorus, with her hands clasped above her head, wailing out her inexpressible despair.' It was not too great an exaggeration. The private apartments in the Osborne Pavilion were filled with cries.

Virtually all public business came to a stop. The Queen was too distraught to attend properly to her boxes. The little she did was at the persuasion of her half-sister, Princess Feodore, Princess Alice, Lady

Augusta Bruce and her intimate friend, Miss Skerrett. It was no exaggeration to say that, for a short time, the sovereign's authority in the
realm was virtually vested in this quartet of ladies.

At the beginning of the year the Queen saw one member of the
Ministry, the Duke of Newcastle, giving him an audience in the Prince
Consort's dressing-room; a harrowing experience for both because,
following custom, everything was left as though the dead man might
walk in at any moment to make use of the room. It was 6 January before
a very necessary meeting of the Privy Council could be held and then
only by the contrivance of the imaginative Arthur Helps who had
succeeded Charles Greville as Clerk. He decided that the Council
Room should not be used. Instead he and two Councillors stood in
the Prince Consort's dressing-room while the Queen sat in her sitting-
room with the door open and gave silent approval to business with a
nod of the head, and Helps announced: 'Approved.'

Uncle Leopold stayed at Osborne for some weeks, occasionally
going up to London; and his quiet sympathy and advice did much to
restore the Queen's sense of proportion. She wished, above all things,
to show the strength of her love for Albert by the strength of her
mourning. She had the natural interest in death that in her day was by no
means abnormal. All ages have had their special preoccupations. For
example, the first Elizabethans showed an excessive interest in their
bodily evacuations, and the second Elizabethans show an excessive
interest in sex. The Victorians took the keenest interest in death. Queen
Victoria, in fact, had a less morbid view of death than many of her
contemporaries. She planned that the Blue Room at Windsor should
not be a shut-up, cobwebby death-chamber, after the custom of some
Middle-European countries; but kept clean, provided regularly with
fresh flowers and linen, and painted up when necessary as 'a living
beautiful monument'. Before the day of the funeral she had already
planned that her husband's remains should lie only temporarily at
Windsor and afterwards be transferred to a new mausoleum at Frogmore. It should be well-lighted, designed by Ludwig Gruner and have
one sarcophagus for them both. Baron Marochetti should sculpt two
sleeping statues as soon as possible.

The Queen neither expected nor hoped to live. She made her will,
appointed guardians for her children, and waited for death. When it did
not come, she was driven to exclaim: 'Oh. – oh! I can't bear to live on
so! I shall never live on! – God cannot mean to tear me alive into pieces!'
Had she guessed how many years stretched ahead she might have found
it insupportable.★

★ So long a time passed that, when it was required, Marochetti's sculpture of her made in
1862 could not be traced until at last it was found in a wall cavity at Windsor.

While, as she thought, she eked out her remaining months, she made plans for monuments, both private and public. There was to be a statue of the Prince Consort wearing highland dress for Balmoral. The water-colour painter E. H. Corbauld, had made a drawing of the Prince Consort on his death bed. This treasure was kept securely locked in a special case and circulated round the family. A death-mask had been cast after the Prince's death. The Queen would not look at it, but she refused to allow it to leave Osborne House. Photographs were taken of the Queen and her daughters gazing at a bust of the departed; dramatic monochrome studies that emphasized the black of their clothing, the pallor of their grieving faces, and the white of the marble sculpture and plinth. The Prince Consort's speeches should be edited by Mr Helps who might perhaps write a biographical introduction under the Queen's direction. This was done at express speed, published in December 1862 and at once translated into German. There was talk of a full biography. The Prince Consort's librarian, Dr Becker, the Windsor Librarian, and young Baron Ernest Stockmar who acted as secretary to the Crown Princess, were consulted about this project. Eventually an account of the Prince's early years was published in 1867 'compiled, under the direction of her Majesty the Queen, by Lieut.-General the Hon. C. Grey'. This was followed by Theodore Martin's monumental life in five volumes.*

For a time all the Queen could concentrate on was 'Memorials, which will be numberless.' Then it became distressingly clear to her that she was to be denied the right of all widows to nurse her grief quietly and alone. In her first rush of grief she proposed that, with the exception of infrequent meetings of the Privy Council, she could not see her ministers. Instead she would communicate with them in writing. Eventually, under pressure, she compromised. But it was not until 29 January, forty-six days after the death of the Prince Consort that she gave an audience to her ageing Prime Minister.

Lord Palmerston found the journey by train and steamer trying, and his jade-green gloves stood out conspicuously in jet-black Osborne, but he was kind and said what he believed, that her husband's death had been a real calamity. The Queen was touched but the old gentleman's visit did not alleviate her distress at having to deal with despatch-boxes and attend to business that she often found inexplicable. She admitted to her friend Lord Clarendon that for years she had done nothing but depend on her husband and sign her name. It was unnerving to have to

---

* The German Emperor William II was the only one of the Prince Consort's grand-children to remember him and he was very proud of the fact. His set of the official biography, inscribed by the Queen 'To darling Willy with love from Grandmama', went with him into exile in Holland. The leaves, though, remained uncut to the end.

do everything for herself. She did not even have the advantage of a confidential Private Secretary. General Grey had been her husband's Private Secretary and had no standing in her Household beyond the fact that he was one of her Equerries. Sir Charles Phipps, officially the Keeper of her Privy Purse as well as the dead Prince Consort's Treasurer, did his best for her, giving advice and writing letters on her behalf. It was through him that she proposed to Ministers that it might be useful if one or other of the Secretaries of State ran down to Osborne every week either for the week-end or on a Wednesday. He would be the equivalent of a Balmoral Minister in Attendance. For a time this was tried; but, encouraged by the King of the Belgians, General Grey began to work unofficially as the Queen's Private Secretary, and though they would not give him the title for five more years, the Ministers recognized his usefulness and discretion. The General saved the Queen from unnecessary blunders. and he saved the Ministers from making the sixteen hour journey to and from Osborne.

The Queen had ample energy and thus time, when she was not writing letters or working on despatch boxes, to brood deeply on her loss and on all that it meant. She was a devout Christian but fitted into no slot of churchmanship. Within the Church of which she was supreme Governor she disapproved of the Ritualists only a little less than she did the Evangelicals, and she sat very lightly to orthodoxy. The Church ordered that she should receive Communion at Easter and on two other occasions in the year. She adapted this to suit herself, communicating twice, on Good Friday and just before Christmas. Parliament fought frantically over the illegality of such things as Crucifixes. She had one beside her bed at Osborne and it was buried with her. Possibly more than most people she was not entirely consistent and, if she disliked a dogma, she simply ignored it. For example, the Protestant prohibition of praying for the dead was abhorrent to her. She prayed for Albert energetically and continuously and urged her daughter in Berlin to do the same: 'Always pray for him, as before – never make any difference, I don't and won't and treat him as living, only invisible to us.' One of her Private Secretaries was later to ask the Dean of Windsor: 'Do we officially believe in purgatory?' and the answer was no. But the Queen believed in something very close to it. She thought it absurd that the dead sleep until the day of judgment. 'The spirit cannot be asleep for a moment, but there must be a progression, and the means and the power of gradually redeeming the past.'

The Crown Princess was a liberal and a seeker and doubtless she might well have questioned such a view, but when at last, in February, 1862, she was permitted to travel to Osborne she would not have had the heart to deny her mother any form of consolation. She found her desolated but very determined, and especially on four matters: that she would have nothing to do with the Prince of Wales who was sent off on a tour of the Near East already planned by his father to keep him out of her sight; that she would live perpetually in retirement, work dutifully at her despatch-boxes, but see the world very little; that she would alter nothing the dead Prince Consort had made or decreed and always make future decisions in light of what she believed he would have wished; and, finally, that nothing should or could be joyful ever again; thus Confirmations and Weddings were for a long time described as 'awful' or 'dreadful', even 'fearful'.

The Crown Princess spoke up for her brother. Typhoid had killed their father, although it might have been aggravated by a chill caught at Cambridge and anxieties about what the Queen termed 'Bertie's fall'. But she was unsuccessful. She realized her mother would not be really content until the Prince of Wales was married and thus totally away from her, living at Marlborough House in London, or Sandringham House that his father had bought for him in Norfolk or at Birkhall. At one time Barton Manor had been thought of as a possible residence for the heir to the Crown but the idea had been given up even before the death of the Prince Consort. Now the Prince was to be told that he could have the use of a suite of rooms on the second floor above the Council Chamber and Audience Room and the Privy Purse's Room. But his sister knew how unlikely it was that he would accept the offer. The David–Absalom relationship was frequently repeated in the Royal House of Brunswick. She knew the kindest thing she could do for everyone was to concentrate her efforts on arranging a marriage as soon as possible.

Not until March did the melancholy court at Osborne move to that *'living grave'* at Windsor. Within three weeks it had returned to Osborne where the Queen received Tennyson, one of the Prince Consort's favourite poets, and as his *In Memoriam* showed, a man with infinite capacity for knowing how she suffered. The poet remarked on the little Queen's statuesque self-possession, the sadness and sweetness of her voice, and rather quaintly on 'a stately innocence about her, different from other women'.

In order to avoid the Exhibition in London that would have painfully reminded her of the Great Exhibition, the Queen determined to travel north to Balmoral on 30 April. It was her first visit in springtime when the larches were at their best, but the weather was not congenial. She and her daughters, with Prince Alfred who was on shore-leave, arrived in pouring rain. Out of respect for her grief everyone kept out of her way and she was received only by Dr Robertson at the door and John Grant in the hall. But it vexed rather than soothed her. She wrote to the

Crown Princess: 'Oh! darling child – the agonizing sobs as I crawled up with Alice and Affie! The stags heads – the rooms – blessed, darling Papa's room – then his coats – his caps – kilts – all, convulsed my poor shattered frame.' Her disjointed, piteous account showed the true state of her mind. Far from bringing her the relief that possibly she had secretly hoped for, she was utterly shattered at Balmoral. And still, inexorably, the despatch-boxes arrived.

Two of the children became unwell, Princess Alice with a serious chill, Princess Louise with a stye on her eye. Things were altogether too much for the Queen. She believed she was going mad. Years later, she admitted that she had been tempted again and again to kill herself. It was Dr Macleod, the Glasgow minister whose sermon had so pleased her during the Crimean War, who brought her from the brink. She had reached the greatest depth of grief in the whole of her life in Scotland. Thereafter, wherever she was, whatever she suffered, it could never be as bad again.

Chapter 20

More marriage and death

When the Court left Balmoral six of 'our Balmoral people' travelled south to go to the Exhibition – 'as I felt beloved Papa would have wished it'. 'Dear Papa's original plan' for the Prince of Wales's return to England had been that he should return through Paris. Therefore, although it was inconvenient because his Governor, General Bruce, had been taken ill, Sir Charles Phipps, not feeling quite well himself, was sent off to see the Prince safely through 'that Sodom and Gomorrah'. Then, because it was felt that the Prince Consort would have approved, his German Secretary, Dr Becker was asked if he would accompany Princess Alice to Hesse as her permanent secretary. The mausoleum was quickly going up and Baron Marochetti had already finished his recumbent marble statue of the Prince Consort. 'How I long for it to be in its place! It will be such an object and such a comfort to go and sit by it.'

Then another death struck the court. General Bruce died in London. All Osborne seemed to dissolve in tears and it was but four days before the wedding of Princess Alice, an event that had to go through simply because the date had been chosen by the Prince Consort. Lady Augusta, upon whom the Queen had come to depend a great deal, was desolated by the untimely death of her brother. The Queen wailed to Vicky: 'This last blow has quite crushed our poor dear Alice . . . this poor, unhappy marriage is more like a funeral than a wedding.'

From all accounts it seemed as if this was the Queen's intention. The ceremony should take place at a temporary Altar placed before Winterhalter's portrait of the Royal Family in the dining-room. This put a full-size portrait of the dead Prince Consort in the most conspicuous position possible. Next to this picture was a portrait of the Queen's dead mother. At the ceremony the gentlemen should wear black evening-coats, the ladies half-mourning of grey or violet; though not the Queen herself or her closest ladies. The bride should be given away by her uncle Ernest for, though he had been working hard to upset the Prince Consort's plans for a marriage between the Prince of Wales and Princess Alexandra of Denmark, he was the Prince Consort's brother. The ceremony should be conducted by the Archbishop of York, an emotional man who had lost his wife only four years before, assisted by Dean Wellesley of Windsor and the local Parson of Whippingham, Mr Prothero, whose wife was a cause for grave concern. After the ceremony the wedding registers should be signed in the Horn Room, a venue that must have aroused a good deal of ribaldry amongst the worldly-wise who used the word 'cuckold' and its synonyms. Then the married couple should take luncheon alone with the mourning Queen, and everyone else manage in a marquee.

All went according to plan. The Queen sat in her armchair, half-hidden by her sons the Prince of Wales and Prince Alfred, gazing at the picture of her husband as he had been fifteen years before. The bride wore flounces designed by her dead father. The Archbishop 'read that fine service (purified from its worst coarseness) admirably, and himself had tears running down his cheeks.' The scene in the Horn Room where the family met was of unrestrained lament. There was no cake, no confetti, no shoe thrown after the four-horse brougham that took the young couple to their honeymoon at St Clare; and the Queen with her half-sister, two of her daughters and the Prince of Wales, called on them within forty-eight hours. After the briefest of honeymoons the couple was back at Osborne.

Hesse-Darmstadt was a minor sovereign-state, but the Queen was having no nonsense about her son-in-law's precedence. She conferred on Prince Louis the dignity of His Royal Highness and, at a private ceremony in the Pavilion, invested him with the Order of the Garter. When the couple left they carried with them a large number of gifts that varied in value and type from a Bible and casket from 'The Maidens of England', or, at least, 5,000 chosen maidens, to opals and diamonds from the dead Prince Consort, a diamond brooch from the dead Duchess of Kent, and a weird gold and diamond bracelet from the living Uncle Ernest that had one of his own eyes painted and enamelled on the surface. 'We all anxiously hope', the Queen wrote to her eldest daughter, 'she may not begin having a family soon and the doctors think it is likely.' The Crown Princess was also told that General Bruce's widow had been appointed Extra Bedchamber Woman in the Household to relieve her sister-in-law, Lady Augusta, from time to time. Her appointment had taken on a more permanent character than most Extra Bedchamber Women, but, unlike Major Elphinstone, she did occasionally ask for leave.

The Queen's practice of appointing relations and friends to attend upon her was not liked by many of her subjects. Yet it was a natural thing to do, and the introduction of strangers always carried with it an element of risk. Thus a fairly clear pattern can be seen in the generations of courtiers and servants throughout the Queen's long reign. Already the Prince Consort's Household had been absorbed into the Royal Household and his staff transferred. Rudolph Löhlein had become the Queen's Personal Attendant in the Lord Chamberlain's Department, and Archie Macdonald sent to the Prince of Wales's household. Gustav Mayet had also been transferred and made valet to Prince Leopold, though later he was to return to the Queen's Household as the confidential copyist of her letters. Annie Macdonald who had been the Prince Consort's 'necessary-woman', or general cleaner, was now the Queen's wardrobe-maid and eventually became her First Wardrobe Woman.

It was Annie Macdonald who had put the grief-stricken Queen to bed on the night of the Prince Consort's death, and she featured prominently in the Queen's life after the departure of Miss Skerrett, who retired in 1862, and the marriage of the princess. Annie was the daughter of the Balmoral blacksmith and the widow of a royal footman, and became so precious that she even featured in a will made in October, 1897 amongst those with whom the Queen especially wished to be re-united after death. 'Good John Brown and good Annie Macdonald' were the only non-royal names in the list.

John Brown himself, as his influence grew, almost formed a dynasty in the royal service. One brother was valet to Prince Leopold and afterwards a Page of the Presence. Another looked after the kennels at Windsor. Another was the royal shepherd at Balmoral. Another kept the Queen's Lodge at Osborne. Yet another was given a farm on the north bank of the Dee. Brown's office as Personal Attendant, though he was always junior to Rudolf Löhlein the Coburger, was held by Browns or their cousins for two generations. It was the same in the Household. Sir Charles Phipps' daughter Harriet became a Maid of Honour and afterwards Woman of the Bedchamber. General Grey eventually gave way to a nephew-by-marriage, who had been an Equerry of the Prince Consort's and, as General Sir Henry Ponsonby, was to serve the Queen for twenty-five years. And Sir Henry's second son was in the Royal Household for three reigns. Towards the end of the reign almost all the courtiers were related by marriage or by blood.

One of the few exceptions was Major Elphinstone but he served Prince Arthur until his death. In 1862 his contract of service was renewed 'in BOTH our names', and in the autumn he and Prince Arthur set up at the Ranger's House Blackheath with a small household. It was to be the Prince's establishment for the next nine years.

Before that they accompanied the Queen to Balmoral where there was suitably subdued jollity on hearing that the Crown Princess had safely been delivered of a second son. The Queen sent her a workbasket plaited with her own hands – 'the first piece of work I touched since December 14!!'

The Queen had spent a good deal of time making pilgrimages to the places where she and her husband had been so happy; chief of them the cairn they had all built in the year he bought the property, and the double cottage at Alt-na-Giuthasach. She and six of her children went to the top of Craig Lowrigan to place the first stones of a memorial-cairn to the Prince Consort. It was not her intention, however, that this should be simply a heap of stones, but a pyramid of considerable size. An obelisk to his memory was put up, and close to it was to be the huge sculpture in bronze ordered from William Theed. A marble replica of the sculpture was to be placed inside the Castle. There, as at Osborne, his rooms were kept clean, always ready for occupation, and often used by the Queen as an extra sitting-room.

The Prince of Wales was still causing trouble. The Queen complained of his 'idleness and "désoeuvrement", his listlessness and want of attention' – all faults calculated to anger an energetic, self-centred woman. He had in principle accepted the idea of marrying Princess Alexandra. He had accepted the officer commanding at Aldershot, General Sir William Knollys as Comptroller of his Household in place of General Bruce, though he had strongly objected to the Queen informing Knollys about the Clifden affair, and actually lost his temper with her. With his Household he had settled into Marlborough House and Sandringham, but when he went to Birkhall, his other property, he declared he did not care for it and much preferred Abergeldie. Rejecting the house chosen for him and bought in his name by his father would have greatly pained the Queen. However, she made no remark, arranged for him to use Abergeldie from time to time and, in 1885, she bought Birkhall from him so that it could not be sold away from the royal estate.

At the beginning of September she went to Coburg, travelling for the first time as Countess of Balmoral, for she was determined to speed on the betrothal of the Prince of Wales, arrange appropriate memorials at Coburg, and let her younger children see their father's homeland. She also took with her Mr Toward, the land steward at Osborne who had collaborated with the Prince Consort in many of his planting schemes, so that he could see the Rosenau and its small garden.

This display of the Queen's organizing ability showed that she was recovering from the helplessness induced by her bereavement. Plans flowed from her. By her arrangement the Prince of Wales met Princess

Alexandra at the Palace at Laeken and became engaged in Uncle Leopold's grotto. Almost immediately she arranged that the Prince should then go on a Mediterranean voyage on the royal yacht *Osborne* with his elder sister and the Crown Prince, thus keeping him out of her way for some considerable time. This would enable her to receive Princess Alexandra at Osborne and teach her how things were done in England. Major Elphinstone found himself saddled with the extra responsibility for Prince Leopold at Coburg, and was instructed on what they should see and do, and that they must take every opportunity to visit old Baron Stockmar. The Crown Princess brought her two elder children to Coburg and William delighted her by riding into her presence on a donkey holding a parasol in his good hand. King William of Prussia also called and was in something of a state about a ministerial crisis, and doubtless the newly organized Queen would have given him encouraging advice if she had not been facing a domestic disaster. Prince Alfred had had a 'fall'. 'Oh! the bitter anguish that followed.' The Crown Princess again tried to help but she was not thanked.

At Osborne the Queen put Princess Alexandra through her paces, and sorted out the problems that a Danish princess would bring with her, and arranged the number and nationality of her personal attendants. The Princess passed the test well.

One aspect of Osborne was altering. Forts were being built to protect Portsmouth; three on the downs inland, but four in the sea, supplied by their own springs of water. They had the Queen's blessing because Lord Palmerston and the Prince Consort had had one of their rare agreements about the need to guard the dockyards. Spit Bank, the nearest fortress was 8 miles away and could only be seen from the top floor of Osborne House when the visibility was good. The next in line, Horse Sand Fort, was 9 miles from the House and could be seen on rare occasions. The other two were invisible from the house.*

In December came the grim anniversary that involved services in the Blue Room, the consecration of the mausoleum and the transfer of the Prince Consort's remains to a temporary sarcophagus there. It was a triduum witnessed by the Prince of Wales, the Crown Prince, Prince Louis of Hesse and Prince Arthur, and inaugurated an annual Blue Room commemoration with its own liturgy called by the family Mausoleum Day. The Court then moved to Osborne for Christmas. Never again would the Queen keep the feast at Windsor if she could avoid it.

---

* After the Franco–Austrian War and Napoleon III's aggressiveness, a war with France was by no means an impossibility. The raising of the volunteers and the defence of certain strategic places was the result. The Spithead forts came to be known as Palmerston's Follies.

To the shocked surprise of both High and Low churchmen the Queen decided that the Prince of Wales should marry in Lent. 'Marriage' she announced, 'is a solemn holy act *not* to be classed with amusements.' She herself remained in black only relieved by her widow's cap of white. She attended the ceremony in a private gallery and anyone who looked up, as Mr Disraeli did, and chanced to catch her eye was instantly made aware that he had made a mistake.

After a honeymoon at Osborne the young couple commenced to take one large burden from the Queen's shoulders. They represented her at the head of society, and thus enabled her to retire still more from the public eye. When in England she tried always to be at Osborne, except for Easter and Ascot and Mausoleum Day when she was at Windsor. She took to going to Balmoral twice a year, and, for a time, though this was soon discontinued, she went to Coburg.

In 1863 Princess Alice kept her promise to be confined of her first child in England and at Windsor on Easter Sunday she gave birth to Her Grand Ducal Highness Princess Victoria of Hesse and by Rhine.* She completed her recovery under the superintendence of her mother at Osborne; then she and the baby and Louis returned home.

The Queen went north to Balmoral. There she wrote to Uncle Leopold: 'A married daughter I MUST have living with me.' A warning of battles to come. She was very pleased with the large pyramid that now crowned Craig Lowrigan, a mass of granite put together without any mortar. She was not pleased with criticism of the text she had chosen for the inscription because it came from the Apocrypha, not recognized as Holy Writ beyond Berwick. Her critic, or rather, her denouncer, was a fiery Free Kirk minister in Edinburgh. She was angry that such a private matter should be the cause of newspaper correspondence and that the minister should actually be supported and her choice condemned. 'My poor birthday!' fell on a Sunday, and Dr Macleod, who might have been disposed to sympathize, had had no time to prepare a proper sermon and preached an improvised and presumably uninspiring one on the text 'All hail!'

Back in England the Queen had to face calamities.

So deep was her mourning, so thick the black edging to her writing-paper, that she was physically incapable of marking other deaths as they relentlessly occurred. Old Baron Stockmar died while she was at Osborne in July. In reply to a polite telegram of condolence from Major Elphinstone she replied: 'The one sustaining thought to the Queen is the *reunion* of two such beings in brighter regions who were so united

---

* Afterwards Princess Louis of Battenberg and first Marchioness of Milford-Haven, mother of the late Admiral of the Fleet the Earl Mountbatten of Burma, Governor and Lord Lieutenant of the Isle of Wight.

already on Earth!' The weather was distressingly hot. The Queen had recently had to dismiss the children's governess for deceit and for leading Princess Louise to be deceitful. A housemaid had hurled herself from the roof at Windsor on to the North Terrace. Tatooed Maoris had been received in the gilded Council Room. And Prince Leopold was unwell. But the Baron's death overtopped all. The Queen wrote to her eldest daughter, burdened with her mourning: 'I have but little to say. I am sitting in the Upper Alcove – expecting to see your dear Papa every minute!! I suppose, dear, you have plenty of the beloved Baron's photographs and also some of his precious hair? If not I can send you some of both.' Here was Osborne at its most exotic, a repository of funereal relics.

Chapter 21
Apt to blaze

The whole family was with the Queen at Balmoral in the autumn of 1863. It had never happened before. It was never to happen again. From Baby Princess Beatrice to the oldest, the Crown Princess, they were all there with their families; crammed into Balmoral with the Queen or with the Waleses at Abergeldie. The Princess of Wales was carrying 'the-heir-but-one'. Not surprisingly there was more fun in the line of parties at Abergeldie.

Mr Gladstone, the Chancellor of the Exchequer, was Minister in Attendance for almost two months and he found only one fault. 'I in vain inquired, with care, about Episcopal Services.' He admired the countryside and was a splendid walker. In addition to his paper-work and dining with the Queen which was obligatory for the Minister at Balmoral, in the first few days he managed a walk of 24 miles and three quarters over rough ground, followed by a Ghillies' Ball at Abergeldie – 'nearby the best fun I ever witnessed'; then a charge on foot up the side of Loch-na-Gar of 19 miles, then more walks of 16 miles, and 25, and 'a measured mile in twelve minutes beside this beautiful Dee'. Eighty-five and three-quarter miles, one of them at high speed, over bogs and heather, and including what he called 'hill scrambles' seemed nothing to him, and he was in his fifty-fourth year. And almost certainly these walks were made in perfectly ordinary country wear with a Piccadilly stand-up collar and a Lincoln and Bennett tall hat.

The Queen suffered a carriage-accident that might have been serious – she was returning from a picnic of broth and potatoes beside Loch Muick, and the coachman, a little drunk, or confused as the Queen generously put it, overturned the carriage and tipped out the Queen, the Princesses Alice and Helena, and Princess Alice's small negro page, Willem, as well as the ubiquitous Brown. It was the last who cut the traces, sent off the coachman to get help, constructed a shelter in the turned-up carriage, produced claret, and comforted the party. The Queen had a bandaged head and dined in bed. Brown had a bruised leg and was the hero of the hour. Mr Gladstone suggested that twilight wanderings in carriages were imprudent. The Queen quickly told him her actions were directed by what the Prince Consort would have wished, and that, in any case, drives filled in the afternoon.

Six days afterwards she unveiled a statue of her husband erected by friendly Aberdonians which was the first major excursion she had yet made into the public eye. The day began badly: 'I was terribly nervous. Longed not to have to go through this fearful ordeal. Prayed for help, and got up earlier.' It was another piece by Marochetti, and the Queen was accompanied not only by her children, and her ladies and gentlemen then in waiting, but also by Rudolf Löhlein and Gustav Mayet, as well as Balmoral servants. Nevertheless the ceremony greatly taxed her nervous resources and, as the *Scotsman* reported on 14 October, 1863, the minister asking for a blessing became carried away with his extempore prayer and made everyone, including the Queen, fidget and fret.

Conceivably having all her large family with her in Scotland began to get on the Queen's nerves. She was a shy, emotional person who, when not low- or high-spirited, had an uncertain temper, and she was quick to flare up. Therefore she preferred to live her own life. It was the protocol at both Balmoral and Osborne that no one should ever propose themselves for one of her excursions. She chose her own company and objective, and she did not like her ladies and gentlemen in waiting to be out of the house before her. It was important to guess where the Queen was going and not go there. So, sometimes, she might be boiling potatoes – a favourite pastime – and making tea over a fire on one side of a hill, with some of her children doing precisely the same on the other side. It was also protocol not to 'see' the Queen. It led to some ludicrous situations, such as when one of the tallest and broadest of her Ministers contrived ineffectually to conceal himself behind a piece of box topiary. And it could lead to painful situations as when Mr Marconi politely raised his hat and bowed to the passing Queen who looked straight through him and afterwards sent a blistering condemnation of his bad manners by a third person. But the idea behind the protocol was that it allowed the Queen to enjoy an illusion of privacy, the necessary rest and refreshment she required after working at her boxes, and that it kept her even-tempered. It was when people made her feel cornered, or when great events from outside upset all routine, that she was apt to blaze.

Just such a great outside event threatened when the family party finally broke up and left Scotland. The Queen was extremely anxious about the possibility of a war between the Danes and the Prussians and

Austrians. She realized it would rend her family – as indeed happened.

And, having come to depend greatly on Lady Augusta Bruce, she was appalled when her friend announced she was engaged to be married and shortly afterwards the ceremony took place. It was the Queen as much as anyone who had brought the couple together for Dr Stanley had been chaplain and cicerone to the Prince of Wales on his tour of the Near East, and after his return had enjoyed the royal favours, being plucked from his fellowship at Oxford and made Dean of Westminster. 'My dear Lady Augusta' wrote the affronted Queen, 'at 41 . . . has most unnecessarily decided to marry (!!).'

At the end of 1863 Sir Charles Phipps wrote from Osborne to Lord Palmerston that, on her physicians' advice, the Queen was totally unable to appear 'in full dress in public' and that a State Opening of Parliament or entering on the London season was quite out of the question. She was however prepared to expose herself to the gaze of felons. On 16 January, 1864 a carriage took her to the Isle of Wight prison at Parkhurst where she visited some of the female prisoners. 'Only five of them in for murder,' she coolly recorded, 'and these not of the worst character as they had killed their illegitimate, newly-born children out of shame.' Good works were one thing, opening Parliament was another. Nevertheless rumours spread that the Queen was about to go out of mourning. Allegedly she wrote with her own hand to *The Times* to say: 'This idea cannot be too explicitly contradicted.'

Then, in May 1864, a peer rebuked her in the House of Lords for her Prussian sympathies in the Danish–Prussian conflict. This was Lord Ellenborough, for long a thorn in the Queen's side and the first husband of the notorious Jane Digby who had seduced, in order, the cataloguer of her grandfather's library, Prince Felix Scherarzenberg, the King of Bavaria, Baron von Vennigen, Count Spyridon Theotky, the King of Greece, the King's Albanian A.D.C., and the Sheik El Barrack, before finally marrying another Arab chieftain who gave her the title of the Sitt. The Queen was at Balmoral when she heard of Lord Ellenborough's impertinence to her in the Upper House and the Castle rang with her rage. She thoroughly lost her temper and objected to the Foreign Secretary formerly Lord John, by now created Earl Russell, who supported her, and she begged Lord Derby, Ellenborough's political leader, to disown him. His reply was less than satisfactory, that Lord Ellenborough held 'himself altogether aloof from any party combination' and was, therefore, beyond control. 'The Queen hopes everyone *will* know *how* she resents Lord Ellenborough's conduct and how she despises him!' Certainly everyone at Balmoral would have done. If he did nothing else Lord Ellenborough put some fire in his monarch's veins. She not only held a Drawing-Room at Buckingham Palace –

now called by Lord Clarendon 'the most dreary looking of jails' – but she drove in an open carriage through the Park to Paddington Station and caused a wild demonstration.

Major Elphinstone for once aroused her wrath by writing from Rosenau in July where, under instructions, he had taken Prince Arthur, to report that it had rained continuously for a week, the temperature was never more than 55 degrees even at midday, and the tutor, the valet and the cook had all succumbed to the damp and taken to their beds.

The double writing-tables in the Osborne sitting-room must have rattled as the Queen penned her reply:

> The *Queen* must repeat that the *Prince and his brother* regularly lived at the dear Rosenau, from the *beginning* of May until October . . .
> Therefore, Major Elphinstone must not be *unfavourably* impressed for the future . . . *Good* air is *good* air . . . The Queen *is* a disbeliever in the effects of climate upon healthy people.

Canute on the East-Anglian shore could not have been more determined to alter nature to suit a regal will.

From Balmoral in the autumn the Queen had a running battle with the Prince and Princess of Wales. The Princess had been delivered prematurely of a child after skating in January, and they now proposed to remove the heir-but-one across the North Sea to Denmark. The Queen lost that brief campaign, as she did that they must travel incognito. But she fired so many salvoes after them that the first thing they did on returning to England was to rush to Osborne to make their peace.

Nothing was too small for the Queen's snapping criticism. John Speke, who claimed to have discovered the source of the Nile, was killed in a shooting-accident – though possibly he committed suicide – and months afterwards the Queen wished to know why he had not been given some honour 'in time'. This was rectified by the College of Heralds. Speke's father was told he might add a crocodile and a hippopotamus to his coat of arms.

So peppery was she that Sir Charles Phipps and Dr Jenner decided something should be done. The physician said that more riding and less driving would do her a great deal of good, but the Queen seldom rode at Osborne. Observably, with the exception of the Ellenborough episode, their mistress was quieter at Balmoral than at Osborne. This, they agreed, was because of the calming inflence of John Brown, her special ghillie, who had a 'No nonsense' way about him that she found soothing, and who always led her pony. They proposed that Brown be summoned for the winter. In December John Brown arrived at Osborne.

Chapter 22

Almighty indiscretions

Queen Victoria's relationship with John Brown has been the subject of endless speculation but another attempt must be made to fathom what was at the bottom of it simply because he was such an integral part of life at both Osborne and Balmoral.

Then as now, the great majority of people had not the least idea that Brown became a regular attendant on the Queen on the advice of her Privy Purse and her Physician in Ordinary. Therefore the gossips assumed the Queen herself ordered the handsome Scot to be permanently at her side. It caused endless talk. There were, as the Queen wrote in her Journal in 1867 – 'those wicked and idle lies about poor, good Brown, which appeared in the Scotch provincial papers last year.' There were the lampoons and cartoons in the irreverent English press as well. The *Gazette de Lausanne* reported that the two were secretly married, cohabited and that, in September 1866, she was carrying a child by him. This almost caused a diplomatic incident but, really, it was impossible for a person in the Queen's position to escape rumour. As a young woman she had been hissed at Ascot and called 'Mrs Melbourne'. As an old woman, bemused by the flashing teeth and dark skin of her exotic Indian subjects, she was again to become a target for calumny. As a middle-aged widow gossip was inevitable, particularly because she was so amazingly indiscreet. In fact her published indiscretions were so blatant that they carried with them an aura of innocence, though not everyone saw them in that light.

At the beginning of 1868 *Leaves from the Journal of a Life in the Highlands* was published and became a best-seller. Helps had proved his name apposite, and was made Sir Arthur for it, by putting the book together from the Queen's Journal while she played a little with the text and added numerous footnotes. There could be no doubting the sincerity of her dedication of the book 'to the dear memory of him who made the life of the writer bright and happy'. Notwithstanding, she was tactless to give such a glowing account of Brown at such a time.★

That same year the Queen published a large work in two volumes entitled *Highlanders of Scotland, Portraits illustrative of the principal Clans and followings, and the Retainers of the Royal Household at Balmoral*. The artist was Kenneth Macleay, the writer of the letterpress, under the Queen's supervision, Miss Murray MacGregor, historian of Clan Gregor, a frequent visitor to Balmoral and, after the death of her cousin the Duke of Atholl, a companion to his widow. The first eight plates were of royal retainers; the second of these was John Brown and was unique in the volume because Osborne House was the background.

When the Queen considered publishing a record of her widowhood in Scotland, she turned for help to Miss Murray MacGregor because Sir Arthur Helps had died. The result was *More Leaves* and more indiscretions. Not only was the volume dedicated to 'My loyal highlanders and especially to the memory of my devoted personal attendant and faithful friend John Brown', but he was mentioned at every opportunity. Presumably Miss Murray MacGregor had no veto and two descriptions of Brown were particularly personal. In her description of a visit from Balmoral to Dunkeld where the widowed Duchess and Miss Murray MacGregor were living their version of a simple cottage life, the Queen confessed herself 'much distressed at breakfast to find poor Brown's legs had been dreadfully cut by the edge of his wet kilt on Monday; just at the back of the knee.' In the same volume she described an expedition to the hotel of Loch Marce 95 miles in a straight line to the northwest of Balmoral, and thrust in a superfluous note about Brown's health because, some time before she had inspected a turretship H.M.S. *Thunderer* off Osborne Pier, on which occasion Brown tumbled down and hurt his ankle.

The chapped legs and barked shins of John Brown were objects of mirth to the majority, and of fascinated horror to a loyal minority. But the Queen's indiscretions were by no means finished. She decided Brown's biography should be written and approached Sir Theodore Martin who had written the Prince Consort's life in five volumes. Somehow Sir Theodore managed to get out of it. Undeterred, the Queen wrote it herself, sent it to Miss Murray MacGregor† for ghost-

---

★ In the biographical notes John Macdonald rated 5½ lines, Löhlein 6, Duncan 7½, John Grant 11¼, and John Brown 20½.

† Miss Murray MacGregor lost her home in 1897 when the Duchess of Atholl died. But the Queen, besides giving her a Diamond Jubilee Medal also appointed her an Extern Sister of St Katherine's Hospital, a medieval charity of which the Queen of England, Regnant or Consort, was the patron. There were also Resident Sisters. Miss Hildyard, governess to the royal children was appointed one on her retirement in 1865. The ten Externs wore a silver badge and had £100 a year. They were 'Ladies to whom, from straightened circumstances and inability to provide for their own maintenance, these stipends would be the principle means of support.'

ing, and proposed to her appalled Private Secretary that Brown's personal journal might be published as a companion volume. The manuscript was passed round to a select but unhappy band who handled it like a hive about to swarm. Sir Henry Ponsonby suggested that such a publication might 'attract remarks of an unfavourable nature', but no one had the pluck to tell the Queen outright that it could never be printed, let alone published, until the new Dean of Windsor, Randall Davidson, a special favourite of Queen Victoria, conceived it his imperative duty to put their friendship and his career at risk, and he spoke up. She was exceedingly cross. For a fortnight things stood in the balance. Then the Queen accepted his judgment, and, although it was to be in the next reign, Randall Davidson ended as Archbishop of Canterbury.

Such almighty indiscretions were part of the cause of a gale of scandal that shrieked for years through Europe about the friendship of the Queen of Great Britain and Ireland and a village boy from Deeside. It ought, almost a century after Brown's death, to be supposed to have died down altogether. But not a bit of it. The gale has reduced in force but there is still a stiff breeze of nonsense blowing. In 1979, claiming he had done ten years' research, and relying almost entirely on what he called 'oral sources', a member of the Queen's beloved MacDonald clan dressed up all the familiar rumours in different clothes. It seems to the present writer unwise to rely overmuch on 'oral sources'. In working on this book he invited the assistance of any who had first- or second-hand information about the Court in the last decade of the Queen's reign. He was given great help by a number of people but also assailed by many 'oral sources' whose claims appeared a little far-fetched and whose opinions were clearly formed more by ancient rumour than by historic fact. The MacDonald 'oral sources' stretch even further back in time. They are recollections of people nearly or remotely connected with Queen Victoria so long after Brown's death that they themselves must inevitably have been aware of and influenced by all the rubbishy old rumours. These 'new revelations' are really romantic hypotheses that reveal an imperfect understanding of the Queen's character and personality, and a regrettable ignorance of the details of her daily life and the ordering of her Court. She always had a dresser within call. Under no circumstances could she have taken Brown as a regular lover, still less have any marital relationship with him and carry and bear his child, and have kept it all secret. But doubtless the rumours will for ever persist, the cinders being blown up from time to time by a reminder of the Queen's 'Hanoverian appetites'. Rather too much has been made of these appetites. Her private papers have firmly scotched the notion that she made excessive demands upon her husband. If she had appetites, they were primarily for food. All her life she gobbled. Towards the end, when indigestion caused her pain, her physician recommended Benger's food and chicken. She simply added Benger's and chicken to her already copious meals. 'She clings to roast beef and ices!' bewailed one of her ladies.

Brown, too, had a primary appetite – for whisky. When he was young and living an active, out-of-door life his drinking made little difference. Brought indoors, and given next to nothing to do, whisky began to affect him. The Queen liked whisky herself and drank it neat, or in her tea, or with apollinaris water. Doubtless her mind was on something else at the time but the astonished Gladstone once saw her lace a very respectable claret with some of Begg's best. She did not drink much herself, but long custom had rather made her come to expect it of her beloved highlanders, and she was especially indulgent to her friend Brown.

Two stories about his drinking went round the Court. At Balmoral he failed to appear one day to sit on the box of her carriage. The Private Secretary went at once to Brown's room and found him totally incapable of climbing onto anything let alone a carriage-box. With great kindness he himself took Brown's place, and the Queen merely ordered the coachman to proceed and made no other comment. On another occasion at Balmoral Brown was tipsy and he stumbled and fell flat. The Queen instantly announced that she, too, had felt an earth tremor. Both stories show her poise and her loyalty. She was not unaware of Brown's faults, but he was her friend. Probably it was this, far more than his proprietorial attitude to the stables and sport at Balmoral, far more than his peremptory manner of speech which made him seem overfamiliar, far more than his direct access to the Queen which so very few enjoyed, that so deeply annoyed her family and many of her courtiers. They could not understand how the Queen and John Brown could be friends. And yet, so very clearly, they were. For Brown the Queen could and did do battle with anyone. It was as incomprehensible as a Japanese garden of raked sand is to western gardeners.

Brown's many enemies made fun of the Queen's order to Dr Robertson to look up Brown's pedigree and see where he came from. Colour surnames like Brown and White and Black were often assumed by attainted clansmen after the Jacobite risings and the Queen wanted to know if her Personal Highland Servant was in reality Mr Somebody-else. Doubtless she was really anxious to put his position in her household on a more easily acceptable formal footing. At any rate, Dr Robertson, who was not an admirer of Brown, strained at his uncongenial task and found a pedigree – something never difficult to do in Scotland – that linked John Brown with the Farquharsons of Inverey.

And so Brown was accepted – by some – as a gentleman of coat armour, and he was listed in the Royal Household as an esquire. It appeared to escape everyone's attention that Rudolf Löhlein was listed as an esquire at the same time, and that, in any case, the Queen had the perfect right to give Brown whatever rank she wished. Neither she nor Brown made pretentious claims about his background. She happily published for all the world to see in *More Leaves* that for a year he had once worked as an inn servant. She was not ambitious for him, nor, perhaps fortunately for the Royal Family, was he ambitious for himself. All he wanted were places for his relations in good service. As royal favourite he could have asked for far more. The Queen built a cottage for him at Balmoral but he never used it, save that his corpse lay there the night before he was buried in Crathie churchyard and then it reverted to the Queen not to his family. He did not leave a great fortune as has been suggested but precisely £6,816. 9s. 11d. in money and £379. 19s. 6d. in personal effects. Nor did he take bribes to misuse his influence.

The Prince of Wales, whose large features empurpled at the mention of Brown's name, had cause to be thankful for that if nothing else. His own Comptroller, Sir Francis Knollys, realized it, remarking after Brown's death 'if he had been an ambitious man, there is no doubt I suppose, he might have meddled in more important matters. I presume all the Family will rejoice at his death, but I think very probably they are shortsighted.'

Sir Henry Ponsonby, who knew Brown so well, echoed and enlarged on this:

> He was the only person who could fight and make the Queen do what she did not wish. He did not always succeed nor was his advice always the best. But I believe he was honest, and with all his want of education, his roughness, his prejudices and other faults he was undoubtedly a most excellent servant to her.

There is no doubt that after Brown's arrival at Court the Queen did become less irascible, more comfortable, healthier and happier. Brown liked his royal mistress because she made him feel useful, which mattered far more to a man of his temperament than merely being important. He was often at the bridle of her horse, and was painted in this position in one of Landseer's paintings done, for a change, against an Isle of Wight background not towering mountains. He chased off prowling reporters, telling them in no uncertain way to respect the Queen's privacy. He sat on her box out driving, physically protecting her from assault and battery by deranged subjects. He took messages to the members of her family and Household, not always conveying the tact and politeness in which they had first been expressed, and when rheumatism locked her joints he wheeled her in her bathchair or, as the contemporary phrase ran, 'he rolled her along the corridors'. And the Queen liked him for his ruggedness, his protectiveness and his directness. Scotland might not have considered it a compliment but, most probably to Queen Victoria John Brown was the personification of all she loved in upper-Deeside.

It is worth remark that when her cousin the Duke of Cambridge was deeply upset at the death of his steward, it was the Queen, more than anyone, who understood his feelings. She wrote:

> Let me tell you how grieved I am at the great loss you have sustained in the death of your faithful and excellent steward and I may add *friend*. . . . Indeed such a loss is often more than those of one's nearest and dearest, for a faithful servant is so identified with *all* your feelings, wants, wishes, and habits as really to be *part* of your *existence* and *cannot* be replaced.

It is said that in her own loss the Queen ordered that a fresh posy be placed on Brown's pillow each day, and that this was done until she herself died. It was a token of her great attachment.

Chapter 23

First independent steps

Lord Palmerston won a General Election in July 1865, largely, it was said, because at the age of eighty-one, he had recently fathered yet another illegitimate child – a feat which won him scores of votes. But the rosy old dandy died three months later having been almost continuously in office for nearly sixty years. The Queen, who had once regarded him as her arch-enemy, was decidedly sorry. In the Gardener's Cottage at Balmoral she wrote: 'The Queen feels deeply, in her desolate and isolated condition, how one by one those tried servants and advisers are removed from her.'

An even more serious loss was her uncle Leopold. He had been a second father and one of her wisest counsellors. When he fell ill she sent Dr Jenner to Brussels. 'The Belgian doctor who had been called in . . . was unfit.' But the bewigged and rouged old gentleman was beyond any medical aid, and, three days before Mausoleum Day in 1865, he died. The Queen did not care for her cousin, now Leopold II, but the Belgian envoy M. Van de Weyer was at Osborne at the beginning of January 1866 giving 'satisfaction at home and abroad'. The words were Lord Clarendon's, once again, although only temporarily, Foreign Secretary, who was a fellow guest on the island. He had arrived in a Solent storm. Seeing it blow up the Queen considerately telegraphed him not to come but the wind flattened all telegraph-posts and the message did not arrive. Lord Clarendon did. He noted that the Queen was in excellent spirits 'but thinks she can make no exertion'.

There was a ministerial crisis and Lord Russell suggested that it would be a great help if the Queen opened Parliament in person. She shrank from the idea of being the cynosure of all eyes for such a length of time and in such a formal way for the first time since her husband died. After so long a period of seclusion it was not surprising. Her critics claimed she was foxing. When, at last she forced herself to do as the Prime Minister asked, they cynically observed that this was because her third daughter was betrothed to a genial but uninspiring German princeling, Christian of Schleswig-Holstein, who had agreed to come and live at Windsor, and a dowry was required from Parliament. But the Queen had been trained in her duty by the beloved dead: her husband, Uncle Leopold, and Baron Stockmar.

Less than a month after the opening of Parliament Sir Charles Phipps died at Osborne. The Queen begged that, before appointing a successor to 'her valued and deeply lamented friend', Lord Russell should regularize General Grey's position as her Private Secretary. Her intention was also to make Sir Thomas Biddulph her Privy Purse, and Sir John Cowell, unmarried and therefore able to be permanently in residence, her Master of the Household. The Government did not oblige her. The General and Sir Thomas Biddulph became Joint Keepers of her Privy Purse. There was a certain amount of wrangling at Osborne about precedence; while the Queen put Prince Christian, her prospective son-in-law, through his paces. Even her cousin Mary Adelaide's betrothed, Prince Teck, was invited for observation. No one ever married into the British Royal Family without this preliminary scrutiny at Osborne or Balmoral.

War threatened between Prussia and Austria. The Ministry continued to slide from crisis to crisis, and the Queen was seriously upset because government business prevented her from spending her birthday as usual at Osborne. Because it had never been necessary before her bereavement none of her beloved mentors – her husband, her uncle or Baron Stockmar – had heavily underlined her duty to make herself visible to her subjects, and she believed her primary role as Queen was to work at her despatch-boxes and maintain, at least in her own Court, a high standard of conduct. The nagging of officials grated on her nerves and she sometimes suspected they were using her for their own party purposes. When Lord Russell suggested she forego her Balmoral spring holiday, she made a gesture of independence by moving from Windsor to Clivedon House which was still within easy reach of London, and she warned him that the present weight of her work was too much and any day she feared a complete breakdown.

Then, against his wishes, she went off to Scotland and took possession of yet another new retreat, a bothy built up Glen Gelder and called the Gelder Shiel. Formerly there had been stepping-stones across the burn, but a bridge had been built at the Queen's order. The cottage had two rooms, a kitchen and a stable and, over the door, was a Gaelic inscription that, in translation, meant The Queen's House. Optically the cottage must have seemed oppressively small because all the walls, the sofa and chair coverings, and even the table cover were of the Balmoral tartan.

Though the tartan had been the invention of the Prince Consort, the Queen had at last taken an independent step at Balmoral. Her husband had not stepped foot in Gelder Shiel. During the next year she took her first independent step at Osborne, acting on her land steward's advice and selling the southernmost tip of the estate, the piece of sloping ground called Mount Misery. Simultaneously she made it possible for her sons and sons-in-law and their guests to smoke at Osborne by providing a special establishment at a great distance from the Pavilion. It was a one-storey structure built onto the south-west end of the Household Wing and contained a convenient room reached through a vestibule with a washhand basin on one side and a water-closet on the other. The view faced south-west. There was also an open garden alcove that faced south-east. Smoking was still not easy for there was no access door into the house and it was some distance from the nearest entrance; and, on arrival, the smoker took his choice of smoking in the enclosed smoking-room or the open alcove. Still, it was a concession and an innovation. Another Queen Victoria was slowly emerging.

Whilst she was at her new shiel in the fastness of Glen Gelder, Prussia went to war with Austria. Like the war over Schleswig-Holstein it split her family down the middle. She did not indicate where her sympathies lay, possibly because the Crown Princess's two-year-old son Sigismund died of meningitis in the first fortnight of the campaign. Then Lord Russell's Ministry was defeated in Parliament. Apprised of this by General Grey, the Queen telegraphed that she considered it 'the bounden duty of her Government, in the present state of the Continent, to set aside all personal considerations, and to continue at their posts . . . The Queen could not accept their resignations'.

Five days passed before she consented to move south to Windsor. Even then she did not wish to accept Russell's resignation. But at Windsor she was obliged to do so. Lord Derby was asked to form a government. Simultaneously Königgrätz was fought and won by Prussia. The family repercussions were considerable. The Grand Duchy of Hesse-Darmstadt and the Kingdom of Hanover had fought on the Austrian side, and, with other Austrian allies, they were heavily penalized. The great possessions of the Kingdom of Hanover, many from the old British Royal Family were swallowed up by Bismarck. The Duke of Cambridge, heir-but-one to that Kingdom, was clamant to the Queen. So was her daughter Princess Alice. Her eldest daughter grieved for Sigismund, yet was proud of her husband whose timely arrival with reinforcements had made the Prussian victory possible.

Queen Victoria's realm was neutral. She herself also tried to be. The Hesse children were temporary refugees who played at Windsor and in the nurseries of Osborne, but their cousin, the seven-year-old Prince

William of Prussia, was also made welcome at Balmoral, and it was then that, despite the boy's handicap, old John Grant produced a small rifle and taught him how to use it so well that eventually he became as proficient with a gun or rifle as he was with a sabre.

Although she had faced the official opening of Parliament in February, the Queen still showed diffidence at appearing in public even at the Braemar Gathering. She could be sure of what she called 'the same people' being there; in other words, the gentry of the neighbourhood; and she was under no political or social pressure to do so, but she had not attended since 1861, and she was in a dither about it. One of the letters that circulated so freely at Court, often by the hand of Brown, was addressed to one of her senior equerries on the matter:

> The Queen felt *too* nervous to tell Lord Charles this evening what she meant, viz.: *that* unless it were a really rainy day, she had made up her mind to make the great effort of going for a short while this year to the Gathering.

This did not sound as if she were trying to avoid an unpalatable duty. Evidently she still shrank from making any formal appearance in public. But, apparently, it was not 'a really rainy day' on the date of the Gathering and her attendance was a success. Afterwards she paid a second visit to the Duchess of Atholl and Miss Murray MacGregor, accompanied by Princess Louise and Prince Arthur, and as a sight-seer she appeared indefatigable. In a single day accompanied by Princess Louise, the Duchess and Miss Murray MacGregor, John Grant and John Brown, she made a 70 mile journey by horse and carriage, partly in darkness and mostly enshrouded in mist and drizzle.

Made confident by her reception at the Gathering and freshened by her hectic holiday with the Duchess, the Queen braved the business of opening the Aberdeen waterworks, though she confessed it made her very nervous. Her answer to the loyal address 'was the first time I had read anything since my husband was taken from me.'

It was the Ministry of Lord Derby that at last met the Queen's wishes, and from May 1867 the sovereign was gazetted with a Private Secretary for the first time. General Grey, as Private Secretary, now officially took precedence over the Privy Purse.

But it was also Lord Derby who firmly grasped the nettle of John Brown. An ephemeral paper, the *Tomahawk*, published a crude cartoon copy of Landseer's picture of Brown standing at the Queen's pony's head at Osborne with the caption 'All is black that is not Brown', and anti-Brown stories were circulating throughout the kingdom. The Queen was due to appear at a review in Hyde Park, and intended that Brown should be on the box. Taking a reluctant Duke of Cambridge with him, for the Queen's cousin was the Commander-in-Chief, Lord Derby asked for an audience and advised her to leave Brown at home on that particular day; otherwise he could not answer for her servant's safety. The vials of her wrath poured over the unhappy pair. Fortuitously a calamity some three and a half thousand miles away caused the Court to be plunged into mourning, the review cancelled, and the matter was dropped. The Emperor of Mexico, brother to the Emperor of Austria, was shot by rebels and his Empress, Uncle Leopold's daughter, driven raving mad. But, though haunted by the disaster in Mexico, the Queen had not quite finished with Lord Derby. She told him she was being expected to receive royal private and state visits that were beyond her, and she sent Dr Jenner to inform him of the exact state of her nerves. In the event, she did receive the Sultan of Turkey aboard the *Victoria and Albert* off Spithead. He spoke nothing but Turkish, but being said to be interested in naval affairs, he was given a Naval Review. However, there was a distinct sea-swell and the Queen, who often suffered from seasickness, on this occasion did not, though she noted that the Sultan did. 'He was continually retiring below,' she commented, 'and can have seen very little.' At the conclusion the poor man was invested with the Garter, and sat down to luncheon in the deck-saloon of the *Victoria and Albert*. Directly afterwards the yacht weighed anchor and steamed for Osborne and, by some misunderstanding as they were passing through a lane of ships, they all saluted simultaneously, and the noise was tremendous. The Sultan, as usual, was below; and only came up to say goodbye and be transferred to another ship off Osborne Pier. He returned to Turkey to the leisurely pursuit of ruling the Ottoman Empire, amusing himself by trying to catch live chickens in his harem. His visit had cost £8,922. 14s. 10d.; most of it for furniture replacements at Buckingham Palace, and no less than £18 for twenty-four pints of eau-de-Cologne and seven pints of the strongest scents.

The Queen's next visitor was the Empress Eugénie who arrived at Osborne for the first time since the death of the Prince Consort. She came for sympathy. Everyone in France believed, and quite rightly as it happened, that her insistence that Maximilian take the Mexican throne had moved him to do so; and she felt the dreadful weight of his assassination and his widow's madness. After a few days she left Osborne.

'Greatly relieved the visit was over,' noted the Queen in her Journal. The next day she suffered one of those losses which, though the royal establishment was large, particularly affected her. When she drove out privately at Balmoral or Osborne, and especially the former, there were a coachman and a highlander on the box, and an outrider in livery coat and top hat to lead the way, open and shut gates, look out for good places to light a fire for boiling potatoes or a tea-kettle, and always be on the watch for the Queen's safety. As a result the Queen became attached to her outriders, selecting them with care and generally choosing them because they were related in some way to her old and well-trusted servants. William Head was just the sort of outrider she most valued; the son of a Sussex schoolmaster and son-in-law of her old coachman and thus related to a family that was in the royal service from the reign of George III. He had travelled with her for scores of miles in Scotland and on the Isle of Wight, but, on the day following the Empress's departure, having the afternoon off, he joined in a game of cricket for an hour, then went to the mews hall, asked for a cup of tea, and collapsed. When he recovered consciousness he was given a little whisky and water and carried to his bed. The surgeon to the Household who lived in West Cowes was telegraphed at 5.20. Such was the speed of telegraphing in those leisurely days that he arrived to see his patient at 5.40. By then William Head was dead. The Queen was told. She was very distressed. According to the *Isle of Wight Observer*, there was an inquest 'at the Sanatorium, Osborne Palace'. The jury returned a verdict of 'Death from natural causes'. The registrar wrote in the cause of death as 'Visitation of God'. The latter almost certainly coincided with the Queen's feelings. No one could more quickly become sorry for herself than Queen Victoria at this stage of her life; she was a regular royal Mrs Gummidge. She would have had a personal sense of grievance at the loss of a favourite postilion.

Before going on to Balmoral in August, 1867 the Queen made a tour of the Border Country. She had her family with her, and Princess Helena and her portly bald husband Prince Christian with their small baby, and the Duchess of Roxburghe who welcomed her and gave her every attention was one of her most particular friends. But she was in low spirits. 'I thought so much of all that dearest Albert would have done and said, and how he would have wandered about everywhere, admired everything, looked at everything – and no! Oh! must it ever, ever be so?'★ At 'our dear Balmoral' she cheered up, and with Princess Louise and Lady Churchill and escorted by Sir Thomas Biddulph, went on an expedition, roughing it in the best style, missing turnings, losing the luggage, being bitten by midges, comforting her daughter who had toothache throughout, enjoying moments of great happiness, Sharp her Collie bounding beside them, Lady Churchill reading aloud *Pride and Prejudice* after dinner each evening, sighting eight stags – 'Oh! had

★ At one point, whenever she saw anything particularly interesting or beautiful she began the curious practice of holding up the small portrait of Albert she always wore so that he could enjoy it too.

dearest Albert been here with his rifle!' – good, simple food and ample of it.

On the twentieth anniversary of her engagement day, Theed's statue of the Prince Consort was unveiled at Balmoral. A psalm was sung, a prayer extemporized 'in pelting rain', a detachment of soldiers presented arms, pipes were played, Dr Robertson made a short and apposite speech, the soldiery fired a *feu de joie*, and everyone spontaneously sang 'God Save the Queen'. With one hand on the head of a deerhound, a gun in the other, the bronze figure, soon to turn green, gazed sightlessly upon the estate he had created.

Then there was Hallowe'en to keep, with bonfires, burning torches, shouting, jumping and almost certainly whisky, on 'the Catholic Day', 31 October – the Protestant Day being apparently 12 November. And yet, though life was full, the Queen was showing signs of certain restlessness. Possibly the news from Dr MacLeod that he was off to India for six months induced it. Whatever the reason, she asked Prince Arthur's comptroller, now Lt-Colonel Elphinstone who was on a sketching and climbing holiday in Switzerland, to find her suitable lodgings, please, for a continental holiday in the spring. She listed her requirements carefully: bracing air, a hot sun and hot days 'but there must nevertheless be *fresh* and cold air besides,' quietness, true mountain-scenery, and, again, '*bracing* air'. The colonel set out on this exacting errand and found what he hoped might be a suitable pension in Lucerne. He returned to England to discover that Prince Arthur was ill. He had travelled from Balmoral to return to work, for he had chosen an army career and had passed into Woolwich, and a chill proved to be smallpox. The Queen was sent daily bulletins and her son soon was well again despite the unusual invalid-diet prescribed: partridge, pheasant, roast beef, peaches and claret. The Colonel was thanked for his '*maternal* care of our precious child during this trying business, short though it has been'.

The daily round at Balmoral was dotted with extensive drives of exploration, and the Queen herself took part in a fishing expedition on Loch Muick, taking two large hauls of fish, over two hundred fish 'in the first few seconds'. Then there was a sudden and very unwelcome excitement. The Home Secretary, Mr Gathorne Hardy, sent a warning to General Grey. The Fenians were planning to seize the person of the Queen. They were starting from Manchester. Special precautions must be taken.

Chapter 24

'Too foolish!!'

The Queen's reaction to General Grey's plans for the defence of Balmoral were characteristic. 'Too foolish!!' she wrote in her Journal. Balmoral was to be surrounded by troops; the police guard much multiplied; all railway and road approaches watched. To the Queen these precautions seemed excessive. She even said it showed distrust of her faithful highlanders. But she was sufficiently pressed and she gave her reluctant consent. To Colonel Elphinstone she enlarged: '*She* believes the danger *entirely* an *exaggeration* and that the *precautions* were really *not necessary*.' Any any rate, she could no longer consider her life at all humdrum.

The Fenians, or Green-ribbon Men, a body determined to get the English out of Ireland by force, had decided on a *coup de main* in England itself. Public offices and officials should be attacked. No greater enterprise could be envisaged than the capture of the Queen. There were confused reports from Manchester where, in September, the Fenians had plotted the rescue of two of their fellows from a police van, and a policeman had been killed.

The reports turned out to be rumours. No Irishmen appeared from Manchester or anywhere else. Nevertheless the authorities considered the Queen would be unwise to travel south by night and she was formally advised to alter her arrangements. 'The foolish alarms have compelled the Queen to travel by day which is very fatiguing for her.' As long as she was at Windsor the Government was content, but she determined to go on to Osborne at the usual time.

Her advisers were appalled. Mr Gathorne Hardy strongly advised against it. She turned the tables by saying that as Home Secretary he himself was very much at risk and must take good care to run no risk. When the Fenians blew up a wall of Clerkenwell Prison killing several innocent people, the Queen sent Dr Jenner up to visit the wounded and he gave her a report on those who had been disfigured for life. But still on the appointed day she went to Osborne.

At this, General Grey became extremely excited. He pleaded with the Queen in a long letter to leave the Island. He enclosed with his appeal letters from the Home Secretary, the Duke of Cambridge as Commander-in-Chief, copies of anonymous threatening letters. Quite carried away, he wrote: 'he would be on his knees beseeching your Majesty to consider whether it would not be better for your Majesty to be at Windsor.' A page carried this letter along the Osborne corridors to the Queen in her private sitting-room. The Queen at once wrote a courteous refusal, saying that she thought 'any *panic* or show of fear would be most injudicious as well as unnecessary.' She mentioned that she had agreed to extra precautions being taken – 'and must ask *not* to have this *again* mentioned.'

The Prime Minister, Lord Derby, then tried to persuade his stubborn royal mistress. 'The *house* at Osborne may, by extreme care, be protected; but your Majesty's unattended late drives afford an opportunity for desperate adventurers.' The Queen told him his apprehensions about 'late and distant drives after dark' were quite groundless.

The fleet encompassed the Isle of Wight. Extra police from Division A and a detachment of the Brigade of Guards were despatched to Osborne. No one could move into the estate at any point without a written pass. 'What *extraordinary* and really *absurd* precautions' remarked the Queen.

Just before Christmas the Duke of Marlborough arrived at Osborne having asked for an audience. He reported that news had come from Canada that eighty people had embarked on two ships at New York with murderous intentions against her and some of her ministers. Intercepting ships would be sent out. He urged her to take care and not to allow her children to go about unprotected. When he had gone she walked with Princess Louise down to the Swiss Cottage, and afterwards went for a drive in the woods. She strongly objected to her liberty of movement being in any way curtailed, and complained to the Prime Minister: 'Such precautions are taken here that the Queen will be little better than a *State* prisoner.' It was not for this that the Prince Consort had built her her island paradise.

An acknowledgment from the Home Secretary on Twelfth Night that the immediate risk was over, sparked off a triumphant reply from Osborne. The Queen wrote: '*She never* for one moment credited the absurd ideas of *danger* either *here* or at *Balmoral*, from the *utter impossibility* of the plans being carried out.'

The Queen was highly indignant with the American statesmen who gave vote-catching support to the Fenians, and she regarded them as unscrupulous agitators. Her lack of concern for her own safety was either very brave or very unrealistic. There was considerable danger, both then and thereafter. The Green-ribbon Men were as great a menace in the nineteenth century as in the twentieth. The officers of Divsion A made extra plans for the protection of the Royal Family. The single policeman of Charles Greville's day was no longer possible. A barracks was built at Ballater and there was always a Queen's Guard when she was in residence. A detachment of Balmoral Volunteers was also formed.

The Queen no longer found it easy to sympathize with the Irish. She never forgot how they had treated the Prince Consort in the last months of his life. They shot her son Prince Alfred in the back, though not fatally. They threw curses and worse at her eldest son on a visit to Cork. They knifed to death one of her Chief Secretaries for Ireland and his Under-Secretary. They established an explosives factory in Birmingham and there were many bomb outrages. They blew up the gasworks in Glasgow, the Local Government Board buildings in London, part of Victoria Station, St James's Square and Scotland Yard, an arch of London Bridge, and caused great damage in two parts of the underground railway. They tried, and they often succeeded, to obstruct the business of Parliament. It seemed evident they enjoyed sedition and took it in with their mother's milk. Only in the last year of her life when the Irish regiments had done well in South Africa did she form the Irish Guards and re-visit Ireland.

As early as the beginning of 1869 the offer of a fine country estate was made to her so that she might regularly visit her realm of Ireland, and Gladstone who conveyed the offer, recommended that she accept. But, while appreciating the 'noble' offer she did not accept it, explaining that Balmoral was necessary for her health.

Since then several historical commentators have speculated on the possible difference to the courses of Irish history had the Queen decided to live beside the Liffey rather than by the Solent and the Dee. None so far has suggested that most probably she would have been shot.

Chapter 25

Titania and her ageing Puck

The Queen enjoyed the female privilege of changing her mind about her Prime Ministers. With most of them she liked them better as she became used to them. So, at first, she had no time at all for Mr Disraeli. He was the traitor who had pulled down and then danced on the grave of poor Sir Robert Peel.* He was a romantic novelist. He shamelessly married a rich elderly widow for her money, though he was lucky there for Dizzy, as they called him, and his Mary Anne were undoubtedly suited and very happy. He was a Jew. Baptised, yes; but nonetheless a recent Christian. But time was to alter her opinion.

As Leader of the House of Commons and Chancellor of the Exchequer under Lord Derby he had had the duty of sending her daily reports. They amazed and delighted her. He said the most encouraging things. 'The Chancellor of the Exchequer . . . feels quite certain there will not be a May crisis, and that your Majesty's Highland home will not be disturbed.' She almost anticipated the red boxes with pleasure. She sat beneath the cedar at Osborne and read his fascinating report on the passage of a new Reform Bill:

> This has been a very remarkable day . . . It has been known by the Government, though most strictly and secretly arranged, that an attack, contemplated as fatal, would be made on the Reform Bill. It was a *conspiration des salons*, but powerfully equipped. When all was ripe, *The Times* thundered . . . 'But your Majesty's Government was in a majority of eight!'

When Lord Derby's gout got the better of him in February, 1868, he retired, and Dizzy was her Prime Minister. The difference was startling. A letter preceded him to Osborne where he was due to arrive and receive his seals of office. It contained the dramatic expression: 'He can only offer devotion.' An extravagant declaration very typical of the

* And Peel she had at first disliked for replacing her beloved Lord Melbourne.

man. He liked elderly ladies and he liked to flatter them. The Russian Ambassador spoke of 'all his grandmothers'. He was only too happy to flatter the plump little Queen, 'to lay it on with a trowel' in fact. She was also very happy to receive it. But neither in the least was taken in. They enjoyed the game, the romance, the striking of attitudes. It really made no difference to the management of the State. When she received him in the Council Room as Prime Minister, the Queen offered her hand and bade him kiss it as a token of accepting office. He was the first of her ministers to fall on one knee to do so. Her Private Secretary must have had interesting thoughts for, thirty-six years before he, Charles Grey, the Prime Minister's son, had defeated Disraeli in a Parliamentary election at High Wycombe.

Whether or not Disraeli's phrase 'We authors, Ma'am' was apocryphal did not matter. It was typical and it was appropriate for *Leaves* had just been published, and was described by him as 'innocent and vivid'. He presented his royal mistress with all his novels. History has not recorded if she read them.

Theirs was an instant romantic friendship and he played a *rôle* in her life not unlike that of John Brown, providing her with something that she needed. Brown gave her steady dependence, protection, and a critical tongue. Disraeli shared with her his pleasure in fantasy. And the two men, realizing how they complemented each other, had a common regard. Brown sent the Prime Minister a Dee salmon. The Prime Minister thanked him in his own hand and invited him to fish for trout at Hughenden. With each the Queen could laugh and feel emotions more intensely. Tennyson was near at hand, but it took Disraeli's magic to make Osborne even more attractive to the Queen. Once he had described it as 'a Sicilian Palazzo with garden terraces statues and vases shining in the sun, than which nothing can be conceived more captivating.' Now it became the Faery Isle inhabited by Titania. This much wrinkled and ageing Puck snapped his fingers and Osborne House, East Cowes in the county of Hampshire became embued with a new patina of beauty and charm, even mystery. Almost at once the Queen began to send him boxes of Osborne primroses, a favourite flower that, ultimately, was to enter the vitals of party organization.

The Queen was not in the least pleased when Dizzy returned to Osborne in less than three months to offer his resignation. The Conservatives had been soundly beaten over an important issue in the Lower House. She refused to accept his resignation and, presumably on his advice, told him to carry on until public business allowed for the dissolution of Parliament and a general election.

Part of this public business was the prosecution of a war against the self-proclaimed Emperor Theodore of Ethiopia, an odd monarch who once celebrated Queen Victoria's birthday with a salute of twenty-one guns and a banquet of raw flesh cut from living beasts. But now he had thrown her Consul and an envoy into chains, and not obeyed her direction sent from her Royal Court at Balmoral to behave in a civilized manner. Far from this, and vexed because a letter he had written to the Queen was mislaid by a Foreign Office clerk, the Emperor added her messenger to his collection and put all the prisoners in an impregnable fortress which was the plug of an extinct volcano. The British lion was not having this, and a huge and very expensive military expedition was mounted. Disraeli continued in office to the vexation of the Liberals, and sent the Queen highly entertaining accounts of the proceedings of Parliament. They arrived regularly at Osborne, followed her to Balmoral in the spring, and back to Osborne once more, thence to the Pension Wallace at Lucerne where the Queen travelled in August as Madame la Comtesse de Kent – and very small she found it, too. 'We have no room to *spare* for a *mouse*,' she complained to Colonel Elphinstone.

Disraeli himself went to Balmoral as Minister in Attendance in the late summer. The Deeside Railway had reached its furthermost point at Ballater the year before. Therefore, being a creature of comfort and not robust, it was strange that the Prime Minister did not use it. He chose instead to leave the train miles before in Perth. His adoring wife, Mary Anne, had given him hampers for the long journey: 'a partridge breakfast and a chicken and tongue dinner with plenty of good wine.' Thus fortified, he took the long slow journey by carriage to Balmoral round the intricacies of the Devil's Elbow. On arrival he dined in his apartment, and the next night with the Queen and her family, Lady Churchill and Lord Bridport the Queen's permanent Lord-in-Waiting who also had Nelson's exotic Neapolitan title and was Duke of Brontë. As had been customary since 1861 the dining-room was only used for great occasions. Disraeli enjoyed dining in the library – 'a small, square room, very cosy.' He did not, however, care much for his official rooms. Though lizard-like in appearance, he shared the Queen's loathing of stuffiness. The September weather was unusually warm and humid. He opened the windows and let the fire go out. Possibly this was unwise. He did not feel particularly well throughout the visit. He was liverish and made himself worse by drinking nothing but sherry. But he had little time to brood on his health. His work followed him and there was a great deal of it. He confided to a friend in England: 'Carrying on the Government of the Country six hundred miles from the metropolis doubles the labour.' Church patronage vexed him as it had vexed Lord Melbourne. He wrote to his secretary from Balmoral: 'Send me a Crockford's directory; I must be armed.'

There were long morning talks with the Queen, with much to discuss; Church preferment, an honours list when Parliament was dissolved, a revolution in Spain, and most important, there was the war in Ethiopia. The campaign had lumbered to success. One English officer had been accidentally killed whilst shooting partridges, and two had died in action. Seven hundred Ethiopians had been killed; Theodore had shot himself; and General Napier, soon to be raised to the peerage, had marched into the plug of the extinct volcano to the music of bands playing 'See the Conquering Hero Comes'. It was then necessary to march out again. Disraeli announced: 'We have hoisted the standard of St George on the mountain of Rasselas,' but, as he admitted to the Queen, who had colonial ambitions, it was necessary to leave the mountain. It would be inconvenient to seize such an out-of-the-way part of Africa. These and like matters filled the mornings though Disraeli did find time and energy to take a short walk round the policies. He described the gardens to Mary Anne: 'An expanse of green and shaven lawn . . . singularly striking in a land of mountains; but H.M. told me that it was all artificial, and they levelled a rugged and undulating soil.' In the afternoons there were expeditions, some especially arranged for the Prime Minister so that he had to go. He was taken to a waterfall 'with such lovely accessories, such banks of birches, woods and boulders of colossal granite.' He was taken to Braemar: 'I was glad there were no Games.' However, he approved of the picnic arrangements and told Mary Anne: 'One might take many hints for country luncheons from this day, for our friends have great experience in such matters.' There were no great bursts of enthusiasm for Balmoral. Possibly he had an old fashioned view of 'horrid crags'. But he was courteous and kind and the Queen enjoyed his brief stay. She gave him two volumes of views of Balmoral, a box of photographs of the Royal Family, a full length portrait of the Prince Consort, and a knitted shawl for Mary Anne. He received an accolade in her Journal: '28th September – Took leave of Mr Disraeli, who seemed delighted with his stay and was most grateful. He certainly shows more consideration for my comfort than any of the preceding Prime Ministers since Sir Robert Peel and Lord Aberdeen.'

Two days after his departure the Queen withdrew to the furthest point yet from the seat of government. It was also another indication that she was not quite so wrapped up in the Prince Consort, for she had built a new house unseen and unblessed by him, that had a single bed and no place for immortelles. This fifteen-roomed 'bothy' was named the Glassalt Shiel and was situated two and a half miles beyond the double house at Alt-na-Giuthasach at the further end of Loch Muick where a burn, the Allt, ran into the loch. It was a silent place, the quietness only broken by the trickle of a waterfall high above the house and the cries of water birds. In all the highlands where midges are a scourge – Prince Charles in his year of hiding was nearly driven demented by them – Loch Muick was actually famed for these tormenting creatures, and the north end of the loch known as the worst part. Fishermen were advised to wear red or yellow to discourage their attention; to keep in the wind or hot sun and avoid shady places. The Glassalt Shiel was backed and shaded by precipitous screes. Ammonia was known to alleviate irritation once stung; paraffin oil and tobacco smoke known to deter them. There was no question yet of the Queen smoking cigarettes. Indeed that summer she gave an order at Balmoral that the smoking-room used was to be closed sharply at midnight. But eventually she took it up, smoking with Lady Churchill to keep off the midges. Possibly it was Glassalt Shiel that drove her to it. When she took possession with her son Prince Arthur, and Princess Louise and Lady Churchill, the servants and officers from Divsion A had a house-warming party with whisky-toddy and plenty of reels. 'I thought of my happy past', the Queen wrote in *More Leaves*, 'and my darling husband whom I fancied I must see, and who always wished to build here in his favourite wild spot, quite in amongst the hills.' Assuredly she was recovering slowly from her great loss.

What an autumn it was. Now that Mr Disraeli had gone his successor as Minister in Attendance, the Lord Chancellor, scarcely merited a mention. The Queen went to see the sheep-dipping, and a couple of local Christenings. She visited the sick and dying. Her four younger unmarried children were with her, as were Prince and Princess Christian. The Van de Weyers were at Abergeldie and many visits were exchanged. Then the Queen's cousin Princess Mary Adelaide arrived with her husband Prince Teck. She was not a great favourite of the Queen's but undeniably a colourful relation. The Princess was a formidable eater and massive, the only Princess of Great Britain and Ireland who smashed alpenstocks merely by leaning on them; so enormously extravagant that she had to be sent into exile for a time to economize; so full of fun that any party at once lighted with her presence; so good-natured that charity flowed from her; and of all the Royal Family she was possibly the most popular. The crowds called her 'Fat Mary' and no one could receive their plaudits more regally or with more obvious pleasure. Four years before she and her brother had been guests at Abergeldie but had been warned off from Balmoral Castle though they visited the villagers. This, then was their first formal stay.

The long sofas in the saloon they took for travelling overnight were far far too narrow for the colossal Princess, and the Prince and her dresser constructed a make-shift bed across two seats of the next compartment. They reached Ballater at 4.45 p.m. to be met by the acting Master of the Household with the odd request that they keep away until dark. Uncomplainingly, the Princess filled the time by eating oatmeal cakes and currant jam at a Ballater inn. The reason for being kept waiting became evident when they arrived at the Castle. The Queen, her children and Court were all at the main entrance to welcome them, a huge bengal light flamed away on the flag tower, highlanders greeted them with lighted torches and then danced reels. After dinner in the library the gentlemen went to the billiard-room and the ladies accompanied the Queen to the Prince Consort's room whither, apparently, she went each evening to do her needlework or plait hats and listen to music or reading aloud.

On her first day the Princess was charmed, as Disraeli had been, by the picnic arrangements. At four in the afternoon, having explored wild country, water-splashed boulders and a Jacobite's refuge, they had a late luncheon. Princess Mary described it thus: 'We then . . . took our share in watching the potatoes, which turned out first-rate, and were done ample justice to; cold meat, cheese and shortbread completing the repast.'

The water-splashed boulders had been inadvisable and Princess Mary took to her bed with a chill but soon afterwards. She recovered in time to have yet another luncheon at Gelder Shiel of boiled potatoes, cold meat, cheese and cake. Before their departure they enjoyed a ball; 'a grand performance of Christy minstrels (fifteen in number)'; dinner with the Van de Weyers; a snack, between breakfast and luncheon, of scones and jellies at Mrs John Grant's in a room set always apart for the Queen's use; and so many boiled potatoes out in the heather that that ubiquitous vegetable was almost the hallmark of Balmoral.

The Queen spent the last few days of her holiday in the north in the coils of finding a successor for the throne of St Augustine, the Archbishop of Canterbury having died. She proposed the Bishop of London for a variety of reasons, the most curious being: 'His health, which is not good, would be benefitted by the change.' Doubtless Disraeli was amused, but it was the last plum of patronage he had to offer, the Dissolution of Parliament being so very close, and he mentioned other names to the Queen. She still pressed for the Bishop of London and good naturedly he gave way. The Queen was gratified; but then dreadfully cast down when, as had been anticipated, the Conservatives lost the election. Disraeli would accept nothing for himself but asked that Mary Anne might be Viscountess of Beaconsfield. His resignation meant that she had to send for Gladstone to form a Ministry. She accepted the necessity. The seals of office were handed in and bestowed at Windsor and then the Queen went off to Osborne.

Chapter 26

Prising open the oyster

Mr Gladstone was warned by his old friend and Eton contemporary, Dean Wellesley of Windsor, on how to treat the Queen: 'You cannot show too much regard, gentleness, I might even say tenderness towards her.' And Mrs Gladstone told her husband: 'Pet the Queen.' But it was not in his nature to do so. Instead of petting her he tended, as she bitterly observed, to treat her as though she were a public meeting.

'Our little English rose', as the Queen had been called at her coronation, had been a reigning monarch for a long time when Gladstone first came to power, and she had an intuitive mistrust of his political ideas – the disestablishment of churches, home rule for Ireland, and so forth. In this she showed uncommon shrewdness because these ideas were to shatter Gladstone's party and, in the end, he had to be tidied away out of office by his own Cabinet. Nor did she care to be instructed in her imperative duties. After the considerate politeness of Benjamin Disraeli, Gladstone's manner was guaranteed to congeal her stubbornness and self-will and make her bristle. Yet, no sooner was he in office than William Gladstone did the very thing most likely to anger his royal mistress. He decided it was time she came quite out of her shell and he set about prising open the oyster. Preceding pages have shown how far she had already gone towards appearing in public. That same year she held a Levée and a Drawing-Room, and she called informally on Lady Augusta at the Westminster Deanery to meet some of her friends. But that was as far as she would go for the present. She refused to open Parliament and, in her Speech from the Throne, involve herself personally with something she detested, Gladstone's project to disestablish the Irish Church. She sent Dr Jenner to tell him so.

Gladstone saw this as a flagrant refusal to do her duty. But instead of doing as he had been advised by his friend and by his wife and spoiling the Queen; taking the trouble to go down to Osborne where she felt most at home and talking the matter over, he was devious. He approached General Grey in order to get to the bottom of things. The remarkable thing was that Grey responded. Although obviously his first duty as the Queen's confidential Private Secretary was to her and not to the Prime Minister, the General consistently betrayed the Queen all through this discreditable episode. Moreover he involved the twenty-one year old Princess Louise who as the oldest unmarried princess still at home was therefore in her mother's confidence. She was the most beautiful of all the Queen's daughters, but she had defects of character that enabled her to break that confidence with a defiance that was almost arrogant.

Balmoral Castle, the Queen's dear paradise, became the scene of what was virtually a conspiracy against her. Her own daughter and her own Private Secretary held secret meetings, and sent private messages to her Prime Minister.

On 1 June, 1869, General Grey assured Gladstone: 'Princess Louise is *very* decided as to the ability of the Queen to meet any fatigue . . . Dismiss the thought of there being any weight of work from your mind, and this the Princess *emphatically* repeats.' This sort of encouragement was exactly what the Prime Minister required. He wrote to Grey in a letter marked 'Private': 'There is no doubt that Osborne during the Session is the great enemy; absence there is almost the same thing for the world as absence at Balmoral . . . This is a mischief I should like to see abated.' Grey's disloyalty became still more marked:

> I am fairly certain that *nothing* will have any effect but a strong – even a peremptory – tone . . . It is simply the long unchecked habit of self-indulgence that now makes it impossible for her, without some degree of nervous agitation to give up, even for ten minutes, the gratification of a single inclination, or even whim.

Gladstone sent salvo after salvo from Carlton House Terrace, where he lived in preference to Downing Street, upon Osborne House and Balmoral Castle. He suggested the Queen be at hand, which meant Windsor, in case her Ministers needed to consult her. The Dean of Windsor was asked to point out to her the urgency of the crisis and the distance between London and Osborne House. 'The Queen', she snapped, 'has had repeated Crisises *there*, in the PRINCE's *time*.'

Gladstone was adamant. As her Prime Minister he formally advised her to move to Windsor. She knew her constitutional duty. For the first time, at the order of her Prime Minister, she left Osborne.

Even then he would not leave her alone. Like the importunate woman of the parable the Prime Minister hammered at the Queen to prise her out into the public eye. It did not endear him to her. Significantly her autumn holiday at Balmoral began halfway through August and lasted until 3 November, the longest she had yet spent in Scotland. In August Gladstone pressed her to sanction the creation of more peerages than she thought justifiable, amongst them Nathaniel Rothschild. He received his reply through Lord Granville then Minister in Attendance at Balmoral: 'to make a *Jew* a *Peer* is a step she could not consent to.' She had nothing against the Rothschilds and nothing against Jews as a race as she showed in her friendship with Disraeli but, unlike Disraeli, the Rothschilds were Jews by religion. The Queen deprecated their admission to the Commons. She agreed with Archbishop Tait who had prophesied with almost uncanny accuracy: 'If you destroy the groundwork of Christianity upon which this legislation is based . . . you will destroy Christian England.'

For ten days the Queen did without a Minister in Attendance. She went to Drunkie House in south Perthshire which had been lent to her. Colonel Elphinstone was with Prince Arthur in North America and could no longer be used as a prospector for holiday places in the Alps. Therefore J. J. Kanné, an experienced courier, had been appointed to the Queen's Household with the Pooh-Bahish title Director of Continental Journeys. His expertise was not restricted to the continent and he made all the arrangements for this expedition to the house beside Loch Vennachar in south Perthshire, that included the Queen, Princesses Louise and Beatrice, Lady Churchill and General Grey's nephew-by-marriage, Colonel Ponsonby, fourteen Balmoral servants, three cooks sent from London, the Queen's dog, ponies, including Sultan who had carried her right to the top of the Righi near Lucerne the year before, and even the sociable that had carried her to the top of the Furca Pass. For reasons of delicacy, which were considered unnecessary, Kanné had changed the name of Drunkie House to Invertrossachs. He was not, however, able to show them over the house or supervise the daily excursions, as he lay ill in an inn 4 miles away at Callandar. The second master cook Jungbluth stood in for him as steward.

On returning to Balmoral the Queen was obliged to meet her Prime Minister who had proposed himself Minister in Attendance. He had arrived in her absence and was ill. On the day after her return he had recovered sufficiently, to emerge from his apartments, dine with the Queen, and in the following days he had some discussions with her. But his main points were written in his official room and sent to the Queen. On 22 September he wrote an immense screed about ecclesiastical appointments with a barbed sentence towards the end. 'As Mr Gladstone has the honour of being under your Majesty's roof, he forbears to trouble your Majesty with any further written explanation.' He returned to London and there worried the Rothschild bone once more. On 28 October he wrote to ask her to reconsider, ending loosely that he would not think of pressing the Queen. She seized on this and replied quickly, expressing gratitude for his undertaking not to press her further because she really did not wish Sir L. Rothschild to have a peerage. The only subject on which these two forceful characters seemed to be in accord was 'the *so-called & most erroneous "Rights of Woman"'*.

In March 1870 General Grey died. She wrote agreeable things about him, but, just possibly, it was a case of *de mortuis nil nisi bonum*. She could not have known the depths of his treachery: that he had told Gladstone she was a 'royal malingerer', but almost certainly she had lost full confidence in the old man. She had more faith in Colonel Ponsonby whom she appointed in his place, and he did not let her down. He was a convinced Liberal and shared many of his wife's uncle's opinions about the Queen's health and Dr Jenner, but he was a more even-tempered and kindly man, ready to advise the Queen if she asked for it or needed it, even to collaborate with Gladstone but only if he thought it was in the Queen's interest. He knew where his first loyalty lay.

General Grey's was the first of a number of deaths during the year. Lady Lyttelton died in April. In June Lord Clarendon and, only two days after she visited him, old Sir James Clark. Little parts of her past were inexorably collapsing about her. 'Really this has been a dreadful year,' she wrote in her Journal, 'and most fatal to those connected with me.'

It was not supposed that a man of Gladstone's temperament would ever cease from his struggles with the Queen. That year he hatched a scheme for the improvement of Ireland, the Prince of Wales and the Queen. The Irish should be governed by the Prince instead of a viceroy and this would remind the Queen of her duty to Ireland, a country Gladstone himself had not yet visited. It would also be good for the Prince to have some responsibility and keep him out of scrapes.

The Queen dismissed the idea, but Gladstone set about perfecting the scheme so that she should find it irresistible. He was more than a little concerned about the Prince of Wales who, earlier in the year, had appeared in the witness box at a divorce hearing. Gladstone had once informed Ponsonby that he wanted to see the Court as pure as the Round Table. Ponsonby, who knew the Arthurian legend rather well, doubted if this was setting their sights very high.

At Balmoral in June the Queen was also worried about her heir. She stood by him in public scandals all through her reign. But privately she was anxious. She wrote from Balmoral suggesting that at Ascot he might be wise to go to the races only on the Tuesday and Thursday. 'Your example can do *much* for good and may do an immense deal for evil, in the present day.' He replied almost by return of post. With great politeness he told her he knew what he was doing. On the first day of Ascot the Queen was out early to watch the shearing of her sheep. Her shepherds took them out of the pen one by one, tied the legs and slung them on to the laps of the four female clippers who sat on the ground in an arc and held the struggling sheep between their knees. The fleeced sheep were then marked and ingrowing horns were attended to. 'A very picturesque sight, and quite curious', noted the Queen. Six hundred miles to the south-west the Prince of Wales, like his mother before him, was hissed as he drove up the Ascot course. Popular as he was, not even he could get away from the disgrace of being in any way associated with a public divorce case.

The Queen was at Osborne while Europe boiled up over the succession to the throne of Spain. The Pope had been declared infallible by the first Vatican Council, but he very soon lost the Papal States. The French withdrew to protect the Empire and the Italians moved into Rome. Telegrams and letters and despatch boxes poured in and out of the Queen's tent on the lawn or her sitting-room at Osborne as Bismarck gulled the French into a trial of strength. On 18 July the French declared war.

Once more the Franco -Prussian war split the Queen's family. France became a republic. Paris was bombarded. The King of Prussia found himself acclaimed German Emperor. Stringent peace terms were agreed upon. Asylum was offered to the French Imperial Family in Kent. A bloody revolution broke out in Paris and lasted for two months.

Admiration of the new French Republic inspired the foundation of many republican clubs in Great Britain and Gladstone, deciding he was faced with a Royalty Problem, once more engaged with the Queen over her quasi-oriental seclusion.

In fact, she had been much more in the public eye than usual, opening Parliament, being present at the inauguration of the Albert Hall, and St Thomas's Hospital, and giving away her daughter Princess Louise to Lord Lorne at a grand Windsor marriage in March. On this occasion she even wore rubies as well as diamonds and jet over her weeds. Almost certainly she was delighted to be rid of her artistic temperamental daughter.

There had been some objection from the Prince of Wales and from Berlin about her marrying a commoner, but the Queen had squashed them all. Later Clan Campbell complained that their future chieftain's wife was barren and they had been foisted off with a princess who never experienced the regular cycle of menstruation. If this was true it ought to have been made clear to any potential husband, but it has not been substantiated. Princess Louise was always stormy and tempermental.

Her marriage was a failure. She and Lorne lived separate lives, he not
unhappy, she seldom content. But at the time of the wedding, freeing
herself of such a daughter was one of the few enjoyable moments in a
terrible year for the Queen.

She was plagued with anxieties – about Duke Ernest of Coburg who
arrived for the inauguration of the Albert Hall and whose unsavoury
reputation much offended her; about the Princess of Wales who gave
birth to a child that died in April; about her favourite son, Prince
Arthur, who, while talking to Prince Christian after dinner at Buckingham Palace one evening, fell out of the billiard room window onto two
policemen in the courtyard below. He had bad concussion. Agonised
letters arrived from Balmoral to Elphinstone.

> The Queen can hardly imagine *what* the kind and devoted Colonel
> must have felt and indeed Prince Christian and *all* on seeing darling
> Arthur vanish and even now the Queen can hardly dare to think of it.
> It causes her to shudder.

Her suggestion that he be sent to Balmoral to recuperate was tactfully
dealt with. May on Deeside was not exactly warm, and rattling over
hundreds of miles of railway-line could not be good for a man recovering from concussion. In a letter of more than a thousand words Elphinstone dared to say he really believed Windsor would be better. Prince
Arthur agreed. The important thing was that Dr Jenner, now Sir
William, also agreed.

Sir William was in an unenviable position. The Queen had definite
ideas about her health with which he largely corroborated. At any rate
he was in the best position to see the effect upon her nervous system
when newspaper articles and Members of Parliament attacked her as a
fabulously rich miser who paid no taxes. None of it happened to be true
but the criticism inflamed the Queen's nerves and affected her whole
system. And now he found that, in addition to the Prime Minister, the
Queen's children believed there was a Royalty Problem that could best
be solved by her showing herself more often to the people. There was a
family conspiracy at Osborne in the early summer of 1871. The Crown
Prince and Princess and their children were there with the Prince and
Princess of Wales. Whilst she did not know the details the Queen could
hardly have missed the conspiratorial aura that filled her home. She was
very tense. She permitted her Prussian grandchildren, Willy and Henry
to fire off brass cannons, and sent them off to look over the dockyards
and go down in a diving-bell. But she did not care for Charlotte, and
when the smallest boy, Waldemar, quietly laid a crocodile at her feet,
she was given a nasty turn. Meanwhile Vicky was secretly writing a
document in the name of the family that is still preserved in the Royal

Archives at Windsor, itemized in the Victoria Additional Manuscripts as AI/16. The round robin was to the signed by all the Queen's sons and daughters and presented to 'our adored Mama and our Sovereign' at an opportune moment. The Prince of Wales reserved the right to decide when that moment had arrived.

The Queen became unwell. Sir William Jenner informed the Princes and Princesses, the Household and the government through Mr Gladstone. It was reasonable to suppose that her nervous system was agitating under the prolonged attacks on her seclusion. Possibly she interpreted them as a mischievous campaign against the privacy on which she and her husband had always insisted, and therefore against the homes he had built for her in Scotland and on the Isle of Wight to ensure that privacy. This would account for her dogged defence of them and of her right to go to them as and when she pleased. 'Nerves' was often believed to be an imaginary malady and doubtless Mr Gladstone and her children considered she was shamming and trying to shore up her claim that she was not well enough to do what the Government asked. But then she was stung by an insect on the forearm. It did not respond to usual treatment and became inflamed and painful. After three days there was no improvement and at that very time Gladstone asked her to postpone her departure from Osborne to Balmoral until Parliament had been prorogued. He later suggested she prorogue Parliament in person. The Queen became almost hysterical. She found Lord Hatherley, the Lord Chancellor, one of the most congenial of Gladstone's ministers, and she sent him a frantic appeal from Osborne:

> The Queen is feeling extremely unwell & if this heat lasts, every day she loses in getting to Scotland will add to this . . . The Queen will not remain where she is, worked and worried and worn, if she is to become the Servant of Parliament and to be responsible to them for all she does! . . . It is really abominable that a woman, a Queen, loaded with care & anxieties, public & domestic which are daily increasing should be unable to make people understand that there are limits to her powers.

She then clearly stated that overwork had killed both the Prince Consort and Lord Clarendon, and unless her Ministers supported her she would abdicate.

Ponsonby put in a good word for his royal mistress in a letter to Gladstone. He suggested that the Queen thought the matter of prorogation minor and that the Ministry was trying to get her to stay in England for political reasons, in other words to help the Liberals. Gladstone hastened to correct this misunderstanding. In his correspondence over this matter – and he was a man who, in office, wrote 12,000 letters a year – he would construct grand phrases because he conceived the struggle was an epic one: '*Worse* things may easily be imagined; but smaller and meaner causes for the decay of thrones cannot be conceived. It is like the worm which bores the bark of a noble oak tree and so breaks the channel of its life.'

On 17 August four days before Parliament was prorogued, with a sore throat and a painful arm the Queen left for Scotland. She felt she was no longer fighting for her private homes and her private life, she was fighting for life itself. Her Journal told the story. On 22 August: 'Never, since a girl, when I had typhoid fever at Ramsgate in '35, have I felt so ill.' Sir William Jenner attended her. So did a Dr Marshall. They decided to send for one of the Royal Surgeons in Ordinary in Scotland, Joseph Lister, as she now had an abscess on her arm. On 4 September: 'Mr Lister thought the swelling ought to be cut; he could wait twenty-four hours, but it would be better not. I felt dreadfully nervous, as I bear pain so badly.' There, in her bedroom, Dr Marshall held her arm firm, Sir William Jenner gave her whiffs of chloroform, and Lister froze the abscess, 6 inches in diameter, before lancing it. 'In an instant there was relief. I was then tightly bandaged and rested on my bed.' Lister stayed at the Castle for another week. By then the abscess was better but the Queen had rheumatic gout. A week after that the gout was at its worst. She was rolled into her sitting-room to see her daughter Princess Alice. Brown carried her downstairs and she went for a short drive. But her foot continued swelling and she returned to sit in her room all day. 'By degrees agonies of pain came on which continued almost without intermission, the foot swelling tremendously. Sir William Jenner tried to encourage me as to its not lasting long . . . was very depressed.'

Her distress and her pain were very real. The fiat went out from the Prince of Wales at Abergeldie that the family plea, AI/16, should not be presented. The Prime Minister in announcing his arrival at Balmoral as Minister in Attendance, 'intreats your Majesty after so serious a de-rangement of health on no account to make any effort for the purpose of seeing him during his stay'.

The Queen did, in fact, see him; but very infrequently, and he had been warned by Ponsonby not to raise any issue that might excite her. The Prime Minister was invited to Abergeldie and found himself playing whist for shillings and half-a-crown on the rubber with the Prince of Wales. There was an unsuccessful attempt to interest him in deerstalking. He went off on his long tramps, covering 50 miles in three weeks. He and Colonel Ponsonby took another semi-official walk in a downpour. The Private Secretary must have raised his eyebrows to hear his companion confide 'he did not think the Queen's absolute retirement a serious matter but was concerned about the stories of the Prince of Wales gambling at Baden'. If it had not been a serious matter, those streams of letters attacking the Queen's seclusion over such an extensive period bore a touch of malice.

Still unwell, drugged with chloral, her hands now attacked by rheumatic pains, and, most probably, at the worst stage of the menopause, the Queen dictated her Journal to Princess Beatrice and attended a ball for a short time seeing all her four sons together, 'all grown-up and so different from one another'. None of them gave her much solace though. Prince Alfred was offensive to Brown. Even Prince Arthur was not all that polite to him. The Queen's chief props and stays during this dreadful time at Balmoral, when she finally won for herself the right to stick to her annual round, were Jenner, Löhlein, Brown, Annie Macdonald and Emilie Dittweiler, a faithful Badener who had been her dresser for thirteen years and was to be so until 1892. In other words, with the possible exception of Lady Churchill, she took her greatest support from men and women of the people, not from the ladies and gentlemen of her Household.

Jenner as a doctor, for all that he had been knighted, stood in that peculiar state between the members of the Household and the staff of royal servants. Like Rudolph Löhlein, John Brown, Gustav Mayet and J. Kanné, all of whom were esquires, he was not one of the Queen's gentlemen. Nor had Sir James Clark been. Nor was her favourite physician, Sir James Reid, to be. Indeed this was underlined by a memorandum from the Queen to the Master of the Household towards the end of the century: 'The gentlemen and Sir James Reid are to come this evening to the drawing-room.' When Reid married one of her Maids of Honour and thus out of his class the Queen was decidedly cross and he only restored her good humour by promising not to do it again. She would scarcely have relished the idea that one of his grandsons would found and edit the magazine *Private Eye*. The fact was that until well into this century doctors, solicitors, governesses and tutors, unless the last were clergymen, were not received in society. They were required to use the side doors of great establishments just as tradesmen went to the rear. It was the moment of birth that mattered, not the moment of death. And to the Queen these were unalterable laws of the structure of society and that was that.

But she still liked people, was not afraid to show it, and from her olympian position could befriend and be befriended by whom she wished.

She could also be extremely unfriendly when she wished. Gladstone, before he went out of attendance at Balmoral, felt the weight of her animosity. He confided to the Foreign Secretary, Lord Granville: 'The repellant power which she knows so well how to use had been put in action towards me.'

Nature provided one solution of the Royal Problem. The Queen emerged from her illness white, wide-eyed, strained, and having lost two stone. The Prince of Wales contracted typhoid at a Saturday to Monday and almost died of it on Mausoleum Day itself. His children were cared for at Osborne, but the Queen was at his bedside until the crisis passed.

A sudden wave of popularity washed over the throne. The Prince of Wales went with his wife to convalesce at Osborne. Afterwards, driving with the Queen, they went to St Paul's for a service of public thanksgiving. Two days later yet another Irishman made an attempt on the Queen and she was saved by Brown's quickness. He was rewarded with the Victoria Devoted Service medal in gold and was the only recipient in history of that honour. The event further charged the cells of public loyalty to the crown. The Republican clubs became things of nothing.

The Queen was on top, and she was determined to be at Osborne and Balmoral as and when she wished.

Chapter 27

The lot of 'essential daughter'

Prince Leopold, being the Queen's youngest son and in need of con-stant care, remained under his mother's roof for many years. He had inherited the Prince Consort's intellect and thus helped the Queen as an unofficial Private Secretary being given a key to despatch boxes, a privilege long denied to the heir to the throne. Eventually he was created Duke of Albany, married, and was given Claremont by the Queen.* As had always been expected, he died prematurely, but there were two children of the marriage, the first, Princess Alice, who is still the longest lived authority on all things at grandmama's Court; and, the second, his heir, who was born posthumously straight into the purple as HRH Prince Charles Edward, Duke of Albany.

Before his marriage, while he still lived with the Queen, he naturally chafed at the restrictions that haemophilia placed on him. Equally naturally she worried about his longing to get up to London, even Paris, and endeavoured to prevent him. So thwarted was he that he committed what to her was a gross enormity. In May, 1878 he told her he had an intense aversion to Balmoral and refused to go there. The Queen responded characteristically, urging all her children to put pres-sure on her recalcitrant son and especially the Prince of Wales who was to exclude him from dinner parties and balls, theatre parties and race-meetings. 'He must be made to feel that such conduct to a mother and Sovereign cannot be tolerated.' This was hard on a young prince especially at the beginning of the London season but the Queen sus-pected, rightly, that the majority of her children agreed with Leopold. The only exception was 'darling Beatrice . . . for she is like a sunbeam

---

* On the death of the King of the Belgians the estate reverted to the Crown. Later it was bought by the Queen from the Crown Estates and thus became her private property to dispose with as she wished. She gave it to her son as a wedding present with life remainder to his wife. At one point thereafter it became a school for Christian Science girls founded by that controversial American, Lady Astor.

in the house and also like a dove, and angel of peace . . . who is my greatest comfort.'

The Queen had hoped that Princess Helena would provide that essential 'daughter at home'. But though she and her husband amiably accompanied her to Scotland and accepted invitations to Osborne, their real home was Cumberland Lodge in Windsor Park where they retreated as often as they could. This was not what the Queen wanted or had expected and Princess Helena fell from favour. A stark comment from Balmoral to Berlin: 'Helena is 26 today. She looks much older!' gives an indication of this. A year later Princess Helena 'is very difficult to live with.' Prince Christian liked roses and breeding doves and shooting and smoking shag tobacco, but he had no conversation, and the ponderous habit of counting to thirty before ever coming to a decision. When Prince Arthur, the soldier of the family, managed to pepper his brother-in-law out shooting near to the Swiss Cottage and blind him in one eye, it at least gave the solemn old German something to talk about. When conversation flagged at meals he would send for his case of glass eyes for general admiration.

The lot of 'essential daughter' fell upon the youngest, Princess Beatrice, the Queen's 'Benjamin', who should always be with her and love Osborne and Balmoral just as she did. It was her fate as the youngest child, but she had strong feelings for the Isle of Wight that continued all through her life and doubtless she thought of herself more as an Islander than as an Overner. From 1870 she had the duty of accompanying her mother in the royal railway saloon on special journeys, with Emilie Dittweiler and Annie Macdonald within call. There she had to lie like a log for fear of disturbing Mama, opening and closing the windows at her command, ordering in fresh supplies of ice as it melted and sloshed about in the cooling apparatus.

'I keep her young and child-like as I can,' the Queen admitted in 1873.

Apparently Princess Beatrice did not greatly mind. She was then fifteen, at the stage Shakespeare called 'standing water' and Flora Thompson, with a more womanly appreciation, 'an ok'ard age, neither 'ooman nor child, when they oughter be shut up in a box for a year or two'. She was a sensitive girl, aware of what it had meant to her mother when Brown gently broke the news that Dr MacLeod was dead. She was not unintelligent. She quite understood Mama's resentment when Gladstone persisted in his plan that the Prince of Wales and not a Viceroy should rule Ireland, and added a new one that the Prince of Wales should 'deputize' for the Queen in London during April, May and June. The Prime Minister was told no. 'The plan must be considered as *definitely* abandoned.' She could sympathize with her anxieties when old Baron Stockmar's biography was published by his son and proved to abound in 'extreme imprudence and indiscretion'. Certainly she took great pleasure in her mother's imaginative expeditions. She went with the Queen and Prince Leopold on a notable visit to Dunrobin when Annie Macdonald was inadvertently locked in a dressing-room in the royal railway saloon; their host, the Duke of Sutherland, was on the footplate as driver north from Inverness; and Brown slept at Dunrobin in a room that had formerly been a dungeon.

This was but the first of many lengthy trips from Balmoral to Inverlochy, to Inverary, to Broxmouth, even to a hotel on Loch Maree, that Beatrice made with the Queen.

If contiguity and a shared love of Osborne and Balmoral were the chief bind between the Queen and her youngest daughter a common romantic affection for Mr Disraeli did not come far behind.

Lady Beaconsfield died in 1872 and her Dizzy was temporarily overwhelmed with grief. She left him instructions to re-marry, but he had little fortune, and she had only had a life interest in their London house. He still had Hughenden but was forced to move into a London hotel. Through a letter from Lady Ely to Disraeli's Private Secretary, the Queen conveyed her grief: 'Poor Mr Disraeli, I feel for him so much.' Friends rallied and helped to lighten the first and worst part of his sorrow; and, though his tender feelings for Mary Anne never altered, he did as she would have wished and returned to normal life as soon as possible. Within a year he was being pursued by the relict of Lord Cardigan who had led the charge of the Light Brigade; an eccentric who wore trousers and was rowed about during Cowes Week playing a guitar in the stern of a gig. Disraeli hurriedly refused an offer of marriage with this odd peeress. She frightened him greatly and the Queen much disapproved of her. However, not long after he became enamoured with Lady Bradford who was fifty-four, and a grandmother, but as Lord Bradford was very much in evidence he wooed her by correspondence through her widowed sister Lady Chesterfield who was seventy-one. He even proposed to the elder sister. She thought this would not answer and preferred to remain his good friend.

The delight of the Queen when a general election returned the Conservatives in February, 1874 can be imagined. Her *bête noire*, Mr Gladstone, was replaced by enchanting Mr Disraeli. His formal submissions were either pithy and not at all fatiguing or they were lyrical. That September he proposed himself for Balmoral, and once more took the long and quite unnecessary carriage journey by Devil's Elbow. On his first day he had the opportunity to visit the gardens and see in the principal, half-span greenhouse a splendid collection of roses in pots – among them Gloire de Dijon, Madame Falcot, Madame Margottin and Maréchal Niel – and to dine with the Queen, before he felt the effects of his long journey and was taken ill. He kept to his room, had a mustard plaster slapped on him by Sir William Jenner, and the Queen paid him a visit. 'What do you think of receiving your Sovereign in slippers and dressing gown?' he demanded of Lady Chesterfield.

Disraeli never saw Scotland again. But he was often on the Isle of Wight.

It was at Osborne in the Audience Room, below the porcelain chandelier of convolvuluses, that in 1878 the Queen invested him with the Garter. For stage-managing an undeniably brilliant diplomatic *coup*, she made him a belted earl and, had he wished it, he could have been a duke. He chose Mary Anne's title, and became Lord Beaconsfield. From the first two letters of the name, not from any illusions of Napoleonic grandeur, he formed a private Order of the Bee, and gave his chosen members a brooch in the form of a golden bee. All the recipients were grandmothers, except for the unmarried Princess Beatrice, who, by her Mama's special permission, was allowed to accept it.

Lord Beaconsfield gave the Queen genuine sympathy and understanding, a lot of flattery and fun, and great happiness.

It seemed as if he presented her with the Suez Canal and the Imperial Crown of India as personal gifts. When an edited version of Charles Greville's *Memoirs* was issued that the Queen found 'full of truth' but nevertheless abominable, he said it was 'a social outrage'. When the Queen was travelling north in August 1875, and, at the beginning of the journey, the royal yacht *Alberta* rammed and sank a private yacht, drowning three people, he was instant and sincere in his condolences. When she built a special cottage for John Brown at Balmoral he admired her thoughtfulness. He himself had been left homeless. When, in 1877, a railway station named Whippingham was built three miles from Osborne, he did not regard it as a desecration of the Faery Isle but encouraged the two widows, his own Queen and the Empress Eugénie, to use it for a tour of the island by railway; a novelty they both appreciated though neither renewed the experience. He again condoled with his sovereign when the *Eurydice*, a fully-rigged training ship, foundered on a Sunday in March off the Isle of Wight and she went down with three hundred and twenty-six of her complement, most of them cadets.* That summer the Queen achieved an ambition by buying

* Admiral Foley, who was put in command of her beaching and clearing, went to dine at Osborne a week after this had been accomplished and reported progress. He also committed two memorable faux pas: first, he presented his monarch with a grisly trophy, a book carved in wood from the wreck; and second, being a little deaf, he mistook an inquiry from the Queen as to the health of his sister for a question as to what was to happen to the hulk of the *Eurydice* and replied that she was to be turned over, her bottom examined, and well scraped.

from the Farquharsons the Forest of Ballochbuie for rather more than
£100,000 and with it went yet another cottage for picnics and boiling
potatoes, the Dantzig Shiel. Her Prime Minister congratulated her on
purchasing 'the bonniest plaid in Scotland'. No one was more understanding than he when the Queen lost her Privy Purse, old John Grant,
a granddaughter, and her daughter Princess Alice all within the space of
four months, and only six months later she heard that the Prince
Imperial had been killed in the Zulu War fighting for her Army. She
was at Balmoral but left at once for the south though Deeside was at its
best – 'the lilacs just preparing to burst' – and she travelled for the first
and only time over the Tay Bridge that so soon was to collapse in a
winter storm and hurl a whole train with upwards of eighty passengers
into the estuary below. In the autumn she took the desolated Empress
Eugénie to Scotland to spend a holiday at Abergeldie. The two took an
afternoon drive together and at teatime in the Gelder Shiel ate freshly
caught trout cooked in oatmeal, the Queen evidently regarding it as a
between-meal snack, the Empress declaring the delicious fish would
stand in well for her dinner.

The Queen had an eccentric touch that Lord Beaconsfield found
appealing, and he, in turn, had a similar touch of eccentricity that
appealed to her. As he walked haltingly on the lawns of Osborne, his
ringlets pomaded, his face cavernously wrinkled, the clothes that
covered his gauntness almost as *outré* as his gestures, talking in his
charming way, he was as exotic as an eastern bird. He managed to make
everyone at Court live just a little more intensely, so much so that his
defeat by the Liberals in 1880 and his death a year later was bitterly
lamented by the Queen and her daughter.

The Queen felt she was getting old. Whippingham Church remained
always her parish church when she was on the Island. But she found it
increasingly difficult to get there every Sunday. Therefore an unimpos-
ing chapel was attached to the east end of the main wing. As if to prove
her religious contrariness, whilst she had in her bedroom a Crucifix and
there was an elaborately gilt-framed *Redeemer Enthroned* by Nicola
Barabino, her new chapel was constructed as plainly as any dissenting
Ebenezer or Bethesda. It faced west, not east, and the principal article of
furniture was a pitch-pine pulpit which stood in the middle of the west
end. Selected preachers had the misfortune to find themselves elevated
only a few feet away from their sovereign who fixed them with a
basilisk stare. In theory the organist of Newport Parish Church was the
Queen's private organist, but generally Princess Beatrice played a
harmonium to accompany the singing. If, as so often happened, the
Queen was suffering from rheumatism, John Brown rolled her up the
long ramp that had been specially built to the corridor of the Main Wing.

Rudolf Löhlein was the senior of her Personal Attendants but he was a married man, and often with his wife and family at Windsor. Princess Beatrice and John Brown being unmarried were always at hand. More and more the Queen depended on them, but one March day in 1883 Prince Leopold had to inform his shrinking Mama that Brown had just died. She took his death very badly indeed.

One result, amongst many other memorials in metal and stone, was the publication of *More Leaves* early in the following year. The Prince of Wales did not care for it at all. Nor did his eldest sister. By the public it was received with very mixed feelings. Miss Murray MacGregor did not have the skill of Sir Arthur Helps in ghosting the Queen; but, then, hers was a far more difficult task. *Leaves* recalled the happy holidays and adventures of the Queen and her husband. *More Leaves* was a record of bereavement, the tale of a bolthole. And who could have attempted any sort of literary *tour de force* with the mourning Queen virtually looking over her shoulder? Naturally the book was lampooned and, in New York, a parody was published entitled *John Brown's Legs or Leaves from a Journal in the Lowlands*. And it was then that the young Dean of Windsor earned his mitre and eventually the primacy by courageously advising against a memoir of Brown.

Just after the first anniversary of Brown's death the Queen heard that her son Prince Leopold had died at Cannes. She was stricken but royal protocol decreed that arrangements must proceed and so the marriage of her granddaughter, Princess Victoria of Hesse to Lieutenant Prince Louis of Battenberg RN, at Darmstadt should proceed. Royal trains from all over Europe converged on the little state, and there Queen Victoria was informed that her son-in-law, the Grand Duke Louis, had been consoling himself for some time with a divorced adventuress and, at the last moment, had married her. His new consort was totally unsuitable and an annulment was arranged by common consent on the spot. Queen Victoria was not having 'that dreadful woman' in the family, though, with unexpected breadth of mind, she told her grand-daughter Victoria: 'If dear Papa should feel lonely when you 3 elder are married – I should say nothing (tho it must pain me) if he chose to make a morganatic marriage with some nice, quiet, sensible, & amiable person.' Grand Duke Louis meekly accepted the family judgment, the marriage was dissolved, and his mother-in-law returned to England.

Then Princess Beatrice plucked up the courage to say she had fallen in love with Prince Louis's younger brother Henry, who was twenty-six, a year younger than she, and that at Darmstadt they had come to an understanding.

The Queen was stupefied.

Possibly Lord Beaconsfield might have mollified if not prevented what followed and which surely was one of the most extraordinary incidents that ever occurred at Queen Victoria's Court. He had had that influence. Perhaps John Brown might have managed it, too, with some of his outspokenness and cold doses of common sense. But both were dead. Therefore, impulsively, acting without advice from anyone, the Queen promptly refused to speak to her love-struck daughter. She was put into Coventry for six months. Essential communication was made in writing. The Queen made only one mention of Princess Beatrice in her Journal between June and December.

It is not as if there was nothing to talk about. There were unlimited family interests to discuss. Prince Louis of Battenberg had been appointed to the Royal Yacht *Victoria and Albert*. He and his wife lived near Chichester and so were conveniently close to Portsmouth and Osborne. That summer they travelled to Russia for the marriage of Victoria's sister Ella to the Russian Grand Duke Serge and were received coolly because Louis's younger brother Sandro, as the elected Sovereign Prince of Bulgaria had recently defied Russia and lost his throne as a result. Moreover to the Russians the Battenbergs were unacceptable being the children of a morganatic marriage between a Prince of Hesse-Darmstadt★ and a Polish Countess of mixed Danish, French and Hungarian stock, afterwards created Princess of Battenberg in Hesse. The distinction was made clear at the reception after the marriage by separating them at table. Victoria was put with the royal princes and Louis with his fellow officers of the royal yacht. To Queen Victoria, who disapproved of divorce but made no distinction between regular and morganatic marriages, such an insult would have been an explosive talking point. Then her eldest daughter with all her family were on the Isle of Wight during late August using Osborne Cottage and the Hohenzollerns shared much the same views as the Romanovs about morganatic marriages. And Princess Louise was no longer cohabiting with Lord Lorne. She had returned from Canada where Lord Lorne had been Governor-General and where, according to one source she was the victim of a sledging accident in which she had lost an ear, and by the autumn of 1884 the Queen was forced to accept their estrangement as a fact and realize they could not be 'forced' to live under one roof. Finally, the chastened Grand Duke of Hesse went to see the Queen at Balmoral, and Princess Louis of Battenberg announced that she was carrying a child and undertook to have her confinement managed by the Queen just as her mother's had been. With the possible exclusion of the last item such matters were exactly the sort of thing mother and daughter would have talked over in the finest detail.

★ The Grand-Duchy had this name until 1866.

Moreover plenty was going on in the world outside. There was an outburst of Fenian outrages, and the sensational rush to relieve Gordon at Khartoum took place largely within this period. Osborne was thrown into a state of excitement by the arrival of envoys from John, King of Abyssinia. They were received on the lawn, presented their credentials and a number of gifts amongst them a young male elephant and a large monkey.* Mr Gladstone made speeches in Ballater 'on the Queen's doorstep', and called at the Castle with Lady Dalhousie. The latter's remark that she had never seen a more uncomfortable home or one she coveted less was unlikely to have reached the royal ears, but the Queen would certainly have heard that the old man's disciples were now beginning to decorate their tables with sweet william flowers.

These topics of conversation must have been a hard test of the Queen's determination to remain silent and her daughter's equal determination not to give way. The imagination might well ask how they could possibly manage it. Balmoral's library, where the Queen and her family and her ladies dined, was lined with books, stuffed with furniture à la mode, and was only twenty-six feet by twenty and a half feet. The meals must have been purgatorial for everyone. At Osborne there was more space in the dining-room or out of doors under the Queen's tent, but the atmosphere can never have been congenial. The silence between the wrathful mother and her daughter must have been palpable.

Doubtless it eventually affected the Queen's digestion. She was a stubborn woman but six months' discomfort was too much for her and she had to give way. But her terms were harsh.

Prince Henry, or Liko as he was known in the family, was to live with her – the Queen, wherever she might be. Suitable apartments would be provided. Princess Beatrice's daughterly duties should continue. They were not to travel and leave her alone. The family, of course, should be invited to the wedding, but it should not be at St George's. There would be a village wedding in Whippingham Church.

To everyone's amazement, possibly even the Queen's, the terms were accepted. Prince Henry was invited to Osborne for Christmas by his sister-in-law Princess Louis of Battenberg who had been lent Kent house, and they dined with the Queen on 23 December. On the 29th he went through the ordeal of being interviewed in the Prince Consort's dressing-room and 'all was satisfactorily settled'.

---

* A tank was let into the ground so that, until it was dispatched to a zoo, the elephant could take a daily bath. This later became a pond and a feature of the primitive three-hole golf course.

Chapter 28

Triumph, exhaustion and anxiety

Once she was committed, the Queen defended her 'Baby' like a tigress. She was outspoken in her condemnation of the Courts of St Petersburg and Vienna and Berlin with their narrow view on the eligibility of a Battenberg to marry her youngest daughter.

The following July, Osborne House, the estate lodges, hotels, and royal yachts were packed for the wedding. Curiously, for there were royal confectioners who could have matched and bettered it, Messrs Buszards of Oxford Street were ordered to fashion a cake that weighed more than 4 hundredweight and stood 9 feet high.

Princess Beatrice's 'village wedding' turned out to be something far grander than her sister's 'wretched marriage' held in the Osborne dining-room twenty-three years before. It was conducted by the Archbishop of Canterbury, the Bishop of Winchester, the Dean of Windsor, and Canon Prothero. The organist and choir were sent from Windsor. The island was festooned with bunting, flowers, flags, and streamers. Small guns popped; larger ones thundered. The weather was sublime. And politically everything was in order because Gladstone had fallen from power the month before. He was not amongst the guests. Nor were any members of the ruling dynasties of Germany. At a stroke the Queen swept aside the Almanach de Gotha protests. She invested Prince Henry with the Garter and conferred on him the dignity of Royal Highness.

Supported by two of his brothers, and dressed in the superb white and gold of the *Garde du Corps*, and wearing the Garter, he drove from Osborne to Whippingham, accepting the salutes of the Isle of Wight Volunteers at the Sovereign's Entrance and a detachment of the Argyll and Sutherland Highlanders outside the church. The bride was dressed as her mother had been in white satin trimmed with orange blossom and the Honiton lace veil worn by the Queen at her marriage in 1840. She had ten bridesmaids, all nieces. After the ceremony the many carriages returned up through the Sovereign's Entrance, along the Royal Drive past the reservoir mount to the carriage ring and the Portico Entrance. The registers were signed in the Horn Room as they had been at Princess Alice's wedding. Then, like her, they were given a two-day honeymoon before coming home for good.

Neither the Queen nor her son-in-law could have guessed how well this unlikely situation would work out. There must have been moments of stress. The Queen suffered from rheumatism, an uneven temper and was accustomed to having her own way. Princess Beatrice* could be bossy too. Princess Louise was the most regular member of the family at Osborne; painting and sculpting and, allegedly, causing trouble by flirting with her good-looking brother-in-law.

Fortunately however, Henry of Battenberg was not like Francis of Teck, another fruit of a morganatic marriage, who grumbled about the rather meaningless title that the Queen had asked the King of Württemberg to give him, and grumbled that he was only a Serene Highness† and grumbled at having only the Post Office Volunteers to command and grumbled because he had no money and nothing to do, and who eventually went off his head.

Prince Henry could always find things to do.

He acted as host when the Queen required it of him. He was master of the many revels, *tableaux vivants*, amateur theatricals, and concerts which she so much enjoyed. He enjoyed himself on the Continent, for by this time the Queen had added a regular spring holiday in the sun by the Mediterranean or at a watering-place. He took great pleasure in hunting, in tennis and bicycling, in the splendid sport at Balmoral, and in fishing and swimming and sailing at Osborne. And he could escape when necessary on board the *Sheilagh*, a yacht that the Queen gave him.

By 1887, the year of the Queen's Golden Jubilee, the Battenbergs were quite indispensable to her. A son had been born to them the preceding November. *Punch* had proposed he be christened Jubilee, presumably in fun, but no one could be certain. People had quaint notions about names. Florence Nightingale, for example, was eager in her old age that her great-great niece be christened 'Balaclava' – 'one of the most beautiful names in the world.' Fortunately for the young Battenberg prince, he was named Alexander Albert.

Princess Beatrice soon quickened with a second child which made the extra work of Jubilee year a great strain. Besides being unobtrusively at the centre of everything as her mother's Benjamin, she looked after

---

* She was now officially Princess Henry of Battenberg but the Queen directed that she still be called Princess Beatrice on informal occasions at Court.

† At her Golden Jubilee the Queen conferred on him the dignity of His Highness.

such details as the giving and receiving of gifts. It was she who designed the Jubilee brooch for presentation by the Queen to friends and admirers. The highlanders at Balmoral were given theirs in May, long before the Jubilee day, and had suitable celebrations at the proper time.

Even more fell on the Battenbergs when the main celebrations took place at Windsor and in London, and then again at Windsor: luncheons and dinners, audiences, receptions, a great procession to the Abbey, smaller, but no less enthusiastic and tiring processions elsewhere, a garden party, visits, military inspections, bands, firework displays, illuminations, the giving and receiving of addresses.

The Queen's youngest daughter and her son-in-law were almost always at hand to give information if her memory should fail her, or propose that she might reasonably slip off to bed even before the official programme concluded. Her commitments were arranged to make the least possible demands upon the Queen. Even so, they were enormous, and it was a very tired sovereign who reviewed 20,000 officers and men of the Fleet at Spithead and then went home to the Isle of Wight. There she was greeted with loyal banners stretched across the streets of East and West Cowes. They included 'Fifty runs not out', an appropriate English tribute, and 'Better lo'ed ye canna be' that seemed a few hundred miles out of place – though no more so than the bagpipe factory reputedly established in East Cowes during the time of John Brown. Three days after reaching home the Queen visited the island's capital, Newport, escorted there by a detachment of the local regiment and members of the local hunt. In August she knighted the Mayor of Newport at Osborne.

After that the Queen was able to rest and reflect in her tent or in the alcoves or beneath the cedars or down by the sea-shore. Now, at a respectful distance, she was attended by two silent servants dressed in scarlet with white turbans who had been brought by a Dr Tyler from India in June to attend their Empress.

Osborne was redolent of a strange mixture of the triumph of the jubilee celebrations, great exhaustion, and equally great anxiety.

Undeniably the most impressive figure in the jubilee procession had been the Queen's son-in-law, the Crown Prince of Germany, but, known only to a few, he was almost speechless. The Queen had been told that all, in the end, would be well, but she was troubled. Her eldest daughter and the sick Crown Prince were with her at Osborne. At Dr Morel Mackenzie's suggestion they were to precede her to Scotland, but not stay at the Castle where there would be many guests and a great deal of activity. Instead they should go privately to the Fife Arms in Braemar. They could drive over to Balmoral when they wished and when the doctor advised it. The character of the illness was particularly distressing. It could be that the constriction in his throat was malign. Equally distressing was the Crown Princess's undisputable unpopularity in Germany. Lord Clarendon had once remarked that one needed to be sharp and get up very early in the morning to know more of what was going on than the Queen. She missed very little and knew that her eldest daughter was detested by the Germans for her liberalism and for insisting that a foreign doctor assist the Crown Prince's physician, and that a rumour ran that she and her secretary, Count Seckendorff, were lovers. In those sunny days at Osborne the Queen wept for her old friend Miss Skerrett who had arranged all the robes for her Coronation fifty years before and had stayed with her until a year after the Prince Consort's death. But Miss Skerrett had recently died at the great age of ninety-four. The Queen's son-in-law was still young, and to be eaten up by disease even before he could begin his promised career was too pitiful. She wept for him and for her daughter and their son William who kept himself at arm's length from his parents, and for Germany, with more tears than she could spare for the peaceful death of dear Miss Skerrett.

The move to Balmoral was beneficial for everyone. Rather against her will, because her own physician, Dr Reid, did not have too high an opinion of Dr Morel Mackenzie, she knighted him at the request of her eldest daughter; and, probably, in her heart she was glad when the German party left for the Austrian Tyrol where the air was dryer and less bracing. Their future was bleak and tragic, and before the Queen returned to England she received confirmation of her worst fears. New investigations had found the Crown Prince had incurable cancer of the throat.

There was a constant stream of visitors to Balmoral. They included the Prince of Wales who went there specially to unveil a statue of the Queen erected opposite Theed's statue of the Prince Consort to commemorate the Jubilee. But the greatest excitement of the long stay was that Princess Beatrice had decided to be confined there. Thus it happened that her only daughter and the first royal child to be born in Scotland since 1600 was born on 24 October, and later she was christened in the Balmoral drawing-room with Jordan water in a gold font sent from England. The Presbyterian rite, conducted by the Dean of the Order of the Thistle, had godparents obtruded into it by Royal Command. The baby should have been named by the old Gaelic name of Eua, chosen by her mother, but the Dean supposed it was a mistake and baptized her Ena.* There was a Ghillies' Ball to celebrate, a function

---

* This could have been corrected when she was confirmed in the Church of England, or afterwards when she was received into the Roman Church before marrying the King of Spain, but she remained Ena all her life.

once supervised by John Brown, now organized and much enjoyed by Prince Henry of Battenberg.

The Queen was not to be deprived of her Hindustani lessons from Dr Tyler's two Indians, and they had been taken north as well, to give the castle an exotic touch and problems in a kitchen unacquainted with oriental eating customs. The year 1887 not only marked the fiftieth year of Queen Victoria's reign. It also marked the beginning of her absorbing interest in the sub-continent of which she was Empress.

Chapter 29

'Mud pies'

The Queen was disposed to be timid. Therefore she appeared to be very blunt. After fifty years on a throne she felt entitled to air firm convictions. With her little chin firmly set she would pontificate on anything and everything from vivisection – 'Butchers!' and government bureaucracy – 'lamentable red-tapery', to ladies hunting – 'wild young women who are really unsexed!' Nor did she often alter her opinions. The residents of Tomintoul in Banffshire objected to her writing in *Leaves* that theirs was a dirty town and evidently expected a correction in any subsequent printing. She scribbled on her Private Secretary's memorandum: '"a Tomintouler" is a byeword & she will *not change it*.' It was the same with the charge often levelled at her that she preferred Scots and foreigners to English servants. She made no attempt to deny it.

The Browns and their cousins held many places in her service both in Scotland and in England. So did the sons of John Macdonald. So did the Thomsons, sons of Crathie's first postmaster who set up a 'Letter Receiving House' in 1842. Four Thomsons were in the royal service. But, while there was a flow south from Scotland, there was no equivalent flow north. This was probably because it was traditional for the Scots to leave their country and seek work elsewhere as the economy of their country could not sustain many inhabitants. For years the majority of the Queen's most intimate and trusted servants were from Scotland, Germany and Switzerland. At the end of the century the butter sculptress and superintendent of the dairy at Balmoral was Welsh.

Lists from *The Royal Kalendar* show that once Indians appeared at Court they gradually outnumbered and outranked the Scots. Only three years after the Jubilee there were four Indians and three Scots in that limbo between the gentlemen and the non-gentlemen of the Queen's household. Ten years later there were still four Indians but only two Scots.

One of the original pair who kissed the Queen-Empress's slipper and taught her snatches of Hindustani, proved himself deft with the blotting paper, always a sign of the Queen's affection. Forty-nine years before she had recorded in her Journal: 'Albert helped me with the blotting paper.' In *More Leaves* she told the world: 'Brown always helping to dry the signatures.' In September, 1889 she wrote to her Private Secretary, who was by now Sir Henry Ponsonby: 'Abdul is most handy in helping when she *signs* by drying the signatures.'

This handy dryer of signatures ended as Munshi Hafiz, Abdul Karim, C.I.E., C.V.O. His leap to fame scandalized or amused the Queen's subjects, was an annoyance to her Ministers, enraged the great majority of her courtiers, and has been the source of very good stories – possibly the most bizarre that at Osborne he was, literally, the cause of a palace revolution. Usually he was not included in the suite that travelled to the south of France. One year the Queen decided that he should go. Her Courtiers realized this would mean him eating with the Household, a prospect that horrified them. They deputed one of the Queen's favourite ladies, Miss Harriet Phipps, to carry their ultimatum. If the Indian went, they would not. Bravely Miss Phipps did this. With a royal screech of fury the old Queen dashed everything from the writing-table in her sitting-room and only with the greatest difficulty was she calmed and ultimately persuaded to change her mind. In any case it made no difference because the Munshi simply travelled alone and turned up a day after the others.

This story, although it sounds Gilbertian, in the main is true, but possibly some other stories about the Munshi make him out to be worse than he really was, and have therefore misrepresented the important role he played in life at Osborne and Balmoral to the end of the reign.

Abdul Karim was not simply a brown Brown. The two royal favourites did have things in common, but only three. They both put on airs. They both accepted presents and cottages and advancement from the Queen as well as her affection. And they both rather ran to seed. Otherwise they were very different. Brown was unmarried, never took any leave, and did not misuse his influence. The Munshi had a wife and other attachments, went on immensely long leaves, and misused his influence by trying to push a lawyer friend at the Queen's ministers. In this he was not successful. Lord George Hamilton, the Secretary for India, dismissed the whole business as a bore. He called it 'the Court's mud pies', and he was exactly right. The Munshi crises were really the concern of the Court, and they occurred because most of the ladies and gentlemen of the Household had the contemporary intolerant view of coloured races; a prejudice that was not shared either by the Queen or by her son and heir.

Karim had his head turned by being upgraded, as Brown had been, from lower servant and the Queen ordered that photographs of him waiting at table should be destroyed because they were demeaning. On first entering her service in June, 1887, he had told the Queen his father was 'a native doctor at Agra'. Later, when his own status had altered and he was the Queen's Munshi or teacher, he told a lie. He upgraded his father and stated he was a Surgeon-General. This was not particularly wicked, but it was stupid because it laid him open to attack from those in the Queen's Household who could not stand him. They suggested to the Queen that his father was not a Surgeon-General at all. Thereupon she telegraphed Sir Henry Ponsonby's son, who was on a tour of duty in India and about to return to be her Equerry, and asked him to call on the Munshi's father. He did so and eventually reported that he was 'only the apothecary at the jail at Agra'.

It was exactly what the Munshi's critics wanted. The Queen was very angry and said she refused to believe it. Her Munshi's credit was lowered. As it happened, young Ponsonby's report was scarcely fair though no one has said so before. It is, of course, necessary to step back a few decades and understand the contemporary view of natives and particularly that of officers who had served in India, but it is equally necessary to understand the difference between British and Indian medical practice and the status given by Indians to their own doctors. The Munshi's father dispensed medicines at the Agra jail as a part-time occupation only after he had finished his military service, and had been given the honorific usually given at the end of service of Khan Bahadeer. In the Indian Army he had been an experienced medical healer, had charge at one time of the hospital attached to the Second Indian Horse and went with them on the famous march to Khandahar. Furthermore the Indian pharmacopoeia with which he would have had to be exceedingly familiar, was larger than the British pharmacopoeia. All this is some extenuation of the Munshi's boast. His father was by no means a Surgeon-General, but he was a retired army doctor of great experience and an honoured Khan Bahadeer who helped out at Agra. This certainly sounds better than the young Equerry's bleak report.

The exactitude of dates does not matter much save in a closed society like a regiment or a Court where seniority and the date of promotion matter a great deal. Yet there is disagreement about the date Abdul Karim was given the honorific title of Hafiz.* Those of the Queen's biographers who have given information on the Munshi state that he was made Hafiz and Indian Secretary in 1894. In fact, as *The Royal*

---

* The Oxford English Dictionary defines this as 'guardian, keeper, observer. A Mohammedan who knows the whole of the Koran by heart.'

Kalendar shows, he was Hafiz before 1890,★ and he was made Indian Secretary with his own staff of clerks in 1892. The year 1894 was when a letter was published criticizing the Queen for surrounding herself with 'low' people. The Queen was sufficiently annoyed about this impertinence to write twice to her Private Secretary on the matter. Old Sir Henry Ponsonby could do little to help her. He confessed: 'These Injuns are too much for me.'

The Munshi's foes in the Household could not give him credit for anything. At root it might be that their aversion was caused not so much by his colour or his manner, as by his apartness. Mrs Bernard Mallet, one of the Queen's Extra Women of the Bedchamber, described him as 'an unctuous oriental', and by royal command she was bidden to visit his wife at Balmoral. She found a fat but not uncomely lady in rich clothes and jewels living in a house entirely surrounded by a 20-foot palisade. It all seemed very odd to her as the house was so close to the Castle. Presumably the same strangeness and apartness obtained at Frogmore Cottage at Windsor and Arthur Cottage on the Osborne estate, both of which were used by the Munshi.

There was endless talk about his zenana. Moreover, 'aunts' were brought from India and Dr Reid declared that every time Mrs Karim fell a new tongue was put out for him to examine. The 'aunts' became famous. Less well known were his 'nephews'. In the royal photograph albums at Windsor there are pictures entitled 'The Munshi with Nephew'; the Munshi standing, the boy sitting. In the photographs the podgy Munshi is constant, the nephews are different. They suggest something quite acceptable in the Moslem world, but horrendous to the male-dominated late Victorians.† Alick Yorke, a Groom-in-Waiting and a great favourite of the Queen's, a worldly man who dressed in an *outré* fashion and wore jewels, rings, huge buttonholes and scent, and was described by his great-nephew the late Sir Victor Mallet, as resembling 'an elderly pansy' would certainly have been aware of the Moslem way of life. Yorke gave 'charming bachelor dinners', and almost certainly he talked.

Though ousted from the nerve-centre of the Court by flamboyant Indians, the Scots have been discreetly reticent about the Munshi. On the Isle of Wight, however, there are people who still remember him and speak of him with affection. He epitomized for them, as he did for his royal mistress, the splendours of the east.

The Queen's absorbing interest in the orient resulted in her making a

★ *Whitaker's Almanack* was slow and did not print his honorific Hafiz until 1891.

† The Queen's grandson, Prince George afterwards Duke of York and Prince of Wales and then George V, had the typically naïve view that all such people automatically shot themselves.

great change at Osborne. Generally she hated change. Her tappisiers, that is, the officials who looked after her furniture and furnishings, covers, tapestries, carpets, upholstery, hangings, curtains, and paper-hanging, took advantage of her regular peregrinations to replace worn work in exactly the same material so that her eye should not be offended the next time she returned. Only the ornaments and bibelots, the photographs and drawings, and the paintings multiplied to conform with the chock-a-block fashion of the day. Nevertheless surrendering to imperial dreams, she had an exotic wing added to Osborne where, so she said, she could entertain properly.

The Country Press, a local newspaper, reported on 21 June, 1890:

> When the German Emperor visited the Queen last year great incon-venience was experienced . . . on account of the want of a State banqueting hall at Osborne House. Her Majesty has now determined to build one of magnificent proportions, the foundations of which will be laid upon the lawn on the west side of the house.

Such a statement must have amused informed circles because, in his visit the year before, the German Emperor had been particularly *mal vu*. On the death of his father from cancer after a reign of only three months, the Kaiser had so mistreated his mother and insulted his uncle, the Prince of Wales, that his Grandmother had only received him on the formal advice of her Ministers. It went beyond belief that she had him in mind when she gave orders for a magnificent hall to be built on the west lawn.

Externally the wing would conform with the rest of the building. Internally it would not. The firm of Cubitts was engaged and furnished plans from sketches done by the Queen's estate surveyor. The wing had no basement and only two floors. On the ground floor was a lobby, and an entrance hall that led to a huge room, 30 feet by 60 feet, with a grand corridor on the east side where Indian trophies and pictures were to be placed. On the first floor, three large rooms were made into a suite for Prince and Princess Henry; a dining-room, drawing-room, and a bed-room with an enclosed bath in the wall; and four smaller rooms, with bathrooms and water-closets. As the Queen aged, a Minister in Attendance became more and more of a necessity even on the Isle of Wight, and it was intended that permanent quarters be kept for him there.

A specialist was summoned to decorate and furnish the banqueting hall, soon called the Durbar Room. It was not to be Indianesque in the late eighteenth-century style that had influenced Brighton Pavilion, but Indian-Saracenic. Moslems like Jews were forbidden to fashion all natural objects. Therefore they made formal but luxuriant twinings and intertwinings of arabesques. It permitted endless flights of fancy, as long as the design was rhythmic and symmetric. Then Moslems, being fatalists, did not work in stone, but in more ephemeral materials such as wood and plaster. They emphasized the importance of form and texture by the use of gilded or coloured raised mouldings or surface ornaments on walls, and intricately designed constructions of plaster and wood, called stalactites, hanging from ceilings.

It has for long been accepted that the expert responsible for the Durbar Room was Lockwood Kipling, the father of Rudyard, who was Principal of the Mayo School of Industrial Art, Curator of the Lahore Central Museum, and acquainted with Sir Howard Elphinstone.★ Certainly Lockwood Kipling designed a billiard-table for the Duke of Connaught at his married home at Bagshot, but considerable doubt has now been aired that Kipling had anything to do with Osborne save at one remove, and that it was one of his many former pupils, Bhai Ram Singh, a scholar of the history of Indian architecture and a connoisseur of the chief building styles, especially Indian-Saracenic, who designed and supervised the work.

This had profuse and elaborate patterns in plaster, wood, and lincustra, a ceiling with stalactites the whole supported by moulded brackets, a peacock in its pride above that necessary gesture to the occident, an open fireplace, and an alcove at one end of the room with a gallery above. Bhai Ram Singh put small oriels beside the peacock, large ones beside the gallery. There was a good deal of gilding and bright colouring to get the fretted, carpet-like effect, and the end result was a white and gold apartment jewelled with bright colours. A portrait of Bhai Ram Singh was placed above the entrance to his creation.

The room has earned rather more praise than otherwise, but it is no longer exactly as he left it.† Nor was it always suitably treated. As a picture from Princess Alice's albums shows, it was not the right place for tinsel and evergreen Christmas decorations, a pair of trees with candles and baubles, and tables heaped with presents. The mixture was over-rich. Probably the Queen's Moslem attendants failed to appreciate the obtrusion of a number of Buddhas and elephants into the decora-

---

★ Barely three months before the building of the new wing began, Sir Howard Elphinstone, on a private cruise to Tenerife, was swept overboard in a storm off Ushant and his body was never recovered. This terminated thirty-one years in the royal service, and the Queen was so moved that she personally drafted the announcement of his death in the *Court Circular*. In her Journal she wrote: 'I am quite in despair. The whole thing haunts me.'

† For some unknown reason after the Queen's death some of the original polished wood decorations were painted white, and the white gallery ceiling and wall were painted blue. Some of the gilded mouldings were also painted. Restoration is proving difficult and expensive.

tions. But the Queen herself was delighted with her Durbar Room. It was proof of her broad view, Saracenic in style but intended for all her Indian subjects of whatever faith if not of whatever caste.

A concession was at last made to modernity. The Queen had experimented with a telephone, but not had one installed. Now she ordered that the Durbar Room should have twinkling electric lights, and, whilst they were at it, the engineers installed electricity throughout the building. It was supplied from accumulators in a battery-house situated near the Servants' Barracks that were charged when necessary by a gas-driven generator.

A hand-powered lift was also installed to carry the Queen in her bath-chair from ground level to her private apartments, an improvement of which she took advantage whenever she suffered cruelly from rheumatism, but was not absolutely necessary. At Balmoral, where there was no lift, she sometimes had to be carried bodily up the grand staircase in her bathchair by attendants. But it was a rare occurrence and, considering all things, she had an enviable digestion and vitality right to the end.

One evening at Balmoral in 1891 she took a fancy to dance after dinner; the drawing-room furniture was moved, the carpet was rolled back, and she danced a whole quadrille with the heir-but-one, a vapid youth who perhaps fortunately for England died of influenza in early 1892. After a decent interval his fiancée Princess May of Teck conceived it her duty to become engaged to his brother, Prince George which gave the Queen much satisfaction.

The Durbar Wing added yet another non-Prince Albert – Thomas Cubitt dimension to Osborne, and was built at such speed that within eighteen months the Queen wrote in her Journal on 20 August 1891: 'A great dinner in honour of the French fleet was given in the India Room.'

This symbol of Eastern power made not the slightest difference to her Courtiers' dislike for the gentleman already so much talked about that, in the French newspapers, he was called *Le Munchy*. And the Queen never did win her battle for his recognition, although, as long as she lived, she went on trying. His portrait was painted against a background of gold by the fashionable German painter Joachim von Angeli. His name was included in the Court Circular in the official ceremonial at public functions, and on the printed programme of private *tableaux vivants*; with her German Secretary, Hafiz Abdul Karim had his appointed place in the Diamond Jubilee procession; and the last Liberal Ministry in the Queen's reign was persuaded to honour him with the C.I.E. She herself honoured him with the C.V.O. It was to no avail.

The plain fact was that, being in the isolated position of monarch, she could mix with and enjoy the company of whom she wished without any difficulty at all. Those accustomed to the cantonment and the Club could not.

Chapter 30

A champagne quality

In her old age the Queen called Henry of Battenberg 'a bright sunbeam in my home'. It was a sentimental way of expressing the truth.

As a recognition of what he did for her she appointed him Governor and Captain-General of the Isle of Wight and Governor of Carisbrooke Castle. It was a popular appointment on the Island. Prince Henry certainly kept to his side of the bargain made before his engagement to Princess Beatrice, and they and their children made this the best part of the Queen's widowhood.

A fourth child and third son was born to Princess Beatrice at Balmoral in October, 1891. The birth of a prince in Scotland was another historic event. On Craig Gowan where the Royal Family had made its first cairn and the fall of Sebastopol and the victory of Tel-el-Kebir had been celebrated, there was another huge bonfire, a torchlight procession to the top led by pipers, and a good deal of dancing and hallooing and whisky drinking. A battery of Artillery fired a royal salute that echoed and re-echoed from the surrounding hills. After dinner there was an impromptu ball at which the seventy-two-year-old Queen forgot her rheumatism and danced with her son-in-law, every step perfection until the end of a reel. Eight years her junior, Sir Henry Ponsonby was filled with admiration for her 'light airy steps in the old courtly fashion; no limp or stick but every figure carefully and prettily danced'. Afterwards she sat on the raised dais that was always comfortable because it backed on to the chief chimney of the Castle kitchen, but Prince Henry danced right through the ball. Again the golden font was sent from England, and again the Dean of the Order of the Thistle mutilated the liturgy of the Kirk by accepting godparents for Prince Maurice Victor Donald, the last name given in compliment to the land of his birth.

Prince Henry had the gift of bringing a champagne quality into life. He dearly loved all the outdoor sports that the Prince Consort had loved. He loved all the games and indoor pastimes that the Queen so loved. Everyone looked to him as diplomatic reconciler when the Queen was out of sorts with a member of her Household. He even managed to get on with her large family which showed he was a very special person.

It was he who made arrangements for entertainers to come to Court. They ranged in variety from *The Mikado* performed in the ballroom by a D'Oyly Carte touring company, the programme being printed on cream satin bordered with gold braid, and professional performances by the Bancrofts and Beerbohm Tree, to a somewhat moth-eaten travelling circus called in to do its best at Balmoral. This had once enjoyed a European reputation but, Mr Pinder, the owner, had fallen on hard times. Given a water-meadow by the Dee on which to camp his battered caravans and animals, he and his circus made a great effort. He was rewarded with a jewelled tiepin from the Queen herself, a fee that would buy all the paint and tack and smartening gear the circus needed, and royal patronage.

Prince Henry was also a force behind the last important piece of building in upper-Deeside, a new church at Crathie. The old one had not lasted a hundred years but it was too small. In 1893 the Queen laid the foundation-stone of a new building and all her family throughout Europe was pressed into contributing not only cash, but also in kind for a monster bazaar. This was a two-day event and special trains were run from Aberdeen to Ballater for people eager to patronize a bazaar at Balmoral and buy from stalls held by royal princesses. The Royal Family provided gifts they had worked themselves, pictures, carvings, carpentry, embroidered linen. The Queen, despite her poor eyesight contributed some basketry, and was supposed to have smiled wryly when not all of it was sold. The royal grandchildren enjoyed it tremendously. Princess Alice recalls that, whilst driving to the bazaar, her mother's maid decided her fringe needed shortening and proceeded to do it despite the jolting. The result looked 'as if the rats had been at it'. Prince Henry, enterprising as ever, put his daughter Ena in a giant shoe from which she sold dolls. He himself took photographic studies at five shillings a portrait. Almost half the sum needed for the new kirk was collected at the bazaar. A year later the Queen opened the finished building. Her pews had her monogram carved in the wood as well as the rose, thistle and shamrock emblems. Neither the leek nor the daffodil nor the hand of Ulster were represented. The pulpit and Communion Table were of granite and Iona marbles, and had been constructed under the supervision of the artist of the family, Princess Louise.

Prince Henry made another incalculably valuable contribution to the

Queen at this period. It was to him rather than to Princess Beatrice that she turned for real understanding. As her eyesight grew worse and worse, when she lost friends, and especially when Sir Henry Ponsonby had a stroke and later died, she leaned on him. And simply because he was so valuable to her, she forced herself to be patient when he wanted to go off sailing from time to time and, perforce, left her behind. He took his yacht round the north of Scotland and the Isles. He took her to the Scillies and to the Mediterranean.

Then there came a time when he wished to leave her and his wife and family for entirely another reason. He had been trained in the profession of arms at a time when the words 'glory' and 'honour' meant a great deal. In 1895 a military expedition was being mounted to make the new King of Ashanti keep to the treaty made between his predecessor and the British. Young Prince Christian of Schleswig-Holstein was a soldier and requested leave from the Queen to join the force. She gave it. But it was a different matter when her son-in-law Prince Henry of Battenberg did the same. There were only nine years between the two volunteers but the grandson could be spared, the son-in-law could not. Ashanti, with its tropical rain-forests, was notoriously unhealthy. The death of the Prince Imperial had prejudiced the Queen against the trustworthiness of Africans. Her refusal was peremptory. Nevertheless Princess Beatrice realized that this was something her husband wanted very badly. Selflessly she helped to persuade the Queen, trying to minimize the danger, emphasizing it was natural for a soldier to want to use his sword. At last, though with reluctance, the Queen gave her consent. But, only a month after leaving England, the Prince caught malaria and was invalided home on board H.M.S. *Blonde*. Off Sierra Leone on 20 January, 1896 he died. Pickled in rum in a makeshift tank made of biscuit tins his body reached Portsmouth. He was laid to rest, with fully military honours, in Whippingham Church.

The widowed Princess Beatrice was moved to do something she had never done before. For a whole month she and her children left Osborne and the grieving Queen. The suite above the Durbar Room and the nurseries in the Pavilion fell silent. Then, her sorrow disciplined though not diminished, Princess Beatrice re-entered the pattern of duty she had followed all her life. She had a memorial-chapel built adjacent to the chancel of Whippingham Church, where one day she and the ashes of her eldest son were also to rest.* She accepted from the Queen her husband's appointments as Governor and Captain-General of the

* Prince Henry's elder brother, Prince Louis, and his wife Princess Victoria, lie beneath a fine black memorial in Whippingham churchyard, though without their princely title and under their enforced new name of Mountbatten and as the 1st Marquis and Marchioness of Milford Haven.

Isle of Wight and Governor of Carisbrooke Castle. Otherwise she continued as before, her mother's principal adviser, prop and stay.

It was noticeable but not her fault that she lacked the enterprise and high spirits of her husband. Nor was she entirely willing to suppress her own interests when despatch-boxes made claims upon her time. Indeed there was some criticism that, when she took up photography, time spent in the darkroom was lost to the despatch-boxes and this was not in the best interests of the nation, but Princess Beatrice did her best by her mother.

The Queen was agonized by the death of her son-in-law, Henry. Her distress was controlled but very deep. In some degree Prince Henry's death anaesthetized her sorrow when Rudolf Löhlein died soon afterwards at Windsor although he was the very last of all the Prince Consort's intimate servants. Time taught her that the only thing that put any spark in her life were Prince Henry's children, Alexander, Ena, Leopold and Maurice,* and her other younger grandchildren, all of whom played in the places her own children had done, and were as artless, and gave her moments of fun.

At Osborne, they kept pens of poultry, played tennis with the squashed-at-the-top rackets of the period, accompanied her on their ponies or bicycles as her 'guard' as she drove a pony phaeton on the lawns under the evergreens, along the avenue of monkey puzzles, and beside the hedges of ilex and bay, plantations of oak and elm and beech, and one of exotic cork; the sovereign and her guard accompanied by a mass of dogs – collies and pomeranians, pugs, jack russells and blenheim spaniels. The children would wait patiently beside the Queen as she breakfasted or took her tea, all of them hoping for a ration of the special biscuits Grandmama had sent from Germany. They went with her on expeditions under the porchway of old Osborne House into the walled gardens, to pick fruit from the cages and walls, and nibble soily radishes, and pick her flowers. They used the Swiss chalet and the fort; made natural history collections; boated from Osborne pier; and they bathed in the collapsable bathing-pool until a storm blew it to bits in the last year of the reign.†

In Scotland the boys early learned to respect game and were put in the hands of the head ghillie. With walking, climbing, exploring, following the guns until they too could shoot and go stalking, fishing and

---

* The youngest, Prince Maurice, was the only one to die a Prince and a Battenberg; killed in action fighting in the 60th Rifles in 1914. Under a Royal Proclamation of 1917 Prince Alexander became the Marquis of Carisbrooke and Lord Leopold Mountbatten. Previously their sister had been created a Royal Highness by King Edward VII and had married King Alfonso of Spain.

† Some of the timbers were used for making a shed that was still standing in the late 1970s.

playing cricket and tennis, they had plenty to do at Balmoral, but they no more settled there than they did in France in the springtime or in the more formal splendour of Windsor. Osborne was really the Battenberg home.

Of other younger children who spent holidays at Osborne or on the Balmoral estate Princess Alice gives some of the liveliest pictures. Balmoral, she calls a 'granity building' in her grandmother's day and, like her cousin Princess Victoria of Prussia she noticed, as children do notice, that Balmoral had a special smell – a combination of beech wood fire smoke, leather and trophies. Doubtless it was damp and stuffy but she found it delicious. She recalls the extempore prayer at Kirk in which the minister was carried away by royal fervour into a muddle of genders praying that the Queen might 'skip like a he-goat upon the mountains'. She recalls her grandmother working and break-fasting out of doors 'till the snow drove her in', not in the original Gardener's Cottage but in its replacement. And, in her excursions to the Shiels she remembers condoling with Miss Campbell of the Glassalt Shiel because, being toothless, she could not attend a Ghillies' ball. But, later, she saw the old lady at the ball, complete with a set of teeth she had borrowed from Miss Cameron of Alt-na-Giuthasach.

One of Balmoral's most notable visitors was Tsar Nicholas II and his young wife who had been Princess Alicky of Hesse and was the Queen's grand-daughter. So huge was his retinue that a log-cabin village had to be constructed to contain it all. Doubtless the whole suite was as uncomfortable as the Tsar who, accustomed to highly heated palaces in Russian winters, found upper-Deeside intensely cold.* There was also a good deal of wind and rain, and the sport was negligible. Not a stag was shot and only one brace of grouse was seen on the entire visit. Nor did the formal conversations between the two sovereigns and Lord Salisbury amount to much. But the Queen was very happy. There were so many of the family at Balmoral that the new heir-but-one, the Duke of York, and his wife and two children,† plus the old Duke of Cambridge, had to be boarded out in Glen Muick. The anointed Autocrat of all the Russias went cheerfully to the Presbyterian Service at the village Kirk which the Queen doubtless considered a moral victory against her advisers who objected so strongly to her receiving Communion in the Presbyterian Church of Scotland.‡

Amongst the festivities the Queen found something to live for again,

---

* So apparently from previous experience did Lord Salisbury. On this occasion his Private Secretary wrote to the Queen's Private Secretary to ask that the apartments of the Minister in Attendance be 'very warm: a minimum temperature of 60°'.

† Later Edward VIII and his brother George VI.

‡ She had done this annually from 3 November in 1873.

a spirit she had lost since the death of her son-in-law. On the last day of the visit the whole company walked and talked outside the ballroom while they were photographed 'by the new cinematograph process which makes moving pictures'. In November at Windsor she saw the film. 'It is a very wonderful process, representing people, their movements and actions, as if they were alive.' It was an historic film; jerky and spotty and a little scratched, of a self-conscious group reacting or over-reacting to being the subject of such an extraordinary phenomenon. It showed the terrace looking somewhat naked, and the ballroom; young princes and princesses skipping about, plenty of bare knees and 'highland things'; Russian furs and uniforms; the tightly-laced ladies with their long and slightly trained skirts and heavily trimmed, small-crowned hats. Stealing the show, as she always did quite unconsciously, was the Queen, leaning on her cane, beaming at one moment and not beaming at the next, glancing over her huge family, a virtually oval but very regal figure.

Chapter 31

No more boiled potatoes in the heather

When the Queen's Diamond Jubilee came she was a little astonished at the reception she was given.

Even the cousin she liked least of all, Leopold of the Belgians, who exploited the Congo, and tyrannized his family, and had mandarin-like fingernails, travelled all the way from Brussels to Balmoral merely to take luncheon and hand to her, with his felicitations, 'a most splendid erection of orchids, one can hardly call it a bouquet, which he had brought from Belgium'. The Queen received him in the front hall. 'Quelle voyage, cher cousin', she said in astonishment. 'Quelle butte!' he replied.

The Queen received an astounding number of telegrams, letters, formal addresses, and gifts; and, for her age, she accomplished an astonishing amount, probably even more than she had ten years before. The public functions were infinitely wearing and led up to and away from the central event of the year: a procession from the Palace to St Paul's to give thanks. It was vast. The Duke of Argyll wrote in excitement that 'no sovereign since the fall of Rome could muster subjects from so many and so distant countries all over the world.' And there were remarkable manifestations of loyalty. Unable to leave her carriage, the clergy and choirs were on the steps of St Paul's for a short Service. The Old Hundredth was taken up and sung by thousands. So was the National Anthem. At the conclusion of the Service, after a word with the Queen, the Archbishop of Canterbury, fully vested and holding his crozier, called to the crowd 'Three cheers for the Queen'. The roars that followed this somewhat unecclesiastical but sincere lead were deafening. Their little sovereign wept with emotion. To be loved so much. And to have lost so much: her husband, and good John Brown, and Lord Beaconsfield and her two favourite sons-in-law who had ridden beside her at her golden Jubilee. And now there was great anxiety about Annie Macdonald who was too ill to attend her and had

had to stay in Balmoral, and anxiety about Mrs Symon who kept the village shop, Merchant's, and who in January had been declared 'hopelessly ill'.

Annie did die less than a fortnight after the great procession to St Paul's and the Queen, still by no means halfway through her public duties, was greatly distressed. 'I am most deeply grieved, and cannot in the least realize that I have lost not only an excellent and faithful maid, but a real friend.'

It was otherwise with old Mrs Symon who had taken on a new lease of life to enjoy the Jubilee celebrations at Deeside. These were considerable. There was a six-course dinner at the Castle on 22 June, a supper and ball on 9 July, and another on 23 July with a display by C. F. Shirras, an Aberdeen firework dealer and pyrotechnist. People on the royal estate already enjoyed much better food than the family of an average labouring man. Their staple diet was plentiful cold beef, freshly baked bread, and tea. In addition they could expect a complement of vegetables, salmon, roast and boiled beef and mutton, venison and other game. Sometimes there were complaints about the sameness of this diet. Therefore very special occasions such as the Jubilee invited very special feasts. The menu of the six-course dinner in June was made up of two soups, two fish dishes, two entrées, five roasts and salad, eight puddings, and dessert, and contained such delicacies as real turtle, veal cutlets, sweetbreads, fowls, York hams, Victoria pudding and meringues. Even the supper on 23 July before the firework display was lavish. It included mayonnaise-salmon, boar's head, chickens, raised meat pies, tongues, turkey flavoured with truffles, lamb, beef, salad, jellies, creams, cakes, pastries, and fruit; with wines, ale and whisky. Replete with this feast, and dazed with many reels, the party was rounded off by a display of Mr Shirras at his most ingenious. According to his printed programme, he offered 'By the Queen's Command' a display of electric rain rockets, signal aerial shells, jets, jewel wheels and expanding rays of coloured fire, a plethora of rockets from Asteroids to Dragonflies, a pyrotechnic portrait of the Queen and, amongst the ambitious devices, 'Fountains of Fire in Silver and Gold, &c., concluding with Grand Rebound, and discharging Nests of Hissing Serpents, &c.' Balmoral had never seen anything like it before.

Osborne, too, had their treats; fêtes, games, teas and suppers. There was no stinting on this extraordinary occasion.

The Queen's Jubilee duties were onerous and kept her from going to Osborne until long after the usual time. Even these local ceremonies demanded her presence, and the King of Siam paid her a formal visit, taking luncheon in the Durbar Room while the band of the Scottish Rifles played on the lawn outside – a truly international occasion.

Then, at last, she could rest from the celebrations that must have seemed to her endless. But the word 'rest' was relative. She still had her despatch-boxes, and Lord Salisbury went to Osborne to discuss 'William's shameful behaviour', in other words Germany's perverse view of a war between Greece and Turkey, and a rising on the Indian frontier.

Quite soon after she left for Balmoral. The ancient Mrs Symon was still improving but the following winter proved too much for her. The Queen was at Osborne when she heard the news, and wrote in her Journal:

> We had found her and her good amusing husband in the village when we first came to Balmoral in 1848 and we built them their new house and their shop. She was quite an institution; and everyone, high and low, used to go and see her.

Princess Alice agrees that it was an institution and everyone foregathered in the shop, but has stringent views on the Misses Symon who took over Merchant's: 'inveterate robbers.'

Princess Alice also gives another picture of the hushed, oppressively silent, gloomy Osborne that has been painted by so many. She mentions peals of laughter, shouts of merriment, sliding in the Marble Corridor, even sliding down banisters. It is refreshing to know that the house was not wrapped in silence, and that the Queen could sometimes take pleasure in the vitality of her grandchildren.

Yet the history of Balmoral during her last years suggests that she did not enjoy the contented old age that so many of her biographers have bestowed on her.

Alick Yorke had taken on Prince Henry's mantle as master of the revels and when he was in waiting at Balmoral there were entertainments of all kinds to amuse the Queen. But the impression given by the memoirs of courtiers at the end of the century is that their lives were infinitely dreary and inward-looking. It seems that a good row about the Munshi would have done them good, but he was generally on leave in India. There is evidence that the weather worsened in Scotland towards the end of the century. Either that or the failure of estate carpenters to fit new doors and windows at regular intervals, were the cause of jeremiads about draughts, cold rooms, and icy corridors. As the Queen's ladies and gentlemen did not enjoy going to Balmoral they strove not to be in waiting when the court was there. Therefore the Queen was being looked after by people who already had an inbuilt grudge against the discomfort and were not disposed to be sunny and cheer her up when, as often happened, she needed it. She still had her vitality and imperviousness to cold that allowed her to drive out for hours in gales and sleet; but she had bouts of depression, and her circumstances at Balmoral were very seldom what they ought to have been.

One of the most grave of her personal troubles was the failure of her eyesight. To someone with a strong sense of duty about dealing with her despatch-boxes and submissions from her Private Secretary it was a severe handicap. Before the death of Sir Henry Ponsonby she had begged him to write more clearly, and he had experimented with dense ink dried in an oven. But even this she could not see clearly. Professor Pagenstacher the celebrated oculist of Wiesbaden went down to Osborne to give the Queen an examination. He prescribed eye glasses which she hated wearing and they were not especially helpful. Electricity was installed in some of the rooms at Balmoral in 1898, but it was never as efficient as the system at Osborne and the Queen's eyesight being so poor, it almost certainly had to be supplemented with candles and lamps. More and more it became necessary for the Queen to listen rather than read. Reading aloud was the duty of the Maids of Honour in waiting and appointed lectrices; but confidential papers had to be read by Princess Beatrice who became, so it seemed to some, too remote.

Mrs Bernard Mallet, in waiting at Osborne as Extra Bedchamber Woman said the Princess deserved shaking for being 'dreadfully self-absorbed and unsympathetic'. This was almost certainly an ill-considered judgment of someone who spent a lifetime at her mother's beck and call. Even she sometimes had rebellious moments, but no one tried to take her place. No one could. But, to help, Princess Thora of Schleswig-Holstein was more and more at Court attending on her grandmother. She assisted with the confidential work although she had no official standing, and so, equally unofficially, did selected Bedchamber Women whom the Queen trusted and whom she treated as lady secretaries. Sir Henry Ponsonby had for a long time been both Privy Purse and Private Secretary but on his death the duties were again separated. The incumbents of these responsible offices disapproved of so much political responsibility falling to the Ladies. Very probably they were right. Less and less were gentlemen invited to the Queen's dinner.

As the Queen discovered, energy and a good digestion were not sufficient consolation for the loss of old friends. Of her intimate servants only one was left, Lizzie Stewart, who, as a girl, had helped build the first cairn at Balmoral in 1852 and had danced to the pipe music with her long hair hanging down. And, of the intimate friends amongst her ladies, only Lady Churchill was left to her. Lady Augusta, Mrs Bruce, Lady Ely, the Duchesses of Atholl and Roxburghe, all these devoted friends were dead. Their replacements were not the same and, in old age making a friend was more difficult for a Queen Regnant than for anyone. Lady Errol had been with her the longest but she had become fanatical about religion, and was a Calvinist, which made her tedious. She was always trying to hold prayer meetings in the Ladies' Sitting Room at Osborne, pressing tracts upon guests, and she tactlessly compared the statue of John Brown that stood close to the Gardener's Cottage at Balmoral to the idol set up by Nebuchadnezzar. But none of this stood between her and the Queen quite so much as her passion for the Mother's Union. Lady Errol was always urging people to join, including her sovereign. It became such a persecution that sometimes, when it was her turn to drive out with the Queen, she was replaced. The Queen dreaded the Mothers' Union.

On the outbreak of war with the Boers in October 1899 the Queen seemed infused with new vigour. Her daughter, granddaughter and her lady secretaries worked as never before sending telegrams and despatches connected with all phases of the war. The Queen went to Ballater barracks to say goodbye to her guard of Gordon Highlanders who had been ordered to the Cape. Only once did she almost sink under the pressure of work. She returned from a drive with two of her ladies. 'There was a perfect avalanche of telegrams and things to see to when I came home. I feel quite overpowered.' But she was not overpowered and became herself a powerhouse of encouragement in the bad times that followed. She refused to accept any idea of the possibility of defeat. To be closer to the centre of things in the bad December of 1899 she spent Christmas at Windsor. She even went to London and drove about for two days to show herself to the people. Instead of going to the south for her spring holiday she went to Ireland because the Irish regiments had fought bravely at the Cape. She was adamant, as she had been in the Crimean War, that there should be no public criticism by politicians of the general officers at the front.

But, halfway through 1900, she began to feel run down. Her digestion was not what it had been. Francatelli's marrow toast that she had enjoyed for so many years was too rich for her. Rich cakes began to defeat her. Even the white Dorking eggs invariably served for her breakfast could make her feel uncomfortable. Needless to say she did not give way easily. Roast beef and ices still had their attraction. She persevered, and met with small success. She felt unwell from the time she moved to Osborne in July. Sometimes rheumatic pain kept her awake at night so that she slept very late in the morning and it put her whole day out, and added vexation to a person of regular habits. Towards the end of the month both Princess Helena and Princess Beatrice were with her. They knew what she did not, that their brother, Prince Alfred, now the reigning Duke of Saxe-Coburg, was dying of cancer. They leaked small pieces of information to her so that the shock when it came should not be too great. She was very worried. On the 30th she heard that the King of Italy had been assassinated by an anarchist. On the day after Princess Beatrice broke it to her that Prince Alfred had died. The Prince of Wales and the Duke of Connaught and their sons went to the funeral at Coburg. At Osborne there was a memorial service at the same time. A warship, sent round to Osborne Bay, fired minute guns.

Lord James of Hereford had been Minister in Attendance when the Queen kept her birthday at Balmoral that May. He was again in Attendance there much later in the year. He noticed a great difference. The Queen appeared shrunken, and her eyes no longer sparkled. She could eat very little. In her Journal she recorded driving out to picnic near Birkhall – 'which for me consists of arrowroot and milk'. No more boiled potatoes in the heather.

Yet more terrible news poured in. Princess Thora's younger sister Princess Marie Louise, had married Prince Aribert of Anhalt who had treated her badly. Learning of this, and that the Princess was in Canada on her doctor's orders and very unhappy, the Queen briefly telegraphed the Governor General: 'Tell my granddaughter to come home to me. V.R.' Then Princess Thora's brother died of malaria and enteric fever in South Africa. Then the Queen heard her eldest daughter was incurably ill and could no longer even write her own letters.

The Queen bowed under this weight of sadness. 'Her face in repose', wrote one of her ladies, 'is terribly sad.' The Queen had always had a fondness for using the adjective 'poor', and at different times, for various reasons, some surprising people aroused her pity and were described as 'poor'. They included Napoleon III, the Sultan, the Pope, the explorer Stanley, the Mahdi, Dreyfus, even Gladstone. At this stage of her long life the Queen herself might have been described as 'poor'. But, though ill and bereaved, she continued doing her duty. There was no Munshi to help. He was on a whole year's leave and was not due back until November. Allegedly even the Queen's faithful highlanders began to take advantage of a deteriorating situation. In the memoirs of Sir Henry Ponsonby's son[*] it appears the custom of 'larders' or drinking after stalking at Balmoral, when the shot stags were put in the larders, had long got out of hand. So had the annual observance of the Prince Consort's birthday on 26 August. Everyone on the estate attended a memorial service dressed in their best and afterwards accepted refreshment. 'It was no uncommon sight to find a man in a top hat and a frockcoat fast asleep in the woods.' The Queen had always

---

[*] *Recollections of Three Reigns* by Sir Frederick Ponsonby, 1st Lord Sysonby, London, 1951.

been indulgent towards tipsy servants at dinner before a Ghillies' Ball, but towards the end they took advantage of her poor sight. In the letters of Mrs Bernard Mallet to her husband that autumn she noted: 'The footmen smell of whisky and are never prompt to answer the bell and although they do not speak rudely, they stare in such a supercilious way. As for the Queen's dinner it is more like a badly arranged picnic.' She was angry about the slackening in the kitchens: 'I could kill the cooks who take no pains whatever to prepare tempting little dishes.'· Apparently it was as bad at Windsor – 'The cooks should be drawn and quartered and the Clerks of the Kitchen strung from the Curfew Tower; their indifference makes me boil with rage.'

Even if Sir Frederick and Mrs Mallet were exaggerating out of a sense of indignation, they indicated a dismal situation. But, by this time, had the chefs prepared an elaborate meal the Queen could not have eaten it. Before she left Balmoral she visited the cottages on the estate to wish them a comfortable winter. In her Journal on the last day she wrote: 'Felt very poorly and wretched, as I have done all the last days.'

She managed a creditable amount of work at Windsor but continued to run down like an unwhipped top. On 14 December she and her family kept Mausoleum Day. It was the thirty-ninth time they had done so. On the 18th she and Princess Beatrice with her children went home to Osborne. She napped on the train, napped on arrival at the Pavilion. Her days had become dozes broken by meals she could not eat, and drives out were no pleasure. Her nights were spent restlessly and in nervous agitation because remedy after remedy to make her sleep had been tried and failed. But Princess Beatrice and her children were there, and Prince Arthur with his wife and family, and Princess Thora to write up her Journal, and Lizzie Stewart to look after her, and, as always, dear Lady Churchill, her constant companion for almost fifty years.

It was broken to the Queen on Christmas Day that Lady Churchill had died. This was the final blow. Her oldest friend's remains were taken to the mainland by royal yacht after a night of great storms.

The Queen just managed to dictate letters and her Journal to Princess Thora but the despatch-boxes were beyond her. She received Lord Roberts for whom a triumphal arch had been made by estate carpenters and gardeners and placed at the Prince of Wales Gate, and she invested him with the Garter and conferred on him an earldom. Physicians arrived from London. The Queen took her last drive. A bulletin was issued on 19 January to say she was at present confined to the house and not transacting any business. It told the world that she was dying.

Queen Victoria was a long time sinking and had a spectacular end; surrounded by almost her entire family and her Household; receiving

Communion and the last rites of the Church before lapsing into uncon-
sciousness. When she did die, everything was done for her by her maids
and her family and her Household and the men on the estate. She had
wished for a white funeral, and, dressed in white, she was placed in her
coffin by the German Emperor and the Duke of Connaught. The
dining-room was made into a *chapelle ardente*, hung with curtains and
draperies, lighted with tall candles, and decorated with palms and
flowers. She was guarded at first by men of the 60th Rifles and then by
the Queen's Company, Grenadier Guards. On her coffin, beneath a
crimson and ermine pall, were her crown and the Order of the Garter.

On 1 February the Queen made her final journey from Osborne; being
carried down to the gun-carriage by bluejackets from the Royal Yacht;
thence by the Sovereign's Entrance to Trinity Pier where her coffin was
placed aboard the *Alberta*. All the way from Cowes to Portsmouth
stretched a double line of battleships and cruisers. Each warship cracked
minute guns as the *Alberta* steamed past carrying the Queen from the
Isle of Wight for the last time.

Epilogue

By a decision of Edward VII Osborne House was given to the nation, the Main and Household Wing used as a Convalescent Home for Serving and Retired Officers, and the private royal apartments in the Pavilion were kept locked and shuttered. A small Altar furnished with a Cross and candlesticks of crystal glass and silver was placed between the bay window and the foot of the bed where Queen Victoria died, and from time to time members of the Royal Family would visit the room or attend special memorial services. In 1954 by command of Queen Elizabeth II, the Altar was removed and the rooms were opened to the public.

Balmoral passed by will to each succeeding monarch for his use during his lifetime, a legal nicety that obliged the unfortunate George VI to buy Balmoral with Sandringham from his brother Edward VIII for a sum of certainly not less than one million pounds sterling. The Castle has been altered since Queen Victoria died. Abergeldie has returned to the Gordons; parts of the original estate have been sold; some that were sold have been bought back in again. It has become once more what it was in the time of the Prince Consort, a home for the Royal Family for about two months each autumn.

Some sources consulted

Unpublished manuscript material

Memoirs

A memorandum of her recollections of Osborne House and Balmoral Castle dictated by H.R.H. Princess Alice Countess of Athlone on 28 July 1977.

Memorandum of life in the service of Queen Victoria with especial reference to the travelling staff, and work in the royal kitchens, made by H. V. Godfrey Esq., R.I.B.A. on 3 July, 1978.

Archive material, including deposited papers

Aberdeen University Library Archives; MS Collection, Letters of J. Thomas to W. Smith.

Census Enumerators' Returns: Scottish Record Office.

Derby Diocesan Archives: Sudbury Parish Burial Register.

Haddo House MSS: Plans and elevation of alterations and additions to Balmoral Castle, 1848 J. & W. S. (John & William Smith).

Metropolitan Police Office, New Scotland Yard: information relating to the A or Whitehall Division of the force from 1842 until 1869, and from 1869 until 1978, given on 4 July 1978.

The Blachford Papers deposited in the County Records Office, Newport, Isle of Wight.

The Griffiths Papers deposited in the Dyfed Archives, Haverfordwest (part published).

The Royal Commission on the Ancient and Historical Monuments of Scotland, Edinburgh: File – Balmoral Castle Estate, etc., Aberdeenshire; & Architects' File – William Smith.

Files on the exhibits at Osborne House and other MSS by Edward Sibbick.

Some sources consulted

Family papers and miscellaneous manuscripts

Family Papers of A. L. C. Bell Esq. – those not deposited at the National Library of Scotland.

Family Papers of Colin Brookes-Smith Esq.

Family Papers of Geoffrey Head Esq.

Diaries and Albums of photographs, guest lists, disposition of guests, train time tables, dinner lists, and other ceremonial details made and collected by Colonel Lord Edward William Pelham-Clinton, K.G.B., Master of the Household between 1895 and 1901, now in the possession of R. G. Farnham Esq.

Papers collected by Miss Helen Smith concerning her great grandfather, William Smith (part published).

William Smith's Family Bible.

Some notes concerning the Isle of Wight art of making sand pictures and a picture in that medium of Osborne House presented to Lord Edward Percy St Maur by the Prince of Wales and Prince Alfred in 1854, made by the late Oliver Thynne Esq., on 1 June 1978.

Published works

A Form of Thanksgiving and Prayer to ALMIGHTY GOD, Upon the Completion of Fifty Years of Her Majesty's Reign (London, 1887).
A Form of Prayer with Thanksgiving to ALMIGHTY GOD, to be used in all Churches and Chapels in England and Wales, and in the Town of Berwick-upon-Tweed upon Sunday the Twentieth Day of June 1897 (London, 1897).
Adair, Innes, *Balmoral, the Hall of Memories* (Edinburgh, 1901).
Alice, H.R.H. Princess, Countess of Athlone, *For My Grandchildren* (London, 1966).
Ames, Winslow, *Prince Albert and Victorian Taste* (London, 1967).
Anglesey, the Marquess of, *One-Leg, The Life and Letters of Henry William Paget, First Marquess of Anglesey, K. G., 1769–1854* (London, 1961).
Argyll, the Duke of, *V.R.I: Her Life and Empire* (London, 1902).
Argyll, the Duke of, *Autobiography and Memoirs*, 2 vols (London, 1906).
Aronson, Theo, *The Fall of the Third Napoleon* (London, 1970).
Aronson, Theo, *Grandmama of Europe* (London, 1974).
Baillie, Dean and Bolitho, Hector (eds), *Letters of Lady Augusta Stanley* (London, 1927).
Baillie, Dean and Bolitho, Hector (eds), *Later Letters of Lady Augusta Stanley* (London, 1929).
Baily, Leslie, *The Gilbert & Sullivan Book* (London, 1952).
Ball, T. Frederick, *Queen Victoria, Scenes and Incidents of Her Life and Reign* (London, 1886–7).
Balmoral Castle, Guide to the Policies (Balmoral, 1975).
Barnes, Major R. Money, *Military Uniforms of Britain and the Empire* (London, 1960).
Battiscombe, Georgina, *Queen Alexandra* (London, 1969).
Bauer, Ludwig (trans. Paul, Eden & Cedar), *Leopold the Unloved* (London, 1934).
Bennett, Daphne, *Vicky, Princess Royal of England and German Empress* (New York, 1971).

Benson, A. C. & Esher, Viscount (eds), *The Letters of Queen Victoria, A Selection from Her Majesty's Correspondence, First Series, 1837–61*, 3 vols (London, 1907).

Benson, E. F., *Queen Victoria* (London, 1935).

Benson, E. F., *The Kaiser and English Relations* (London, 1936).

Benson, E. F., *Daughters of Queen Victoria* (London, 1939).

Bishop, Roy, *Paintings of the Royal Collection: an account of His Majesty's pictures at Windsor Castle, Buckingham Palace, Hampton Court, Holyroodhouse and Balmoral* (London, 1937).

Blake, Robert (Lord Blake), *Disraeli* (London, 1966).

Bolitho, Hector, *Albert the Good* (London, 1932).

Bolitho, Hector, *The Prince Consort and His Brother* (London, 1933).

Bolitho, Hector, *Royal Progress* (London, 1937).

Bolitho, Hector, *The Reign of Queen Victoria* (London, 1949).

Bolitho, Hector, *Albert, Prince Consort* (London, 1964).

Boyle, Andrew, *The Riddle of Erskine Childers* (London, 1977).

Brook-Shepherd, Gordon, *Uncle of Europe* (London, 1975).

Brown, Ivor, *Balmoral* (London, 1955).

Buckle, G. E. (ed.), *The Letters of Queen Victoria, A Selection from Her Majesty's Correspondence, Second Series, 1862–85*, 3 vols (London, 1926).

Buckle, G. E. (ed.), *The Letters of Queen Victoria, A Selection from Her Majesty's Correspondence, Third Series, 1866–1901*, 3 vols (London, 1930).

Burton, Elizabeth, *The Early Victorians at Home* (London, 1972).

Carr-Gomm, F. C., *Handbook of the Administrations of Great Britain, 1801–1900*.

Cecil, (Lord) David, *Melbourne* (London, 1955).

Carlton, John, *Osborne House* (a Department of the Environment Guide, London, 1974).

Colvin, H. M., *Biographical Dictionary of British Architects, 1600–1840* (London, 1978).

Cook, C. Kinloch, *A Memoir of H.R.H. Pcss Mary Adelaide, Duchess of Teck*, 2 vols (London, 1900).

Cullen, Tom, *The Empress Brown* (London, 1969).

Davies, Hunter, *George Stephenson* (London, 1975).

Diamond Jubilee . . . Sons of England Service to be held in continuous succession through the British Colonies around the World (London, 1897).

Donaldson, Frances, *Edward VIII* (London, 1974).

Duff, David, *The Shy Princess* (London, 1958).

Duff, David, *Hessian Tapestry* (London, 1967).

Duff, David, *Victoria in the Highlands* (London, 1968).

Duff, David, *Victoria Travels* (London, 1970).

Duff, David, *Albert & Victoria* (London, 1972).

Dyson, Hope and Tennyson, Charles (eds), *'Dear and Honoured Lady'* (London, 1969).

Epton, Nina, *Victoria and her Daughters* (London, 1971).

Ernest II, Duke of Saxe-Coburg, *Memoirs*, 4 vols (Eng. trans. London, 1888).

Ernle, Lord, *Whippingham to Westminster* (London, 1938).

Fisher, Helen, *The Balmoral Story* (Aberdeen, 1953).

Fletcher, Professor Banister and Fletcher, Banister F.: *A History of Architecture on the Comparative Method* (5th edn, London, 1905).

Florance, Arnold, *Queen Victoria at Osborne* (Newport, 1977).

Fulford, Roger, *Royal Dukes* (London, 1933).

Some sources consulted

Fulford, Roger, *The Prince Consort* (London, 1949).

Fulford, Roger, *Hanover to Windsor* (London, 1960).

Fulford, Roger (ed.), *The Greville Memoirs* (London, 1963).

Fulford, Roger (ed.), *Dearest Child, Private Correspondence of Queen Victoria and the Princess Royal, 1858–1861* (London, 1964).

Fulford, Roger (ed.), *Dearest Mama, Letters between Queen Victoria and the Crown Princess of Prussia, 1861–1864* (London, 1968).

Fulford, Roger (ed.), *Your Dear Letter, Private Correspondence of Queen Victoria and the Crown Princess of Prussia, 1864–1871* (London, 1971).

Fulford, Roger (ed.), *Darling Child, Private Correspondence of Queen Victoria and the Crown Princess of Prussia, 1871–1878* (London, 1976).

Gernsheim, Alison and Helmut, *Queen Victoria* (London, 1959).

Gernsheim, Alison and Helmut, *Edward VII and Queen Alexandra* (London, 1962).

Gore, John, *King George V; A Personal Memoir* (London, 1941).

Gore, John (sel. and re-ed.), *Creevey* (London, 1948).

Grey, Lieut-General the Hon. C., *The Early Years of His Royal Highness The Prince Consort, compiled, under the Direction of Her Majesty the Queen* (London, 1867).

Grun, Bernard, *The Timetables of History* (New York, 1975).

Guedalla, Philip, *The Queen and Mr. Gladstone*, 2 vols (London, 1933).

Hardwick, Mollie, *Mrs Dizzy, the Life of Mary Anne Disraeli, Viscountess Beaconsfield* (London, 1972).

Hammond, Reginald J. W. (ed.), *The Isle of Wight. Red Guide* (London, 1974).

Harrison, Michael, *Clarence* (London, 1972).

Hibbert, Christopher, *The Destruction of Lord Raglan* (London, 1961).

Hibbert, Christopher, *The Court at Windsor, A Domestic History* (London, 1964).

Hibbert, Christopher, *George IV, Prince of Wales 1762–1811* (London, 1972).

Hibbert, Christopher, *Edward VII* (London, 1976).

Hobhouse, Hermione, *Thomas Cubitt, Master-Builder* (London, 1971).

Holroyd, Michael, *Lytton Strachey; a Critical Biography*, 2 vols (London, 1967–8).

Hough, Richard, *Louis & Victoria* (London, 1974).

Jagow, Dr Kurt (ed.) (trans. E. T. S. Dugdale), *Letters of the Prince Consort, 1831–1861* (London, 1938).

Jerrold, C., *The Married Life of Queen Victoria* (London, 1913).

Kennedy, A. L. (ed.), *'My dear Duchess' Social and Political Letters to the Duchess of Manchester, 1858–1869* (London, 1956).

Knight, Alfred E., *Victoria, Her Life and Reign* (London, 1901).

Lee, Sir Sidney, *Queen Victoria* (London, 1902).

Lee, Sir Sidney, *King Edward VII, A Biography*, 2 vols (London, 1925, 1927).

Lindsay, Patricia, *Recollections of a Royal Parish* (London, 1902).

Longford, Elizabeth (Countess of Longford), *Victoria R.I.* (London, 1964).

Lutyens, Mary (ed.), *Lady Lytton's Court Diary* (London, 1961).

Macaulay, James, *Gothic Revival, 1748–1845* (London, 1973).

Macleay, Kenneth, *Highlanders of Scotland, Portraits illustrative of the Principal Clans and Followings, and Retainers of the Royal Household at Balmoral in the Reign of Her Majesty Queen Victoria*, 2 vols (London, 1868).

McConnochie, Alex. Inkson, *Queen Victoria's Highland Home and Vicinity* (Aberdeen, 1897).

McLintock, Mary, *The Queen Thanks Sir Howard* (London, 1945).

Magnus, Sir Philip, *Gladstone, A Biography* (London, 1963).

Magnus, Sir Philip, *King Edward the Seventh* (London, 1964).

Mallet, (Sir) Victor (ed.), *Life with Queen Victoria* (London, 1968).

Marie, Queen of Roumania, *The Story of My Life*, 2 vols (London, 1934).

Marie Louise, H.H. Princess, *My Memories of Six Reigns* (1956).

Martin, Sir Theodore, *Life of the Prince Consort*, 5 vols (London, 1875–80).

Martin, Sir Theodore, *Queen Victoria as I Knew Her* (London, 1908).

Matson, John, *Dear Osborne* (London, 1978).

Maunsell, G. W., *The Fisherman's Vade Mecum* (London, 1944).

Maurois, André (trans. Hamish Miles), *Disraeli, A Picture of the Victorian Age* (London, 1927).

Middlemas, Keith, *The Life and Times of Edward VII* (London, 1972).

Monypenny, W. F. and Buckle, G. E., *The Life of Benjamin Disraeli, Earl of Beaconsfield*, 6 vols (London, 1910–20).

Moorehead, Alan, *The White Nile* (London, 1960).

Moorehead, Alan, *The Blue Nile* (London, 1962).

Morley, John, *Life of W. E. Gladstone*, 3 vols (London, 1903).

Morton, John Chalmers, *The Prince Consort's Farms* (London, 1863).

Murray's Handbook for Scotland of 1894 (Newton Abbot, Devon, 1971).

Nicolson, Sir Harold, *King George V; His Life and Reign* (London, 1952).

One of Her Majesty's Servants, *The Private Life of Queen Victoria* (London, 1901).

Official Programme of Her Majesty Queen Victoria's Diamond Jubilee Procession, Tuesday June 22nd, 1897 (London, 1897).

Palmer, A. W., *A Dictionary of Modern History, 1789–1945* (London, 1962).

Peel, G., *The Private Letters of Sir Robert Peel* (London, 1920).

Philip, William W., *Crathie Churches and Royal Bazaar at Balmoral, September 1894* (Aberdeen, 1896).

Ponsonby, Arthur (1st Lord Ponsonby of Shulbrede), *Henry Ponsonby, Queen Victoria's Private Secretary, His Life from his Letters* (London, 1942).

Ponsonby, Sir Frederick (1st Lord Sysonby) (ed.), *Letters of the Empress Frederick* (London, 1929).

Ponsonby, Sir Frederick, *Sidelights on Queen Victoria* (London, 1930).

Ponsonby, Sir Frederick, *Recollections of Three Reigns* (London, 1951).

Pope-Hennessey, James, *Queen Mary* (London, 1959).

Pope-Hennessey, James (ed.), *Queen Victoria at Windsor and Balmoral, Letters from her Grand-daughter, Princess Victoria of Prussia, June 1889* (London, 1959).

Pound, Reginald, *Albert, a Biography of the Prince Consort* (London, 1973).

Rae, Lettice Milne, *The Story of the Gibbs'* (Edinburgh, 1961, privately printed).

St Aubyn, Giles, *The Royal George* (London, 1963).

St John, Charles, *Wild Sports and Natural History of the Highlands* (London and Edinburgh, 1919).

Sara, M. E., *The Life and Times of H.R.H. Princess Beatrice* (London, 1945).

Sell, The Rev. Dr (ed.), *Alice Grand Duchess of Hesse, Princess of Great Britain and Ireland; Biographical Sketch and Letters* (London, 1884).

Sitwell, Dame Edith, *Victoria of England* (London, 1936).

Stanley, Lady Eleanor (ed. Mrs Steuart Erskine), *20 Years at Court* (London, 1916).

Steegman, John, *Victorian Taste* (London, 1970).

Stirton, the Rev. John, *Balmoral in Former Times: an Historical Sketch* (Forfar, 1921).

Strachey, Lytton, *Queen Victoria* (London, 1921).

Stuart, Dorothy Margaret, *The Mother of Victoria* (London, 1941).

Sutherland Gower (Sutherland-Leveson-Gower), Lord Ronald, *My Reminiscences* (London, 1895).

Sutherland Gower, Lord Ronald, *Old Diaries, 1881–1901* (London, 1902).

Taylor, Edmond, *The Fossil Monarchies* (London, 1963).

Thomson, David, *England in the Nineteenth Century '1815–1914'* (London, 1950).

Tisdall, E. E. P., *Queen Victoria's John Brown* (London, 1938).

Tisdall, E. E. P., *Queen Victoria's Private Life* (London, 1961).

Turnbull, Patrick, *Eugénie of the French* (London, 1974).

Victoria, H.M. Queen (ed. Helps, Sir Arthur), *Leaves from the Journal of Our Life in the Highlands from 1848 to 1861* (London, 1868).

Victoria, H.M. Queen (ed. Murray MacGregor, Miss Amelia Georgiana), *More Leaves from the Journal of a Life in the Highlands, from 1862 to 1882* (London, 1884).

Watson, Vera, *A Queen at Home* (London, 1952).

Wheeler-Bennett, Sir John, *King George VI: His Life and Reign* (London, 1958).

Windsor, H.R.H. The Duke of, *A King's Story* (London, 1951).

William II, Ex-German Emperor, *My Early Life* (London, 1926).

Woodham-Smith, Cecil, *Florence Nightingale, 1820–1910* (London, 1951).

Woodham-Smith, Cecil, *The Reason Why* (London, 1953).

Woodham-Smith, Cecil, *Queen Victoria: Her Life and Times* (London, 1972).

Wright, Lawrence, *Clean and Decent* (London, 1960).

Wyndham, Mrs Hugh, *Correspondence of Sarah Spencer, Lady Lyttelton 1787–1870* (London, 1912).

Wyness, Fenton, *Royal Valley* (Aberdeen, n.d., c. 1950s).

Zetland, the Marquis of (ed.), *The Letters of Disraeli to Lady Bradford and Lady Chesterfield*, 2 vols (London, 1929).

Standard reference books

Almanach de Gotha
Burke's Landed Gentry
Debrett's Peerage, Baronetage, Knightage, & Companionage
Dictionary of National Biography
Encyclopaedia Britannica
Kelly's Directory of the Isle of Wight, 1897–
The Imperial Calendar
The Royal Kalendar
The Scottish Annual and Braemar Gathering Book
Whitaker's Almanack

Newspapers and periodicals

Aberdeen Bon-Accord and Northern Echo
Aberdeen Journal
Aberdeen Press and Journal
Country Life
Hampshire Chronicle
Hampshire Telegraph

Leopard Magazine
Morning Chronicle
Morning Post
Observer Magazine
Portsmouth Evening News
Scots Magazine
Scotsman
Stamp Collector's Weekly
The *Black and White Magazine*
The *Builder*
The *Examiner*
The *Gardeners' Chronicle*
The *Illustrated London News*
The *Isle of Wight County Press*
The *Isle of Wight Observer*
The *Isle of Wight Times*
The *Scottish Annual, and Book of the Braemar Gathering*
The *Times*
The *Queen's Homes* a collection of articles by Charles Eyre Pascoe with draw-
    ings done by Victor Prout engraved by Swain from an unidentified and
    undated volume of periodicals.
Town & Country
Windsor and Eton Express

Index

Notes: Sovereigns and the members of their families appear under their first names. Non-royal members of the British and continental nobility appear under their titles. The abbreviations V. and A. stand for Queen Victoria and Prince Albert; O. for Osborne and B. for Balmoral. Foreign names have largely been anglicized.

Abercorn, James, 2nd Marquis (afterwards 1st Marquis of Hamilton and 1st Duke of Abercorn), 32, 33
Aberdeen, George Hamilton, 4th Earl of, 34, 35, 41, 69, 72, 86, 150
Aberdeen Journal, 42, 71–2
Abergeldie, 45, 60, 61, 71, 91, 102, 123, 127, 151, 160, 167
Adelaide, Queen (Consort of William IV), 24, 85
Albert, Duke of Saxe, Prince of Saxe-Coburg-Gotha (afterwards the Prince Consort): amiability, 65; appearance (in 1843), 1, (in 1857), 90–1; created Prince Consort, 89; desolation at Anson's death, 57, and at Cart's, 96; dislike of 'monotony of place', 10; emotional scenes with V., 40, 70, 88, 97, 105; enjoyment of coursing, 25; enjoyment of other sports, 43, 51, 52, 73, 98; first separation from V., 9; his *gravitas*, 48, 91; illnesses, 83, 112–13; improvements at B., 44, 48, 54, 66, 67, 71–3, 77–86, 91–3; improvements at O., 12, 15, 16, 17–22, 30, 40; innovations introduced by him, 85; 'overfond of business', 105; pessimism, 30; realism, 41; talents as an organizer, 7, 8; tirelessness, 39–40; unpopularity, 19, 21, 23, 66, 74, 85; (references to him after his death, 114, 115, 116, 117, 118, 119, 120, 121, 122, 123, 124, 126, 128, 130, 132, 138, 141, 142, 143, 150, 152, 154, 163, 177, 182, 195)
Albert, Prince, of York (afterwards Duke of York then George VI), 188
Alberta (royal yacht), 166, 197
Albert Edward, Prince of Wales (afterwards Edward VII), 28, 32, 41, 49, 50, 60, 68, 90, 92, 95, 96, 102, 108–9, 110, 111, 118, 120, 121, 123, 124, 127, 130, 135, 156, 157, 158, 159, 160, 161, 162, 163, 164, 168, 174, 177, 180
Alexander Albert, Prince, of Battenberg (afterwards 1st Marquis of Carisbrooke), 172
Alexandra, Princess, of Denmark (afterwards Princess of Wales and Queen Consort of Edward VII), 111, 121, 124, 125, 127, 130, 158
Alexandra, Tsarista of All the Russias (formerly Princess Alix of Hesse and by Rhine), 188
Alfred, Prince, Duke of Edinburgh (afterwards sovereign Duke of Saxe-Coburg-Gotha), 9, 49, 60, 81 and n., 90, 92, 95, 96–9, 102, 110, 114, 118–19, 124, 161, 194–5
Alice, Princess (afterwards Princess Louis of Hesse-Darmstadt and Grand Duchess of Hesse and by Rhine), 30, 90, 92, 106, 109, 110, 114, 118–19, 120, 125, 127, 139, 160, 167
Alice Mary Victoria, Princess, of Albany (afterwards Princess Alice Countess of Athlone), 163, 181, 185, 188, 192
Alt-na-Giuthasach, 44, 56, 123, 188
Angeli, Joachim von, 182
Anglesea, Henry William, Field Marshal 1st Marquis of, 74

Anson, George Edward, 12, 15, 25, 33 and n., 45, 48, 55, 56, 58, 59
Argyll, Elizabeth Georgiana, Duchess of, 32
Argyll, George Douglas, 8th Duke of, 32, 190
Ardverikie House, 32–4
Arthur, Prince, Duke of Connaught, 50, 61, 81 and n., 90, 102, 103–4, 110, 114, 122, 124, 140, 143, 151, 155, 158, 161, 164, 181, 195, 196, 197
Atholl, Anne, Duchess of, 132, 140, 193
Atholl, George Augustus Frederick John, 6th Duke of, 132

Ballochbuie, forest of, 43, 45, 167
Balmoral Castle (old), 34, 35, 36, 40, 41, 53, 56, 62, 64, 66, 84
Balmoral Castle (new), 66, 67, 71–3, 77–86, 91, 94, 102, 103, 107, 111, 118–19, 127, 128, 129, 130, 137, 140, 142, 143, 145, 149–52, 154, 157, 159, 165–6, 170, 173, 182, 184, 188–9, 192–3, 195, 196
Balmoral Estate, 34, 39, 45, 53, 56, 60, 62–4, 66, 91–2, 98, 103, 122, 123, 146, 157, 187–9, 192
Baly, Dr William, 108, 109
Beaconsfield, Benjamin, Earl of, 3, 64, 125, 147–50, 151, 152, 153, 165–6, 167, 190
Beaconsfield, Mary Anne, Viscountess, 38, 147, 149, 150, 152, 165
Beatrice, Princess (afterwards Princess Henry of Battenberg), 89, 90, 127, 151, 155, 161, 163–5, 166, 167, 168, 169, 170, 171–2, 173, 174, 180, 184, 186–7, 193, 194, 196
Beattie, James, 68, 83
Becker, Dr (A.'s librarian), 64, 98, 116, 120
Begg, John, 98
Biddulph, Sir Thomas, 138, 142
Birkhall, 45, 53, 61, 88, 91, 118, 123, 195
Bismarck, Otto von (afterwards Count, then Prince), 139, 157
Blachford, Lady Isabella, 8, 11, 12, 16, 36
Blair, Willie (royal fiddler), 72, 92
Blore, Edward, 11, 13, 36
Blücher, Countess, 99
Bowater, Sir Edward, 112, 113, 114
Bray (A.'s garderobier), 98
Bradford, Selina, Countess of, 165
Bridport, Alexander Nelson, 3rd Baron

and 1st Viscount, and Duke of Brontë, 149
Brighton Pavilion, 3, 4, 5, 11, 12, 24, 25, 180
Brookes, William, 77–8
Brown, Dr (of Windsor), 112
Brown, John, 53, 104, 107, 122, 127, 128, 130, 131–6, 140, 141, 148, 161, 162, 164, 165, 166, 167, 168, 169, 173, 175, 177, 190, 194
Bruce, Lady Augusta, *see* Stanley, Lady Augusta
Bruce, Colonel (later General) the Hon. Robert, 102, 120
Bruce, the Hon. Mrs Robert, 193
Buckingham Palace, 3, 24, 36, 38, 129–30, 141
Bunsen, the Chevalier, 49
Byron, George Gordon, 6th Baron, 44

Cardigan, Adeline, Countess of, 165
Cardigan, James Thomas, 7th Earl of, 165
Caroline, Duchess of Saxe-Gotha-Altenburg (A.'s step-grandmother), 37
Cart (A.'s confidential valet), 9, 96, 97
Channel Islands, the, 28
Charles, Prince, of Leiningen (V.'s half-brother), 32, 61, 88
Charles XV, King of Sweden and Norway, the Goths and the Wends, 111
Charles Edward, Prince, 2nd Duke of Albany (afterwards sovereign Duke of Saxe-Coburg-Gotha), 163
Charlotte, Queen (Consort of George III), 85
Charlotte, Princess, of Prussia (afterwards Duchess of Saxe-Meiningen), 124, 158
Cherbourg, 91
Chesterfield, Anne, Countess of, 165, 166
Christian, Prince, of Schleswig-Holstein, 138, 142, 151, 158, 164, 186
Christian Victor, Prince, of Schleswig-Holstein, 142, 195
Churchill, Jane, Lady, 74–5, 92, 107, 142, 149, 155, 161, 193, 196
Clarendon, George William Frederick, 4th Earl of, 61, 72–3, 91, 106, 111, 116, 130, 137, 156, 174
Claremont House, 3, 18, 37, 38, 163 and n.
Claridge's, 108
Clark, Sir James, 10, 34, 35, 36, 60.

70, 89, 101, 109, 112, 113, 114, 156, 161
Clark, John, 34
Clifden, Nellie, 112, 123
Coburg, 101, 107, 108, 123, 124, 130, 195
Cole, Henry, 53
Cook, Thomas, 77
Corbauld, E. H., 116
Cornwall, 28
Country Press, The, 180
Cowell, Major (later Major-General Sir) John, 102, 138
Craig Gowan, 62
Cramond, 106
Crystal Palace, the, 59
Cubitt, Thomas, 11, 13–15, 16, 20, 21, 22, 23, 28, 29–30, 36, 37, 39, 40, 45, 46, 60, 65, 66, 68, 75, 76, 78, 182

d'Albertançon, François, 39, 79, 81
Dantzig Shiel, 167
Davidson, the Very Reverend, later the Right and then the Most Reverend Randall, successively Dean of Windsor, Bishop of Rochester, Bishop of Winchester, and Archbishop of Canterbury, 133, 154, 168, 171
Derby, Edward Geoffrey, 14th Earl of, 62, 69, 139, 140–1, 145, 147
Disraeli, Benjamin, *see* Beaconsfield, Benjamin, Earl of
Disrael, Mary Anne, *see* Beaconsfield, Mary Anne, Viscountess
Disruption, the (of 1843), 43, 68
Dittweiler, Emilie, 161, 164
Dyce, William, 31
Drunkie House (Invertrossachs), 155

Eastlake, Charles, 9
Edward, Duke of Kent and Strathearn (V.'s father), 1
Edward, Prince, of York (afterwards, Prince of Wales, Edward VIII, and Duke of Windsor), 188
Elisabeth, Empress of Austria, Queen of Hungary, 108
Elizabeth, Queen, the Queen Mother, 86
Ellenborough, Edward, 1st Earl of, 129, 130
Ellenborough, Jane, Countess of, 129
Elphinstone, Major (later Major-General Sir) Howard, V.C., 102–4, 114, 121, 122, 124, 125, 130, 143, 144, 155, 158, 181 and n.
Ely, Jane, Marchioness of, 165, 193

Ernest I, Duke of Saxe-Saalfeld-Gotha, from 1826 Duke of Saxe-Coburg-Gotha (A.'s father), 8, 9
Ernest II, Duke of Saxe-Coburg-Gotha (A.'s brother), 10, 23, 37, 83, 114, 121, 158
Ernest, Prince, of Leiningen (V.'s half-nephew), 114
Erroll, Eliza Amelia, Countess of, 194
Esterházy de Galántha, Prince Paul, 101
Eugénie, Empress of the French, 76, 90, 108, 141, 157, 166, 167

Fairy (tender in the Royal Yacht Squadron), 32, 44
Farquharsons of Inverey, 43, 134, 167
Feodore, Princess, of Leiningen (afterwards of Hohenlohe-Langenburg) (V.'s half-sister), 114, 121
Fitzclarence, Lord Adolphus, 4, 32, 40, 44
Ferdinand Maximilian, Archduke (afterwards Emperor Maximilian of Mexico), *see* Maximilian, Emperor
Francis, Prince Teck (afterwards Duke of Teck), 138, 151–2, 172
Francis Joseph, Emperor of Austria, King of Hungary, 44, 141
Frederick William IV, King of Prussia, 38, 87, 109
Frederick William, Prince, of Prussia (afterwards, Crown Prince, then Frederick III, King of Prussia and German Emperor), 82, 83, 94, 96, 109, 111, 114, 124, 139, 158, 169, 173, 174
Frederick William Louis, Prince, of Hesse-Darmstadt, *see* Louis, Prince, of Hesse-Darmstadt
Frogmore Mausoleum, 111, 115, 120, 124

Gelder Shiel, 138–9, 152
George, Field Marshal the Duke of Cambridge, 91, 136, 139, 140–1, 145, 151, 188
George, Prince, of Wales (afterwards Duke of York, Duke of York and Cornwall, Prince of Wales, and King George V), 179 n., 182, 188, 195
Gibson, John, 69
Giles, James, 35, 36, 41, 68, 83
Gladstone, William Ewart, 127, 128, 134, 153, 154, 155, 157, 158, 159, 160, 161–2, 164, 165, 171, 195
Glassalt Shiel, 150–1, 188
Goode, Thomas, 92
Gordon, Lady Alicia, 34, 35

Gordon, General Charles George, 170
Gordon, John, 55
Gordon, Sir Robert, 34 and n., 35, 36, 39, 42, 62, 66
Grant, John, 39, 51, 81, 107, 140, 167
Grant, Mrs John, 152
Granville, Granville George, 2nd Earl of, 81, 155, 161
Great Exhibition (1851), 53, 59, 60
Greville, Charles, 21, 25, 56, 115, 146, 166
Grey, Colonel (later General) the Hon. Sir Charles, 58, 64, 91, 103, 107, 116, 117, 122, 138, 140, 143–5, 148, 154, 156
Grüner, Mlle., 30
Gruner, Ludwig, 18, 23, 40, 48, 69, 88, 101, 115

Hamilton, Lord Claud, 33
Hamilton, Lord George, 177
Hardy, Mr Gathorne (afterwards Sir Gathorne Gathorne-Hardy, then 1st Viscount and 1st Earl of Cranbrook), 143, 144
Head, William, 142
Helena, Princess (afterwards Princess Christian of Schleswig-Holstein), 24, 90, 138, 142, 151, 164, 194
Helena Victoria, 'Thora', Princess, of Schleswig-Holstein, 193, 195, 196
Helps, (later Sir) Arthur, 115, 116, 131, 132, 168
Henry, Prince, of Battenberg, 168, 170, 171, 172, 173, 175, 180, 184, 185, 186, 187, 192
Henry, Prince, of Prussia, 158
Highlanders of Scotland, Portraits of the principal Clans and followings, and the Retainers of the Royal Household at Balmoral, 132
Hildyard, Miss, 30, 32, 41, 57, 62, 96, 132 n.
Hitchcock, Professor Henry Russell, 13
Hohenlohe-Langenburg, Feodore, Princess of, *see* Feodore, Princess of Leiningen (afterwards of Hohenlohe-Langenburg)
Holland, Queen, of, *see* Sophia Frederica
Holyrood House, 3, 102, 106
Hooker, Sir William, 49
Humboldt, Frederick, Baron von, 105

Idylls of the King, 109
Illustrated London News, 40
Isabella, the Lady of the Island, 6
Isle of Wight Observer, 142

James of Hereford, Lord, 195
Jane Eyre, 95
Jenner, Dr (later Sir) William, 109, 112–13, 114, 130, 137, 141, 144, 153, 156, 158, 159, 160, 161
John Brown's Legs or Leaves from a Journal in the Lowlands, 168
Jungbluth, C. F., 155

Kanné, J. J., 155, 161
Karim, Abdul, Hafiz (Munshi and Indian Secretary to V.), 177, 178, 179, 182–3, 195
Karim, Mrs, 179
Keats, John, 34
King (A.'s garderobier), 98
Kipling, Lockwood, 181
Kipling, Rudyard, 181
Knollys, General Sir William (afterwards 1st Viscount Knollys of Caversham), 123, 135
Kohler (A.'s valet), 97
Königgrätz, battle of, 139

Lablache, Luigi, 30
Landseer, Sir Edwin, 33, 41, 52, 62, 135
Lausanne, Gazette de, 131
Leaves from the Journal of our Life in the Highlands, 4, 72, 80, 82, 98, 107, 131, 148
Leitch, W. L., 35
Leopold of Saxe-Saalfeld-Coburg, King of the Belgians (from 1831) 2, 8, 9, 12, 39, 40, 60, 61, 63, 88, 89, 90, 91, 110, 111, 114–15, 117, 122, 124, 125, 137, 138
Leopold II, King of the Belgians, 137, 190
Leopold, Prince, Duke of Albany, 70, 90, 112, 113, 114, 124, 151, 161, 163, 165, 168
Leopold, Prince, of Battenberg (afterwards Lord Leopold Mountbatten), 187 and n.
Lincoln, Henry Pelham, Earl of (afterwards 5th Duke of Newcastle), 11, 12
Lindsay, Mrs (formerly Miss Robertson), 43
Lister, Mr (later Sir) Joseph (afterwards 1st Baron Lister), 160
Loch-na-Gar, 44, 53, 60, 78, 127
Löhlein, Rudolf, 9, 56, 98, 113, 122, 128, 135, 161, 168, 187
Longley, the Most Reverend Charles, Archbishop of York (afterwards translated to Canterbury), 121

Index

Lorne, John Douglas Sutherland, Marquis of (afterwards 9th Duke of Argyll), 32, 157–8, 169

Louis, Prince, of Battenberg (afterwards Admiral of the Fleet 1st Marquis of Milford Haven), 168, 169

Louis, Prince, of Hesse-Darmstadt (afterwards Louis IV, Grand Duke of Hesse and by Rhine), 106, 111, 124, 168, 169

Louis Philippe, King of the French, 37, 38

Louise, Princess, (afterwards Marchioness of Lorne, then Duchess of Argyll), 90, 119, 126, 140, 142, 151, 154, 155, 157–8, 169, 185

Louise, Queen of the Belgians, 3, 24, 25, 60

Lyell, Sir Charles, 71

Lyttelton, Sarah, Dowager Lady, 24–30, 37, 38, 39, 49, 57, 58, 60, 156

Mcdonald and Leslie, Messrs, 67

Macdonald, Anne (from Inverness-shire), 97

Macdonald, Annie (from Balmoral), 122, 161, 164, 165, 190, 191

Macdonald, John, 33, 34, 50, 51, 53, 56, 70, 81, 86, 97–8, 106 and n., 176

Macdonald, Archie, 106, 113

MacGregor, Miss Murray, see Murray MacGregor, Miss

Mackay (piper), 3, 50, 63, 74

Mackenzie, Dr (afterwards Sir) Morel, 173, 174

McLeod, the Reverend Dr Norman, 76, 119, 125, 143, 164

Magnus, George Eugene, 29

Mallet, Mrs Bernard, 179, 193, 196

Malmesbury, James Howard, 3rd Earl of, 61

Marconi, Guglielmo, 128

Marie, Duchess of Saxe-Coburg-Gotha (A.'s step-mother), 10, 30, 37, 61, 88, 107

Marie, Princess, of Edinburgh and Saxe-Coburg-Gotha (afterwards Queen of Roumania), 81

Marie Louise, Princess, of Schleswig-Holstein (afterwards Princess Aribert of Anhalt), 195

Marlborough House, 118, 123

Marlborough, John Winston, 7th Duke of, 145

Marochetti, Baron Carlo, 115, 120, 128

Marshall, Dr, 160

Martin, (later Sir) Theodore, 116, 132

Mary, Princess, Duchess of Gloucester, 89

Mary ('May'), Queen (Consort of George V), see Victoria Mary, Princess, of Teck

Mary Adelaide, Princess, of Cambridge (afterwards Princess Teck, then Duchess of Teck), 138, 151–2

Maurice Victor Donald, Prince, of Battenberg, 184, 187 and n.

Mausoleum Day, 124, 125, 137, 163, 196

Maximilian, Emperor, of Mexico, 89, 141

May, Princess, of Teck, see Victoria Mary, Princess, of Teck

Mayet, Gustav, 97, 113, 128, 161

Melbourne, William, 2nd Viscount, 2, 4, 23, 24, 73, 149

Mensdorff-Pouilly, Count, 60

Meyer, Dr (A.'s librarian), 30

Middleton, the Reverend John, 94

Moltke, Helmuth, Count von, Colonel (afterwards Field Marshal and Chief of General Staff), 82, 83

More Leaves from the Journal of a Life in the Highlands, 132, 135, 168, 177

Morning Post, 10

Muick, River and Loch, 44, 54, 56 and n., 71, 127, 143

Murray MacGregor, Miss, 132 and n., 140, 168

Napier, Field Marshal Sir Robert Cornelis (afterwards 1st Baron Napier of Magdala), 150

Napoleon III, Emperor of the French, 76, 90, 108, 157, 195

Napoleon Eugène, Prince Imperial, 157, 167

Napoleon, Prince ('Plon Plon'), 90

Neild, John Camden, 63

Newcastle, Henry Pelham, 5th Duke of (*and see* Lincoln), 115

Nicholas II, Tsar of All the Russias, 188

Nightingale, Florence, 61, 88, 114, 172

Osborne (royal yacht), 124

Osborne Cottage, 7, 169

Osborne House and Estate (new), 11, 12, 15, 16–23, 29–31, 35, 36, 37, 39, 45–6, 48, 49, 69, 70, 75, 76, 78, 80, 88, 89–90, 95–6, 99, 101, 106, 107, 110–11, 114–16, 118, 121, 124, 125, 126, 128, 130, 137, 138, 139, 141–2,

144–5, 147, 148, 149, 154–5, 157, 158, 159, 162, 164, 167, 170, 171–2, 173–4, 177, 179, 180–2, 187, 193, 196, 197
Osborne House (old), 8, 10, 11, 12, 15, 22, 23, 28, 36

Pagenstacher, Professor, 193
Palmerston, Henry John, 3rd Viscount, 48, 60, 73, 101, 112, 116, 124, 129, 137
Pannanich Wells, 44
Paterson, William, 39
Peel, Sir Robert, 4, 5, 23, 24, 28, 34, 49, 50, 59, 147, 150
Persigny, Count de, 98
Philip, Count of Flanders (cousin to V. and A.), 98, 103
Phipps, Colonel the Hon. (later Sir) Charles, 33 n., 48, 53, 58, 61, 64, 98, 100, 110, 117, 120, 122, 129, 130, 138
Phipps, Lady, 110
Phipps, the Hon. Harriet, 122, 177
Ponsonby, Colonel (later Major-General Sir) Henry, 92, 122, 133, 135, 155, 160, 177, 179, 184, 186, 193
Ponsonby, Lieutenant (later Major and Brevet Lieut.-Col. Sir) Frederick (afterwards 1st Baron Sysonby), 122, 156, 178, 195, 196
Pride and Prejudice, 142
Private Eye, 161
Prothero, the Reverend (later Canon) George, 121, 171
Prothero, Mrs, 121
Punch, 172

Richmond and Lennox, Charles Henry, 6th Duke of, created Earl of Kinrara and Duke of Gordon (1876), 103
Ram, Bhai, 181
Reid, Dr (later Sir) James, 161, 174, 179
Roberts, Frederick Sleigh, Field Marshal Earl, 196
Robertson, Dr Andrew, 41, 52, 64, 83, 98, 100, 118, 134, 143
Rollande, Mme, 30
Rothschild, Nathan Mayer, 1st Baron, 155, 156
Roxburghe, Susanna Stephenia, Duchess of, 142, 193
Royal establishments, 2–3
Ruskin, John, 13
Russell, Lord John (afterwards Earl), 23, 47, 48, 50, 56, 59, 101, 102, 129, 137, 138, 139

St Clare, 121
St John, Charles, 51
St Katherine's Hospital, 132 n.
St Maur, Lord Edward Percy, 75–6
Salisbury, Robert Arthur Talbot, 3rd Marquis of, 188, 192
Sandringham House, 118, 123
Saxe-Gotha-Altenburg, Caroline, Duchess of, *see* Caroline, Duchess of Saxe-Coburg-Altenburg
Saxe-Coburg-Gotha, Marie, Duchess of, *see* Marie, Duchess of Saxe-Coburg-Gotha
Scotsman, 128
Seckendorff, Count, 174
Sheilagh, 172
Shirras, C. F., 191
Sibthorpe, Colonel Charles, 59
Sigismund, Prince, of Prussia, 139
Skerrett, Miss, 35, 115, 122, 174
Smith, John ('Sink 'em'), 42, 65
Smith John ('Tudor Johnnie'), 42, 65
Smith, William, 65–7, 71, 77, 78, 79, 80, 83, 86
Sophia Frederica, Queen of Holland, 91
Spa, 40
Speke, John, 130
Stanley, Lady Augusta (née Lady Augusta Bruce), 81, 102, 109, 115, 121, 129, 153, 193
Stanley, the Very Reverend Arthur, Dean of Westminster, 129
Stewart, Charles ('The Princie'), 72
Stewart, Lizzie, 193, 196
Stockmar, Baron, 2, 17, 25, 33, 39, 50, 58, 59, 60, 73, 74, 82, 84, 88–9, 92, 107, 108, 112, 125–6, 138, 164–5
Stockmar, Baron Ernest (the younger), 116, 164–5
Sutherland, George Granville William, 3rd Duke of, 165
Symon, Mrs, 191, 192
Symon, the Misses, 192

Tait, the Most Reverend Archibald, Archbishop of Canterbury, 155, 171
Tennyson, Alfred, 1st Baron, 148
Theed, William, 99, 123, 143, 174
Theodore, (self-proclaimed) Emperor of Ethiopia, 148–9, 150
Thomas, John, 67, 84
Thomsons, the (in the royal service), 176
Thompson, Flora, 164
Thora, Princess, *see* Helena Victoria, 'Thora', Princess of Schleswig-Holstein

Times, The, 129
Tomahawk, 140
Toward, Mr, 123
Tyler, Dr, 173, 175

Victoria, Princess, of Prussia, 188
Victoria, Princess, of Saxe-Saalfeld-Gotha
(afterwards Princess of Leiningen,
then Duchess of Kent) (V.'s mother),
1, 22–3, 24, 25, 45, 49, 61, 81, 102,
106, 109
Victoria, Queen: accident at B., 127–8;
alarmed by Chartists, 38, 39; appearance (in 1843), 1, (in 1857), 90; aware-
ness of what went on round her, 174;
beginning of absorbing interest in
India, 175; emotional scenes (a prey to
her nerves), 70, 87–8, 89, 95, 96,
97–9, 109, 110–11, 119, 128, 158–62;
family conspiracy against her, 158–60;
Fenian threats to, 143–6; first consideration of buying a house in Scotland, 10; first sea-bathe at O., 31;
first separation from A., 9; first visit
to Isle of Wight, 6; first visit to Scotland, 3; gifts to, 62, 170, 190; hatred
of heat, 95, 106; her 'Hanoverian
appetites', 133–4; high regard for
privy councillorship, 21; love of
Osborne, 16, 24, 28, 45, 89–90, 95,
101, 164; love of Scotland, 33, 35, 40,
43, 44, 45, 47, 50, 53, 56, 57, 62, 70,
87, 88, 98, 101, 107, 112, 142, 164;
need for 'a daughter at home', 164;
peppery temper, 130, 154, 177; relationship with Brown, 131–6; relationship with her mother, 1, 22, 109–110;
reluctance to be seen in public, 129,
137–8, 140, 153–4, 158–62; tempted
to commit suicide, 119; timidity, 176;
travel, 123, 165; views on death, 115;
views on feminism, 156; views on
government bureaucracy, 176; views
on the Irish, 50, 146; views on the
Jews, 155; views on ladies hunting,
176; views on morganatic marriages,
168, 169; views on religion, 43, 64,
90, 117, 125, 167, 188, 194
Victoria Adelaide, Princess Royal (afterwards Princess Frederick William of
Prussia, Crown Princess, Queen and
Empress Victoria, and Empress
Frederick), 28, 32, 41, 49, 62, 90, 92,
94, 95, 96, 97, 98, 99, 100–1, 106,
107, 108, 109, 111, 112, 114, 116,
117–19, 121, 123, 124, 126, 127, 139,
158, 169, 174, 195
Victoria Eugénie Ena, Princess, of
Battenberg (afterwards Queen of
Spain), 174, 185
Victoria Mary, Princess, of Hesse-
Darmstadt, then of Hesse and by
Rhine (afterwards Princess Louis of
Battenberg and Marchioness of
Milford Haven), 125, 168, 169, 170
Victoria Mary, Princess, of Teck ('May')
(afterwards Duchess of York, Duchess
of York and Cornwall, Princess of
Wales, and Queen Consort of George
V), 182, 188
Victoria and Albert (royal yachts), 4, 32,
40, 50, 76, 108, 141
Vilain XIV, Madame, 24 and n., 25

Waldemar, Prince, of Prussia, 158
Watson, Dr, 113
Wellesley, the Very Reverend Gerald
Valerian, Dean of Windsor, 113, 121,
153
Wellington, Arthur, 1st Duke of, 61, 86
Westminster, Hugh Lupus, 3rd Marquis
of, and afterwards 1st Duke of, 14
Weyer, M. Van de, 137, 151, 152
Whippingham, 38, 49, 107, 110, 121,
166, 167, 170, 186
White, Edward, 8, 45, 48, 60
Wight, Isle of, 5, 6, 7, 24, 25, 37, 47,
62, 87, 94, 95, 129, 135, 142, 145, 164,
166, 169, 173, 179, 197
Willem (negro page), 127
William, the Prince of Prussia (after-
wards Prince Regent, William I, King
of Prussia and German Emperor), 38
William, Prince, of Prussia (afterwards
Crown Prince, then William II, King
of Prussia and German Emperor), 40,
96, 100, 107, 108, 111, 124, 139–40,
158, 174, 180, 192, 197
Windsor Castle, 3, 99, 100, 108, 112,
124, 125, 126, 139, 144, 154, 173, 187,
189, 194, 196
Winterhalter, Francis, 29, 41, 101, 120

York, Archbishop of, *see* Longley, the
Most Reverend Charles
Yorke, the Hon. Alexander, 179, 192